An Ancient Guide to Good Politics

An Ancient Guide to Good Politics

A Literary and Ethical Reading of Cicero's *De Republica*

Moryam VanOpstal

LEXINGTON BOOKS
Lanham • Boulder • New York • London

Published by Lexington Books
An imprint of The Rowman & Littlefield Publishing Group, Inc.
4501 Forbes Boulevard, Suite 200, Lanham, Maryland 20706
www.rowman.com

86-90 Paul Street, London EC2A 4NE

Reprinted from "*On the Republic*" and "*On the Laws*", translated with Introduction, Notes, and Indexes by David Fott. Copyright © 2013 by Cornell University. Used by permission of the publisher, Cornell University Press.

Copyright © 2023 by The Rowman & Littlefield Publishing Group, Inc.

British Library Cataloguing in Publication Information Available

Library of Congress Cataloging-in-Publication Data

Names: VanOpstal, Moryam, author.
Title: An ancient guide to good politics : a literary and ethical reading of Cicero's de
    Republica / Moryam VanOpstal.
Description: Lanham : Lexington Books, [2023] | Includes bibliographical references
    and index.
Identifiers: LCCN 2022034496 (print) | LCCN 2022034497 (ebook) |
    ISBN 9781793652249 (cloth) | ISBN 9781793652256 (ebook)
Subjects: LCSH: Cicero, Marcus Tullius. De republica. | Cicero, Marcus Tullius.--
    Political and social views. | Cicero, Marcus Tullius.--History and criticism. | Political
    science--Philosophy.
Classification: LCC JC81.C7 V36 2023 (print) | LCC JC81.C7 (ebook) |
    DDC 320.1--dc23/eng/20220818
LC record available at https://lccn.loc.gov/2022034496
LC ebook record available at https://lccn.loc.gov/2022034497

♾️ The paper used in this publication meets the minimum requirements of American National Standard for Information Sciences—Permanence of Paper for Printed Library Materials, ANSI/NISO Z39.48-1992.

To my wife Tami,
and to Laeth, Niels, Clara, Soren, and Joris

Contents

Acknowledgments

The joyful labor I undertook in writing this book could not have succeeded without my family's unfailing support and sacrifice. To my in-laws, who helped hold down the fort, and to my mother, who started my educational journey and sustained me in ways great and small—thank you. To my children, who endured countless hours of boredom—yes, we can play now. And to my wife, Tami, without whom none of this would have been possible—you have given more than anyone else and asked for nothing in return. I cannot thank you enough, but I won't stop trying. You remain, as you always have been, my best and dearest friend.

Beyond this, I am forever indebted to Richard Dougherty for first introducing me to Cicero, for his academic mentorship, and for enduring, through the years, my endless questions and persistent speculations. Likewise, for helping to improve this manuscript, I am particularly grateful to Gerard Wegemer and David Sweet for their advice and conversation over the years. To whatever degree I have succeeded in being a respectful and careful reader, I cannot measure my debt to Leo Paul de Alvarez and John Alvis. They are gentlemen and scholars all.

Many others have supported me along the way. I am grateful to Paul Wolfe, headmaster of The Cambridge School of Dallas, for his unwavering support and encouragement. David Upham, Jonathan Culp, Tiffany Jones Miller, Dan Burns, and other faculty at the University of Dallas helped me in more ways than they know. Mickey Craig and Nathan Schlueter of Hillsdale College first inspired and encouraged my interest in political philosophy, which has definitively shaped the course of my intellectual life.

A number of friends and fellow scholars have helped me inestimably in better understanding and better expressing my understanding of Cicero over the years, at the University of Dallas, at conferences, and through other professional relationships. I have mentioned many of them already. They deserve the credit for much that has gone right with this book. In addition, I must particularly thank the anonymous reviewer for Lexington Books who provided several thoughtful and helpful critiques. Finally, I am deeply grateful to Jana Hodges-Kluck, Sydney Wedbush, and Anna Keyser of Rowman & Littlefield for their patience, attentiveness, and thoughtful help in editing and production along the way.

A Note on Translation and Usage

In this book I have primarily relied on David Fott's excellent translation of *De Republica*. In rare cases when I have substituted my own translation or altered his, I have made a special note in the text. Fott's numbering of certain passages in his translation differs from most recent translations since he relies on J. G. F. Powell's 2006 edition of the Latin text rather than K. Ziegler's 1992 edition. To help readers reference passages in their preferred translation, I have placed both numbers in the citation whenever they differ.

Throughout the text, when citing Cicero's various works, I have used shorthand to denote the text to which I am referring. The list of initials used is below.

DA   *Laelius De Amicitia* (*Laelius on Friendship*)
DD   *De Divinatione* (*On Divination*)
DF   *De Finibus* (*On Moral Ends*)
DO   *De Officiis* (*On Duties*)
DL   *De Legibus* (*On the Laws*)
DRP   *De Republica* (*On the Republic*)
DND   *De Natura Deorum* (*On the Nature of the Gods*)
TD   *Tusculanae Disputationes* (*Tusculan Disputations*)

Introduction

Reading Cicero forces us to read between the lines. Cicero was a practiced orator as well as a great statesman, and he did not simply aim to speak his mind when he addressed his fellow Romans, but to change their minds. He wished to bequeath to his fellow Romans a trove of worthwhile and transformative reason in his published speeches and dialogues, and so grasping his nuance—or, in some cases, discerning his rhetorical dissembling—is worth our effort and care. But beyond this, we are forced to read between the lines because too many of the original lines in his manuscripts are missing. Whole swaths of Cicero's political and philosophical writing have regrettably been lost to antiquity. His words cannot be recovered in these instances, but fortunately his argument, broadly speaking, can be. Where there are gaps, enough remains in most cases to ask educated questions and find educated answers, which has made the recent decades of renewed scholarship in Cicero all the more exciting.

Cicero is not lost to us, then, and this is fortunate. Setting aside his political and historical significance—which by themselves merit him a place in history—in Cicero's writings we find a thinker who could reasonably lay claim to being the greatest conveyer and unifier of political thought in antiquity, and all the more so given the fragmentation of sources that have survived the centuries. *De Republica*, the focus of this book, serves as a good example. It is a self-conscious emulation of Plato's *Republic*, but freely engages Aristotelian political thought along with Stoic and Epicurean teaching. Rather than simply restating opinions, however, Cicero weaves them together into a dialogic tapestry as he roams from the Earth to the Heavens and back again. He writes about justice, glory, and much more besides; about institutions and laws, and also about education and mores; about Plato's gold-souled man, not inquiring as a philosopher only, but as a man who is engaged in the thickening of the political plot during Rome's greatest trial. If Cicero possesses the insight and art, he has in his grasp all the elements needed to craft a truly great work.

If Cicero is a great statesman and accomplished in deed what others only wrote about, it is reasonable to ask why he would attempt to set his insight down in theoretical teaching. "Why not?," of course—but how many statesman have tried to write a dialogue in imitation of Plato? Why not simply compose his own memoirs? One simple possibility is that Cicero was particularly convinced that wisdom was worth writing down; or, beyond this, we might suppose that emulating Plato tickled his vanity. These explanations are both likely parts of the truth, but they do not give Cicero his due. He was a deep thinker who believed that wisdom, as such, could not actually be written down, although good writing could point the way to wisdom; his works are meant to serve as signposts to *sophia*.[1] Certainly, it is likely true that a kind of pride or ambition drove his work; after all, he imitated Plato because he believed himself able to imitate Plato. However, Cicero had a more fundamental and beneficent purpose: he believed in the truth that knowing the unchanging things mattered a great deal for dealing rightly with the changing things, and so he set himself to the work of becoming a philosophic guide to his fellow Romans. Politics in practice could be improved by good theory, he believed; moreover, bad politics could be saved by good theory. Cicero also hoped that good politics could do something to encourage good philosophy, since he thought Romans were doing philosophy rather poorly.

Whatever else we might say about Cicero's motives, grand or not, it all comes down to this: the most important reason Cicero wrote *De Republica* was to bring the insight of philosophy to bear in a very particular context, which was Rome in the last throes of the republic. Of course, in the 50s BC when Cicero writes *De Republica*, he cannot know with certainty the momentous events the next ten years will bring: the end of the Gallic Wars and Julius Caesar's return home; the crossing of the Rubicon in 49 BC and the civil war between Caesar and Pompey, in which Cicero grimly determines to cast his lot in with Pompey; Cicero's robust period of writing in the twilight of the post-constitutional conflagration; Caesar's victory and condescending forgiveness of Cicero, followed by the brutal assassination of Caesar; then Cicero's continued writing as the fallen republic decays into the tyranny of the Triumvirate, and his Philippic orations against Marcus Antony; and finally Cicero's brutal murder at the hands of Antony's henchmen, along with the death of his brother Quintus. As history records, Antony was so offended by Cicero's persistent defiance that he ordered his hands cut off along with his head and placed them on the rostra in the Roman Senate. It was a grotesque gesture by Antony, an attempt to vitiate the power of Cicero's example through gruesome intimidation. It was also, in an unintended way, the tyrant's greatest compliment to the virtue of his fallen enemy.

Because Cicero was killed—because he could not stop the Triumvirate, and he could not stop Caesar, and could not save the republic—it is easy to conclude that Cicero failed. One might wonder, though, whether Cicero's enemies, given a glimpse of the millennia to come, might not wish with chagrin that they had been Cicero. Though he was ultimately prevented from preserving the republic, it is no more the case that Cicero failed than that Aristotle failed because one of his pupils, Alexander the Great, became a great conqueror who then succumbed to decadence, or that Plato failed because his own interventions in Syracuse did not flourish. Certainly, Cicero regretted that he had not been able to stop the collapse of the republic, much less bring about its genuine revival. He didn't only write in hopes of transforming his present moment, however, but to dispatch the vital spark of his insight beyond the liminal strivings of his mortal life. In this endeavor, Cicero spectacularly succeeded. His writings not only inspired great Romans and great Church Fathers to come, but ultimately served as a critical touchstone for the revival of classical thought in the Renaissance and beyond. Cicero could not save his own great republic, but he helped breathe life into a hundred more and he reigned for some centuries as one of the singular exemplars of duty, rhetoric, and virtue. Indeed, it is only in the last century-and-a-half that Cicero's works have fallen out of fashion—a short respite after such a heady reign—but he is already enjoying rediscovery among scholars today. If Cicero will be broadly rediscovered and enjoy a second sailing remains to be seen; but, if the handful of serious, reflective books published in the last decade alone are any indication, he is already being rediscovered by a new era of scholars and thinkers. This book is part of that happy effort by a happy, but now-increasing few to revisit his neglected library shelves, to shake off the dust from the bindings of his old books, and to crack open the pages of Cicero's insight once again.

Turning more particularly to the subject of this book, it could be said that Cicero's wide-ranging writings, in *De Republica* and across his corpus, are united by a kindred concern: "How should a good man live?" The ancient world was criss-crossed with opinions on this question, rustic, religious, and philosophic. Notwithstanding his religious offices in the Roman state, Cicero's inclination always ran in the philosophic direction, with Greek ideas like Epicureanism and Stoicism defining the ends of the popular philosophical spectrum. Although he admired the Stoics a good deal more than the Epicureans—the Epicureans embracing the body and its pleasure, rejecting the soul, and the Stoics emphasizing the soul and reason, devaluing the body—Cicero somewhat eclectically embraced what was good wherever he found it, taking into account both our bodies and souls, our cosmic abode and our earthly dwellings. After all, we are all born in a land, one with a people, and reared in a family; our flourishing depends on parents, on friends and neighbors, on laws and institutions, on city temple and kitchen table. Our well-being depends on all of these things being in a good condition, and on their being good. Cicero's ethical teaching about how a good man lives thus centers on the active life and man's duty to be just, to be temperate, to be brave. All this seemed to him to be quite reasonable and most probably true—even if he couldn't be quite sure. In framing the matter in this way, Cicero took his stand with the New Academy, a philosophical school claiming to embody the original Socratic skepticism. But there was one question that vexed this school perhaps more than others, and that was the question of the best way of life.

The life of duty is noble, but it has a competitor in the life of contemplation. The philosophical way of life requires setting aside human troubles to pursue a more fine and divine end, an alternative that is all-the-more tempting in light of the unsettling realities of human life. It is true, unfortunately, that our lives are often deeply troubled by corrupt laws, bad friends, and broken families, not to mention feuds, wars, and revolutions. Whereas in Cicero's view the Epicureans adopted the path of least resistance, pursuing pleasure or untroubled existence, the way of life that strives upward to the divine through an ascetic love and pursuit of wisdom—this way of life simultaneously concerns itself with the best things and with the rarest delights. The life of contemplation would thus obviously recommend itself to any thoughtful individual. Problematically, this life of contemplation would seem incompatible with the aforementioned life of duty, for wisdom does not readily reward the fickle or halfhearted suitor. Devotees of the contemplative life—if they give their all—have little time to spare for duty, honor, and country, or so it would seem.

The active, noble life and the contemplative, divine life thus seem incompatible, but rather than contenting himself with this fracturing of life, Cicero in his dialogue *De Republica* presents an exploration of human and political life that draws together virtue and wisdom, politics and philosophy. Ambitiously, he declares toward the beginning of his work, "There is nothing in which human virtue more nearly approaches the majesty of the gods than either founding new cities or preserving ones that are already founded."[2] This book explores how Cicero strives to unite the active and contemplative lives into a single life of alternating centers, and how this endeavor outlines the possibility of a philosophic politics. There are many competing claims to our affection and affirmation, in fact—what is law and what is just, what is ours and what is other, presents good and eternal goods, and so on. Rather than ideologically justifying his choice for one side or the other of these dualities, Cicero will counsel a prudence that helps us find what is fitting in every moment. That is, though he cannot tell us what is good in every instance, he aims to change us so that we'll be able to see the truth ourselves. To read

Cicero respectfully and profitably, then, requires reading with all the attention we have to give.

The two-part organization of this book moves from a philosophical and literary study of the two ways of life in *De Republica* to Cicero's political teaching as revealed, more and less openly, over the course of the dialogue. With one major and some minor exceptions, I discuss the major topics as they arise in the ordering of the dialogue. The major exception is that the famed Dream of Scipio should be understood as an interpretive key for the whole work and, in an academic study of the dialogue, should be treated earlier rather than later. Thus, readers will find in chapter 1 a discussion of Cicero's own introduction to *De Republica*. He begins with a stalwart defense of Roman civic duty against the enervating influence of Epicureanism and philosophy generally—a critique that comes as something of a shock to his modern readers, naturally—but his final judgment is not so devastating. From the rubbish heap of philosophical rejects Cicero plucks a handful of philosophers and, I argue, concludes by suggesting the salutary unity of the two ways of life. Although he merely foreshadows this more profound conclusion in his introduction, by the end it will become clear that this unity is essential, and that the philosophic life and the political life forget each other at their mutual peril. The only kind of philosophy that Cicero meant to critique in his preface, then, was the vain kind that concerns itself with abstract speculation about things divine (such as the appearance of phantasmic second suns) while neglecting to consider how men should live under the light of the true sun, to note the concern of Laelius, the dialogue's advocate for the political sphere. Still, if the laws are to be just and good for men, they must be informed by wisdom's insight into the nature of things above and things below, and Scipio becomes the dialogue's oracle for this "political" philosophy. With the question of the two ways of life in hand, chapter 2 forays briefly into the thought of select scholars on Cicero's understanding of the two ways of life and offers a tentative defense of the idea that Cicero ultimately refuses to partition these ways of life. Rather, he champions the unified life characterized by alternating modes or centers of political practice and philosophic inquiry. To bolster this argument, chapter 3 takes a different tack and explores how the Dream of Scipio serves as a hermeneutical key to *De Republica*, both in structure and content. There particularly, by means of a literary and structural argument, I defend the idea that Cicero attempted to unite the active and contemplative ways of life. Though he initially forces a distinction between Socrates' ethical concern and Plato's more Pythagorean, theoretical bent, Cicero casts both of these famous Greeks as leading Romans, embodying Socrates in the character of Laelius and placing Plato's mantle on Scipio. Instead of preferring the opinion of one or the other, it will prove to be the tension and dialogue between these two that best illuminate justice, duty, and the good, thereby enabling both good politics and insightful philosophy. Not content to stop there, Cicero crafts an earthly analogy to the Heavens in the persons of the dialogue's nine interlocutors by corresponding the nine speakers to the nine heavenly spheres in the Dream of Scipio. This analogy highlights the significance of Laelius, the central figure, as the guide of action in the dialogue, but simultaneously emphasizes the significance of Scipio as divine wisdom's interjection in terrestrial life. Laelius and Scipio together, whether viewed as Socrates and Plato or as the Sun and the Earth or Heavens, mutually support and reinforce noble thought and thoughtful deed. These men are exemplars of thought and action whose interplay helps reveal that the distinction between active and contemplative lives is not as stubborn in fact as it is in theory, and it would be rare for any person to engage exclusively in one mode. For most human beings, these two modes of living meaningfully coexist and are, in some sense, in conspiracy, orienting and fulfilling one another. The complete life is in fact characterized by alternating, reinforcing junctures of contemplation and action. To further round out the argument, chapter 4 explores the unity of active and contemplative lives from yet another angle, noting the gap that exists between established law and the true justice that is known only to the wise. Through exploring the orbs of Gallus as discussed in the dialogue, I suggest that Cicero does not consider this gap an unbridgeable chasm, but that philosophy and poetry (united, perhaps, in history) become modes of revealing *ius* (justice or right) more or less dimly. Finally, chapter 5 concludes the discussion of the two lives by revisiting the Dream of Scipio to see how Cicero ultimately counsels his readers to embrace a unified life, one that shies away from thinking either too much or too little about the Heavens and the Earth, but rightly about both. Although Cicero's Academic skepticism makes him wary of staking too much on a particular theory, at the culmination of the Dream of Scipio—the literary summit of the whole book—Cicero introduces Plato's theory of the soul as the keystone of the unity between the life of action and contemplation.

Having suggested this rapprochement in part 1, I turn in part 2 to explore select elements of Cicero's understanding of politics. Although there are a few set pieces (in the text that we have) where one character or another exposits a political teaching, Cicero reveals his most important teaching on the origin and preservation of republics through the dialogue between and among characters. Beginning this section, chapter 6 explores Cicero's emphasis on man's natural sociability and his belief that the bond that makes a people one is their shared commitment to *ius*—not to a particular law or set of ideas about right, but their shared commitment to seeking what is right together. Maintaining this republic is a task belonging to political deliberation, the primary task of which is not to enforce right but rather to maintain the bond of human fellowship. Who will undertake this deliberation, however? This raises the question of who should rule, which in turn raises the question of the best "form" (Lat. *status*) of the republic. The chapter concludes with an exploration of Cicero's conviction that political forms breed particular moral constitutions, which leads to the profound recognition that politics is in fact a means by which a whole people may be philosophically oriented to justice, a good which looks for the leadership of a kind of philosopher-statesman. Before turning to this great and mysterious figure, chapter 7 unpacks the cycle of regimes, or *cursus mutationem*, in Ciceronian thought, showing how he seems to suggest both a formal and an informal cycle in *De Republica*. Formally, Cicero deviates from other thinkers in the tradition by denoting a series of probabilities in the decline of regimes rather than a rigid course of certainties. More importantly, Cicero indicates that there is an informal pattern that characterizes the course of every regime and, in revealing this fact, indicates the sort of steps a prudent ruler should take to secure his position and the well-being of his republic. To elucidate this pattern, chapter 8 delves into Cicero's detailed account of the history of the early Roman kingship and republic, arguing that he simultaneously aims to re-frame the Roman story for Romans and to provide an illustration and proof of the *cursus mutationem* for his more careful readers. Once identified, this pattern becomes evident in every iteration of the kingship and the republic and reveals Cicero's retelling of Roman history to be a textbook for would-be statesmen. Finally, chapters 9 and 10 bring together Cicero's teaching on the unified way of life and the meaning of political things to discuss the figure of the Guide (Lat. *rector reipublicae*) and the mixed regime, two elements most conducive to the unified, complete way of life. Since much material discussing the Guide has been lost, I glean from what we have of Cicero's writing what type of person this is, his characteristics and his work, and the sort of position he has in the republic. Cicero does not recommend this man as the heroic type who can save any city, but as the best man to lead the mixed regime. The mixed regime, in turn, is the best form of republic because justice in the city is not tied to maintaining a static order in the city, but is particularly open to philosophy's insight regarding justice in law. The guide and the mixed regime together maintain a prudent balance of power, authority, and freedom in the city to best orient its people toward the just and to the good. Finally I conclude the book by succinctly stating what I take to be the *ratio rerum civilium*, his account of political affairs, that runs like a golden thread through Cicero's crafting of *De Republica*. For Cicero, this teaching is perennial philosophy, always true and always relevant. Indeed, for Cicero writing about politics is a revelatory project, a means to draw back the veil on nature herself. To see these unseen things must require, paradoxically, giving them form, and this chapter highlights how elements of Cicero's teaching on the *ratio rerum civilium* were illustrated in his writing on the history of the Roman kingship and republic.

In writing a book about as fragmented a work as *De Republica*, it is always uncertain how far one should go in filling in the blanks. As far as possible, I have tried to infer what can be said about missing material from what we have, but I have avoided indulging in speculation. The most significant ellipsis in this book, regrettably, is any substantial discussion of Cicero's theory of natural law as it might have been undertaken in *De Republica*. Although we have notable portions of Book 3, which seems to focus on natural law, we are missing far more material than we have preserved, and it is a perilous thing when interpreting a dialogue to make assumptions about such content. For this reason other scholars turn to dialogues such as Cicero's *Laws* to discuss natural law, but to interpolate so much content from other dialogues would have been inconsistent with the aim of this project.

As a final word, I should say something about the approach I have taken in writing this book, which comes best in the form of a personal confession: I have wondered from time to time whether Cicero would in fact greatly dislike my book, for several reasons. Inevitably, of course, there are ways I have misunderstood him and important things I have missed: that would be cause enough. But worse than all this, I have wondered whether Cicero would be offended, as a rhetorician and as a philosopher, at a modern academic study of his work. Immediately, I recognize that his vanity would have been tickled by the attention—but I also know that, by and large, in this book I have talked about what Cicero said, but not about what truth and justice really are; I dispute with my fellow Cicero scholars (we happy few), but I do not argue with Cicero himself. My book treats Cicero more like an artifact and less like a man; more like a puzzle and less like a provocation to live a better life. My book, in being faithful to the genre, is to some extent written as though Cicero's thoughts do not really matter.

Strange to say, for this reason, I hope you and Cicero both dislike my book, or are tempted to. But in response to Cicero's disdain I might respond that I have tried, in good faith, to shuck the limits of category and to say something worth saying for human beings more generally. It is my fervent wish that Cicero's writings in *De Republica* become more alive to you as you read or reference this book, and that as a result you will be more deeply intrigued and provoked by what he has to say. And if only because of these good intentions, I suppose it is my hope that Cicero might have liked this book after all.

NOTES

1. As Schofield has noted, Cicero may well have succeeded better than Plato at writing dialogues that are "balanced and open-ended," and thus (along with Plato) succeed in aiming at wisdom as a deep way of thinking and not only a kind of knowledge (*Cicero*, 8).

2. Cicero, DRP, 1.12.

PART 1

The Two Ways of Life

Chapter 1

Making Romans Reasonable

De Republica, 1.1–13

The question driving the plot of Cicero's *De Republica* is, very simply, "How should a good man live?" The fact that Cicero hopes to discover the answer to this question in a dialogue about man in civil society—and specifically in a republic—says a great deal about his philosophical frame. But how important is the active, political life to living a good human life? Is the good life found in giving our all for the city? Or is there a better way? In his preface to *De Republica*, Cicero seems to argue emphatically that the good man is in fact the political man and decidedly not the philosophical man. This strong assertion dominates the preface, but when we turn several pages and read Cicero's prologue to the main dialogue (1.13–19), he confronts us with the very opposite argument voiced by the character Scipio: the good man is the philosophical man who transcends the city, not the political man. Whereas the preface is consumed with justifying the political virtue of the active life, the prologue turns into a peroration in praise of the contemplative life. These two opening parts of *De Republica* begin and end in opposite places, raising an obvious difficulty. These poles also represent Cicero's serious attempt to grapple with the tension between the two lives that, in classical thinking, lay claim to being the best ways of life.

The aim of the first five chapters of this book is to reconcile these turns by exploring Cicero's philosophical and literary attempt to unify the active and contemplative ways of life. This unity of lives turns out to be central to Cicero's purpose to teach us about how to make and keep republics, and so his writing on the unity of lives is central to his teaching in *De Republica*. Understanding how this is so requires reading his text with care, beginning in chapter 1 by discerning Cicero's sleight of hand in the preface, where he takes brutal Romans and, through his rhetorical art, renders them mild enough to receive his teaching, a teaching which in truth amounts to a revolution in what it means to be Roman. He does not do this by making them religious, as Numa did, but by making them reasonable, though they may not know it. Chapter 2 explores the tension between the two lives in Cicero's writings and in the insights of other Cicero scholars before making a tentative argument for his unification of the two ways of life in an overlap of alternating, reinforcing modes. Chapters 3, 4, and 5 illustrate in various ways how this claim is the best way of understanding Cicero's thinking about the unity of action and contemplation. Chapter 3 shows how Cicero smuggled Socrates and Plato into Rome in the persons of Laelius and Scipio, the main characters in his dialogue, and how they embody the unity of the two lives for us. In *De Republica*, Cicero artfully designed the nine spheres of the Heavens to overlay the dialogue's nine interlocutors on Earth, a dramatic touch that helps serve as a hermeneutical key for understanding the relationships of the characters. Chapter 4 unpacks the problem of human ignorance, as discussed in the dialogue, and how it serves as an obstacle to the influence of wisdom and justice in law and society, which is a problem that an Academic skeptic such as Cicero takes very seriously. The chapter argues, however, that Cicero ultimately emphasizes the importance of what he believes we really can know, even somewhat uncertainly, and his teaching in *De Republica* highlights the way in which political philosophy serves as link between the centers of the active and contemplative ways of life. Chapter 5 concludes the argument regarding the unity of lives by revisiting the Dream of Scipio and showing how Cicero, far from giving his readers encouragement to commit to one or the other, would counsel those too concerned with Earth to think a little more of the Heavens and, conversely, those too concerned with the Heavens to think a little more of Earth. The chapter concludes by discussing how Cicero makes use of Plato's theory of the soul as a keystone in his argument for the unity of lives.

INTRODUCING CICERO'S PREFACE TO *DE REPUBLICA*

It is unfortunately the case that much of the actual text of Cicero's opening arguments in *De Republica* is lost. Cicero began Books 1, 3, and 5 of *De Republica* with prefaces in which he spoke in his own voice, the rest of the content being made up of a dialogue among the nine interlocutors. As it is, due to churlish time and indifferent scribes, we only have portions of the first preface left. Fortunately, the pattern of Cicero's argument suggests how he meant to frame both the first two books and the work as a whole.

In the section of the preface that remains to us, Cicero's inquiry springs energetically out of the gate. The heart of Cicero's preface is an argument for civic duty. He holds out to us a definite sense, at least in outline, of what man is. Cicero does not conceive of man as "individual," as the smallest,

indivisible whole, a dignified granule who autonomously deigns to participate in society for his own, idiosyncratic sake. Man is contingent, a part living continually in search of the whole, who unites the good of each and of
all because both persons and communities are fully human. Cicero builds on,
and reveals, this assumption throughout his work. In the preface, he fronts
this claim by holding as one and the same the good man and the good citizen.

At first blush it might seem that Cicero is preaching to the choir: of all the
people in the world, why should he need to convince Romans of the good
of civic duty? But the times are hard, and Cicero thinks that Roman grist is
not what it once was. As Rome spread her pinions across Europe and Africa,
extending her imperium by empowering her generals, she became vulnerable
and weakened as power struggles fractured her political center. Certainly, the
corruption of the people into the mob played its part, but another was that
leading Romans had become cosmopolitan at the expense of virility and virtue. The allurements of body and mind had drawn Romans from their proper
allegiance. In response, and with republican vigor, in his introduction Cicero
makes a stirring appeal to memory, honor, and glory to awaken his Roman
audience to patriotic zeal. In making his case, Cicero seems to be addressing
two sorts of people: first, the Roman who lacks the moral interest or courage
to defend Rome and, second, the Roman whose intellect has excused him
from hard duty because he has been corrupted by philosophy. They must both
embrace the challenge. Cicero notes at the end of his preface, therefore, that
he "spoke many words" because he "first had to remove doubt about entering
public life." His argument "concerning the republic," which takes up the rest
of the book, would otherwise fall on deaf or indifferent ears.[1]

An indeterminate portion of Cicero's preface is lost, but fortunately not
its argument. Cicero's conclusion to the preface, where he pulls together
the strands of his argument, helps a great deal in recovering the lost beginning. Some of the details matter more than others. We learn, for one, that *De
Republica* was dedicated to one of his friends, a practice in keeping with most
of his other works; we discover that Cicero and his dedicatee were, in fact,
boyhood acquaintances, and it is a reasonable inference to think that the book
is dedicated to his brother, Quintus.[2] This detail aside, it's clear that Cicero's
overarching concern is to make an argument in service of the republic against
Romans who are abandoning their duty, and especially against those who are
making philosophical excuses for their retreat. For this reason, Cicero makes
a strong case that Romans should reject such men and their corruption.

In the remainder of the preface, Cicero—or, Cicero-as-narrator—makes a
surprisingly adamant case against philosophers and philosophy in general.
Some interpreters have suggested that Cicero is only criticizing Epicureans
here, but this is part of a carefully crafted rhetorical appeal. Though he rejects
the philosophers—except for one or two, at the very end—in the course of

his doing so he brings in their philosophy in a sleight of hand, making the philosophy itself seem more Roman than foreign, which is a technique Cicero employs throughout the dialogue. Cicero, leader of souls, concedes what he must to Roman prejudices in order to lead Romans subtly to reason.

OUSTING THE PHILOSOPHERS

Which philosophers precisely, then, were the objects of Cicero's wrath? Whom was he gainsaying in his defense of the public life? The partial manuscript doesn't reveal this precisely, but there is reason to think Cicero was not meaning to be very precise. Speaking broadly, he simply addresses those who are avoiding public life for moral or intellectual failings, or both. Cicero derides the "philosophers" who merely prattle on about "piety" and "justice" while lawmakers actually busy themselves attending to these matters.[3]

Based on the portions of the preface we have, Cicero was quite liberal in casting aspersions against philosophers. It would be natural to assume he was targeting the Epicureans, the sempiternal objects of his contempt, but this is not a distinction he makes in the material we have. Rather, despite his own philosophical interests, Cicero paints with an unexpectedly broad brush. In referring to the men he criticizes, Cicero denotes "these disreputable men [*iste*]" or "those men [*illa*]" or "the same men," never specifying more particularly whether he means the Epicureans, for instance, or philosophers generally.[4] While there is no doubt that Cicero generally delights to scorn the Epicureans, he does not seem to have singled them out here, or it is not clear that he has. Toward the end of his preface he once again addresses all "those who are still moved by the authority of the philosophers" without making any explicit qualification.[5] His generalized critique is further confirmed when the dialogue begins following Cicero's preface. Almost right away, Cicero's main character, the reputable Scipio, states his preference for the practical, ethical Socrates over the theoretical Plato, an inclination that seems to underscore the rejection of philosophers generally (at first blush at least). Although Cicero will eventually tuck his definition of the "philosopher" into a narrower form to distinguish between the worthy sort and the unworthy sort, it is important to see that in his opening salvo he's broadly disparaging of the philosophers, and intentionally so.

By beginning his dialogue with such an emphatic distinction—all the lawmakers opposed to all the philosophers—Cicero accomplishes a number of things. His rhetoric was no mistake. Primarily, he establishes his bona fides as a Roman. His education in Greece, as well as the fact that he is setting out to write a book in conscious imitation of Plato, potentially undermine his position as a Roman first and foremost, and as a fit tutor to Rome.[6] Cicero intently captures and calms his down-to-earth Roman readers in the first few pages. Simultaneously, his emphatic criticism would inevitably provoke the engagement of his philosophical readers. Stoicism and Epicureanism had made particular in-roads in Rome's intellectual classes, and Cicero puts them on notice that they must prove their worth. Are they in fact as Roman as he is? Cicero, the former governor and the senator, explicitly frames himself as the model citizen.[7] The men to whom Cicero is appealing are likely to be among the upper crust of Roman life, younger men of family and influence, who entertain philosophy as much by fashion as by conviction. Cicero seems to think that their Roman devotion to honor is the best way to turn their philosophical inclinations away from a seductive, uncivic leisure to an honest virtue.

REFUTING THE PHILOSOPHERS

Cicero responds to three specific philosophic dodges of public duty, offering an unqualified defense of the priority of governance and legislation. Among the list of prominent Romans he praises—the Scipios, Quintus Maximus, and Marcus Metellus, for example—most are known for their military prowess, but Cicero emphatically declares that virtue's "greatest use is the governance of the city [*maximus civitatis gubernatio*] and the completion [*perfectio*] in fact, not in speech, of the same things as these men [*isti*] shout about in the corners."[8] Lawmakers, not philosophers, are the benefactors of mankind.

The philosophers offer a variety of excuses for their refusal to engage in public life. They cite the troublesome labors of such work, the dangers that public life can bring, and the indignity of submitting to "worthless" men.[9] The first two of these frustrations are real problems illustrated in the dialogue itself, as Scipio is forced to carve out what little time he can during the Latin holiday for more philosophical discourse[10] and as the dialogue ends with a foreshadowing of his death at the hands of political enemies.[11] Cicero's argument for dutiful service despite these first two objections depends to no small degree on his own reputation and authority, and so he explicitly appeals to his own autobiography for several paragraphs. His ultimate point is that the philosophers' refusal to undertake labor or danger is indecent and dishonorable, and *ipso facto* unacceptable. Cicero makes significant use of shame in making his case in the preface, but his ability to shame Romans out of navel-gazing philosophy depends on his own standing to shame them. Cicero's *auctoritas*—his authority, his respectability—form the necessary foundation of his arguments, both in speaking knowledgeably to the philosophers and in speaking of the value of being Roman.

If escaping from labors and dangers is dishonorable and indecent, what work is honorable and decent? Cicero's explanation of his own motives for political service is summed up in the aims of "saving [*conservare*] fellow citizens" and "procur[ing] a common leisure [*commune otium*] for all others."[12] This reference to public leisure is unusual in two respects, being an uncommon verbal construction and a provocative blending of philosophic and political concerns. It recalls a similar use of the word in Cicero's "Pro Sestio" (56 BC) and in a letter to Lentulus (54 BC),[13] making reference to "cum dignitate otium" as the aim of the statesman. Chaim Wirzubski helpfully summarizes the literature on the meaning of the phrase, noting in particular Pierre Boyancé's argument that Cicero understands *otium* as "the well-earned leisure which crowns and rewards a long career of action and achievement." Boyancé understands Cicero to be making an argument against those who prefer pleasure to duty, suggesting that duty brings relief in the end and that the two can thus be reconciled.[14] Wirzubski argues compellingly, however, that Cicero's understanding of *otium*—a word Cicero repurposed into a peculiarly political usage[15]—is not characterized by a division between public duty and private pleasure, but a harmonization of the two: "*Cum dignitate otium* was, for Cicero, above all tranquility with dignity in the Roman State as well as in his own life."[16] Cicero's pursuit of a "common leisure," then, is an indication of his desire to reconcile the concerns of both active, political men and contemplative, philosophic men. This is the work the philosophers he condemns are fleeing from, to which he beckons them to return.

The third argument the philosophers make is that involvement in public life is dishonorable given the base character of so many men involved in it as well as the abuses such men will shamelessly inflict even on good men. Why should anyone expose his dignity or his person to such offenses? Why would anyone desire to do so? Cicero simply asserts to the contrary that the "wise man" and the "free man" will indeed submit themselves to conflict with the vicious, whether individuals or the mob. When such men threaten great injustice, it is precisely the thing to do to oppose them rather than to scurry away. Cicero responds on the basis of the dignity, honor, and justice of service: "not to obey wicked men and not to allow these men to tear the republic to pieces" is worthwhile in itself.[17]

Notably, Cicero's response to each of these three objections has been to stress nobility, not utility. In swaying his audience, any orator would be tempted to ground his argument against the philosophers in the need to mind practical matters. After all, even philosophers need to eat, and the well-being of the city is necessary to undergird their leisure. For Cicero, however, the utilitarian argument would undermine his case entirely. He is not interested in persuading men that they should engage in political work as a concession to necessity; instead, he argues that they should engage in the political because that is what a good man does; in fact, it is the best thing he can do.[18] Hence,

Cicero emphasizes *honestum* and *officium*, honor and duty, which center our motivation on what is good and noble rather than on what is pleasant and attractive. As his preface concludes, Cicero has set the stage for the embrace of the goods of political knowledge and inquiry into political affairs. He has worked "the philosopher" and the "wise man" into such an escapist caricature that the sensible, political man opposed to them is, we see, the one who is truly concerned with virtue. Cicero wants to make sure we take his point seriously, however, and so he makes one more assault on the philosophers.

In a final dismissal, Cicero seizes the center and claims for the political man the territory of worthwhile knowledge and inquiry from which the philosophers have ostensibly absconded. The "educated men," he says, deny the value of the knowledge of political things, but then they patronizingly "promise to approach the helm during the greatest floods."[19] Rather than accept such absurd promises, Cicero makes a practical appeal to Romans to attend to the wisdom of those who "have inquired, and written many things, about the republic."[20] Contrary to the absurdity of inexperienced men being able to serve as excellent statesmen because they have studied geometry and clouds, Cicero sets it down that "by no means should the wise man neglect this knowledge of political affairs"—knowledge that the political man rightfully concerns himself with.[21]

Notwithstanding his abuse of the philosophers, Cicero's rhetorical prowess is fully at work in this preface, and so we should not simply accept his dismissive aspersions as representing his own set opinion. Cicero is not, in fact, against philosophy, but against the philosophers who dilly-dally in their schools. As Yelena Baraz notes, Cicero's writings generally "[aim] to counteract Roman distrust of philosophy, and intellectual activity more generally, as an occupation."[22] He is in favor of Romans adopting philosophic reason, but he wants them to believe it is their own wisdom, not that of the Greeks. Ultimately, as we will see, Cicero is very much for the philosophers who have inspired and who share his insight in the service of the common good.

PILFERING THE PHILOSOPHERS

The overarching question that frames Cicero's inquiry, once again, is how to live well. If the philosophers are not reliable guides, Cicero is risking some immodesty in suggesting that he knows better. It turns out that the philosophers may not be so shabby in their conclusions after all, however, even if they themselves are *persona non grata*: in the course of his prosecution of the philosophers, Cicero slyly pilfers several philosophic arguments from the Greeks and uses them as proof of Roman strength, nobility, and goodness. In

other words, Cicero takes philosophy for Rome even while giving philosophers the boot. He doesn't actually rely only on his own insight, then, and
will ultimately prove willing to explicitly defer to the insights of highly select
philosophers by the end of the preface.

Cicero manages this coup d'état of stealing reason for Rome by root-
ing his critique of the philosophers in nature, which is neither Greek nor
Roman. In so doing he actually enters the philosophic fray, subverting some
philosophers with the teachings of others. In his earlier critique, he derided
the philosophers' preference for leisure and he questioned their courage,[23]
their contribution to human life,[24] and their flippant presumption that they
could rule, if need be, in a time of crisis.[25] Pointing out their folly, Cicero
then builds an argument that derives the guide for human action from human
nature, observed through common human activity. In this way, without obvious or explicit reference to philosophical precursors and without asserting
his teleological allegiances, Cicero reveals to his Roman audience the law
of nature rooted in their own experience and he goes on to prove his point
by upholding the lives of great Romans as exemplars of this truth. Hence, to
drive the philosophers out of the forum, Cicero has subtly equipped his fellow
Romans with Greek armaments.

To accomplish this "rationalizing" of Romans, Cicero offers three main
points in his call to duty, two of which are lost from the text but which can
be reconstructed in part from a summary he gives at the end of section 3. The
concluding thoughts in this paragraph seem self-evidently a summary of the
text that came before. This section contains three rapid-fire summations of
an argument regarding human nature, conduct, and virtue, the third part of
which corresponds neatly with the beginning of the fragmented text of *De
Republica* we possess.[26]

Cicero's first argument in the preface thus apparently argued that "we are
utterly gripped by the work of enlarging the weal of mankind."[27] As human
beings, he emphasizes, our efforts are spontaneously and persistently oriented
toward the good of others, and even the good of all. In a similar argument
in *De Officiis*, Cicero notes that man "devote[s] himself to provide whatever
[he] may contribute to the comfort and sustenance not only of himself, but
also of his wife, his children, and others whom he holds dear and ought to
protect."[28] Generosity (derived from "gens," denoting beneficence to one's
own), not competition or conquest, is entirely natural to man. In framing this
point in the way that he does, Cicero suggests that beneficence sprouts from
the native soil of our humanity, not as a result of a particular education or formation or calculation, but because this is what it is to be human. Beneficence
is a human trait, not a Roman one per se. We spontaneously, he argues, strive
to grow the wealth, strength, and ability, and the well-being generally, of our
selves and our fellows, without being taught or told to do so.

Second in his argument for duty, and closely tied to this, Cicero notes that "we take pains to requite this life of man, rendering it safer and wealthier through our deliberations and exertions."[29] English struggles to grasp the subtleties of Cicero's Latin in this passage. He points out that we, by our exertions, strive to improve our lot, which reiterates the main point of the previous argument; however, the important subtlety is found in Cicero's use of the verb *reddere*, which implies a "paying back." We do not shoulder our work on behalf of our fellow man simply because we are kind, but because we are moved by a deep sense of reciprocity. We *owe* our exertions; we owe them to mankind, to our people, to our parents, to our friends, and so forth. Our exertions flow forth as a gift in repayment of a debt, which is the proper response to our *being*, on account of which we care for and cultivate human life. Ultimately, just as in the argument he makes in *De Officiis*, Cicero is getting at the idea that we owe our homeland a particular debt.[30] He reiterates this claim a little later in the same passage by declaring that, "Our fatherland has neither given us birth nor educated us according to law without expecting some nourishment, so to speak, from us."[31] In the course of making this argument, Cicero moves from an observation about the simple character of mankind—beneficence—on to the world (and by implication the cosmos) and its constituent obligations. He establishes that there is scaffolding in our nature that orders our activity to the grateful, or grudging, service of others. But why, one might ask, should we go through the bother of heeding this inclination?

In his final point, Cicero notes, "We are roused to this [wish] by the spur of nature herself."[32] This third part of the argument is the first part of Cicero's argument that is fully developed in our manuscripts. Cicero highlights nature now, but he does so rather curiously. He does not appeal to nature as the ground of order (that is, teleologically), but as a source of compulsion in doing our duty. Nature doesn't simply orient us or draw us, he suggests, but she actually compels us. Cicero's articulation of nature takes a strikingly external character here, being a sort of "strength" or "force" that presses against us (even from within us) to direct us into the course of virtue. As our manuscript text begins after the lacuna, Cicero is appealing to *memoria* and recalling the deeds of several great Romans, including the two Scipios and Marcus Cato. He highlights that "no necessity compelled" Cato to undertake public service, but that "nature has given to the human race such a necessity for virtue and such a love of defending the common safety [*salus*; more broadly, well-being] that this force [*vis*; i.e., nature] will overcome all allurements of pleasure [*voluptatis*] and leisure."[33] Cato was compelled by necessity, then, but it was the necessity of his nature, not of circumstances. To do other than he did would have been unnatural for Cato, and thus inhuman and inappropriate. Cato's dutiful action did not concede to nature, but acceded to it. His actions serve as an example to be followed regardless of our own circumstances.

Here Cicero broaches the central question of *De Republica*: How should a good man live? The answer Cicero gives in the preface, which becomes a significant part of the argument of the work, is that man should live in keeping with his nature, and his nature urges beneficence, duty, and virtue in all that we do. By grappling with this question, Cicero is consciously engaging with the whole tradition of thought that concerns itself with living well, a tradition implicit in any and every philosophical inquiry into the human good and the nature of the good itself. It is a central question for Glaucon in Plato's *Republic*, and necessarily also for Cicero in his *De Republica*. This question is sometimes articulated as a concern over the "best way of life." In his criticisms of the philosophers, Cicero highlights an important difference of perspective regarding the best way of life. There is, indeed, a fundamental tension between the way of life that concerns itself with the human good through prudence and political engagement—the active life, harried and toilsome—and the way of life that concerns itself with seeking knowledge of the good in itself through intellectual engagement, a life engaged in serious reflection—toilsome in its own way—and in leisured conversation; in other words, a contemplative life.

When, after the preface, Cicero begins the dialogue proper and introduces the alleged tension between Socrates and Plato, the tension between these two ways of life will be pushed to the forefront. For now, it's important to see that Cicero has begun laying the groundwork for this conflict already, and from the beginning complicates the question of what is "best" for man by indicating that the necessity that moves men to engage in the active life is not the necessity of troubling circumstance ("that madman [Cato] . . . chose to be tossed about in these waves and storms to an extreme old age—although no necessity compelled him"), but the "necessity of virtue" which is imposed by nature herself.[34] This unity already foreshadows Cicero's ultimate refusal to bifurcate the best way of life into an either/or. Courage and justice are not compelled by necessity, but by our nature, and the best way of life for a human being must be in keeping with our nature. Cicero means what he says in the preface: as Schofield writes, "*On the Commonwealth* begins and ends with argument for the supreme importance of opting for a public life devoted to the service of the commonwealth despite its perils and uncertainties."[35]

ENLISTING THE PHILOSOPHERS

At this point in the book—that is, after the first few pages—Cicero's embrace of the political life as most choiceworthy seems the obvious and necessary conclusion. If we human beings are spontaneously moved to improve our human situation, and we consciously render our service in payment for a debt we feel we owe, and we are moved to do the good despite danger and pain—if these facts sketch out the very scaffolding of our being—then Cicero concludes that those who fortify us in religious observance, in obedience to foreign and domestic law (*ius gentium* and *ius civilis*), in the very principles of right, in continence and nobility, and in acts of virtue must be very great, and indeed the greatest. These men are those who, by "training," "custom," and "laws," shape, confirm, and sanction the right in us.[36] Hence, Cicero argues, "that citizen[37] who compels of all persons, by official command and by penalty of laws, what philosophers by speech can scarcely persuade a few persons [to do], should be given precedence even over the teachers themselves who debate these things."[38] The one who makes laws cultivates good men rather than simply speaking about the good man. Even if the philosophers know anything, Cicero suggests, it is a wasted knowledge, because it is not employed. It is not brought to bear on living. The philosopher is a charlatan; the legislator is the true physician of souls.

Yet, as he draws his preface to its conclusion, Cicero pivots unexpectedly and plucks out a man or two from the ranks of the bedraggled philosophers. What qualifies these select few for Cicero's compliment is that they agree with him and have said useful things about living and governing well. Cicero turns to these philosophers to reveal the error of the many other philosophers. Of course, this was a pre-meditated move: Cicero had already begun to modify his definition of "philosopher" in the course of the preface. In the first reference to philosophers in our extant manuscript, Cicero declares, "the philosophers say nothing—at least of what may be said correctly and honorably—that was [not] accomplished and strengthened by those who have configured laws for cities"—implying that there are in fact things which *are* said "correctly and honorably [*recte honesteque*]" by some philosophers.[39] There are inquiries that are not prattling wastes. But which philosophers are the good ones and which the bad? In concluding thoughts before he begins the dialogue proper, Cicero summons the teaching and examples of "most highly educated men" [*doctissimos homines*] who, despite their lack of experience in political life, fruitfully inquired into political things. Thus, Cicero makes the wise (including some philosophers) allies against the foolish philosophers.[40] Ultimately, Cicero turns to the only philosophers who are worthwhile, in his mind, a distinction which becomes clear as the dialogue commences.

Before he begins the dialogue proper, Cicero gives one final explanation of the nature of his project: "to expound the meaning of political things [Lat. *ratio rerum civilium*]," which was a "kind of reasoning" not "discovered" by him. Given that his book is a self-conscious emulation of Plato's *Republic*, Cicero is likely deferring to Plato here, though Aristotle's influence appears persistently as well. Indeed, as Cicero begins the dialogue by introducing "the most famous and wisest men in our city [*civitatis*] belonging to a single generation," one almost expects him to point to Socrates and Plato, though of course they were not Roman.[41] Cicero must, instead, direct us to their Roman counterparts, Scipio Africanus the Younger and Gaius Laelius Sapiens. These two interlocutors turn out to be Plato and Socrates in Roman dress. His reason for drafting the philosophers into his drama is that Cicero does not, after all, simply wish to give an account of political things. Rather, his design is to root reason deeply in the heart of Roman politics and in Romans themselves.

In his preface, then, Cicero ousted the philosophers from pride of place in Rome and established his own bona fides as a Roman. He did not simply mean to slander the Epicureans, as some might suppose, but philosophers generally. Cleverly, however, in making his assault, he borrowed arguments from the Greeks, stripped off their colors, and redeployed them to inculcate Romans with a mindful, even teleological, defense of duty, honor, and virtue. Ultimately, having rendered Romans reasonable, Cicero redeems a small handful of philosophers to serve as guides, dressed up in togas, in his inquiry in matters concerning the republic.

NOTES

1. Cicero, DRP, 1.12.
2. Cicero, DRP, *1.13.*
3. Cicero, DRP, 1.2.
4. Cicero, DRP, 1.2, 4, 9, 11. Cf. James Zetzel's confirmation of the pejorative use of *iste* (*Selections*, 99).
5. Cicero, DRP, 1.12.
6. Cicero spent more than two years studying under Antiochus and Posidonius (Fott 21).
7. Cicero, DRP, 1.6–7, including the missing biographical material in the unfortunate lacuna.
8. Cicero, DRP, 1.1–2.
9. Cicero, DRP, 1.4, 1.9.
10. Cicero, DRP, 1.14.
11. Cicero, DRP, 6.16; Z6.12.
12. Cicero, DRP, 1.7.
13. Cicero, *Ad Fam.* 1.9
14. Wirzubksi, "*CVM Dignitate Otium*," 2.
15. Wirzubksi, "*CVM Dignitate Otium,*" 5.
16. Wirzubksi, "*CVM Dignitate Otium,*" 13; cf. 4. Cf. *Wood, Social*, 196–99.
17. Cicero, DRP, 1.9.

18. This is Cicero's firm argument in the preface, and I will argue it is a position he maintains throughout *De Republica*. Certainly, Cicero is modulating himself to persuade his audience, and so he is unusually critical of the philosophers, for example. Notwithstanding, he means what he says about the centrality of the political in a fully human life, a center that will unite the practical and theoretical lives.

19. Cicero, DRP, 1.11.

20. Cicero, DRP, 1.12.

21. Cicero, DRP, 1.11.

22. Baraz, *Republic*, 93. See also Atkins, *Politics*, 27.

23. Cicero, DRP, 1.9 and 1.4.

24. Cicero, DRP, 1.2.

25. Cicero, DRP, 1.11.

26. J. G. F. Powell reconstructs the preface somewhat differently, assuming that the summary in DRP 1.3 is only a summary of the point Cicero was making in the portion of the introduction we have (Powell, "Virtues," 19). In terms of my argument that Cicero is slyly booting out the philosophers while stealing their philosophy, it makes little difference whether my view that there are three distinct arguments here is right or wrong. In either case, this summary gives us an indication of Cicero's argument beyond what is in the manuscript.

27. Cicero, DRP, 1.3. This is my translation of the Latin *maxime rapimur ad opes augendas generis humani.*

28. Cicero, DO, 1.12.

29. Cicero, DRP, 1.3; my translation of *studemusque nostris consiliis et laboribus tutiorem et opulentiorem vitam hominum reddere.* I have translated the verb twice in an attempt to capture the shades of meaning in "reddere."

30. Cicero, DO, 1.22, 1.57, 1.158.

31. Cicero, DRP, 1.8.

32. Cicero, DRP, 1.3. Lat. *et ad hanc voluntatem ipsius naturae stimulis incitamur.* This is Fott's translation with one important change, substituting "wish" for "pleasure." I agree with Powell's preference for *voluntatem* rather than *voluptatem*, although Ziegler, Büchner, Zetzel, and Fott all prefer the latter. Their scholarly, majority opinion carries obvious weight, but their preference for "pleasure" follows from Cicero's general delight in needling the Epicureans, in this case perhaps by suggesting that natural pleasure is actually found in duty, not retreat. Their conclusion is eminently reasonable. However, since this sentence is a summary of Cicero's argument concluded in DRP 1.1, and since this translation would contradict that argument both in language and content, it does seem that *voluntatem* (choice, desire, wish) is the better option. In 1.1, Cicero also references the "spur of nature" by saying that "nature will overcome all allurements of pleasure [*voluptatis*]." It would make little sense for Cicero to say that nature will overcome pleasure (*voluptatem*) for the sake of pleasure (*voluptate*).

Apart from this, Cicero often prefers to associate *voluptas* with bodily pleasures and to reserve terms such as *laetitia* for delight in the mind or soul (cf. DRP, 1.7 and *De Finibus*, 2.13–14). It is this sort of soulful delight that Cicero has in view in claiming that we can desire the hardship of duty. An ardent young man who wants to go to war is after a very different sort of thing than when he goes to a bordello. We don't generally feel bodily pleasure in hardship, but we do feel compelled by nature herself to undertake it nonetheless, and are satisfied when we have done so, and this is what Cicero means. Powell's preference for *voluntatem* is more sensible on this score as well.

33. Cicero, DRP, 1.1.

34. Cicero, DRP, 1.1.

35. Schofield, *Cicero*, 64.

36. Cicero, DRP, 1.2.

37. Cicero here makes a first, subtle reference to the "guide" of the republic by noting the central role of a single man, or citizen, in shaping laws and mores. Later in the passage he reverts to referencing "those who are in charge of cities," obscuring the individual reference but not negating it (Cicero, DRP, 1.3).

38. Cicero, DRP, 1.3.

39. Cicero, DRP, 1.2.

40. Cicero, DRP, 1.12. Leo Strauss reasonably takes Cicero to refer to Plato and Aristotle as the wise philosophers, or at least as philosophers who have taken a requisite interest in the study of political things (Strauss, "Transcript," 12–14).

41. Cicero, DRP, 1.13.

Chapter 2

Unifying the Two Ways of Life
De Republica, 1.14–17

At the heart of the concern about how a good man should live are the questions, "What is good?" and "What is good for man?" Cicero's prologue in *De Republica* makes it clear that he understands the potential tension that exists between these two queries. What is good in itself may be high, sublime, and worthy, and yet inaccessible to man due to its subtlety or the imposition of duty or necessity. Thus, requirements of a life lived in pursuit of things divine may make meaningful political engagement or personal commitment to care for human things practically impossible. On the other hand, what is good *for man* involves both noble and mundane things, both the good and the useful, the hard and the utterly pedestrian; but being preoccupied with these things often precludes the opportunity for extended, leisured contemplation. This tension constitutes the dilemma of the two ways of life, since it seems we are required of necessity to make a primary commitment to either the practical or the theoretical way, if we have the means to choose. Since the theoretical way of life emphasizes the work of that part that is distinct and best in man—his intellect—and since its pleasures are so rare, the contemplative life is a particularly compelling choice, though the practical concerns continually impinge on it.

With his prefatory work done—Cicero has ostensibly banished the philosophers and promised to give a thoroughly practical teaching on how to found and maintain republics—Cicero commences the action of the dialogue. He introduces it with a brief prologue between two characters, an exchange that turns out to serve as a frame for the rest of the book. This frame beckons our attention to the critical lens through which Cicero would have us read his dialogue, which is the tension between the theoretical and practical lives, a problem raised by the paradoxical appearance of twin suns. The best way to understand Cicero's argument is through a careful reading of the prologue, a consideration of the problem of the two ways of life, and weighing scholarly perspectives on Cicero's own mind on the matter. Ultimately, the best way of describing Cicero's thinking on the matter is that the two ways of life are really alternating centers of a single, unified life.

HISTORICITY AND MEANING IN CICERO'S FRAMING OF DIALOGUES

Cicero's attention to historical and dramatic detail were often painstaking, which we see in the historical setting he sketches for the conversation in *De Republica*, including a specific time (the three days of the Latin holiday)[1] and place (Scipio's home just outside of Rome). Indeed, Cicero's letters contain a number of requests from friends to do research to provide him with the correct historical details in his argument. His concern for accuracy is not merely historical, but also dramatic: when he writes his book *On Old Age*, a self-conscious emulation of Socrates' conversation with Cephalus in the first part of Plato's *Republic*, Cicero notes that Plato had Cephalus retire from the conversation because it would have been unnatural for Cephalus to linger in the long dialogue due to his old age;[2] consequently, Cicero changes the setting in his *De Senectute* to preserve the dramatic integrity of the extended conversation between Cato (his Cephalus) and Scipio and Laelius.[3] All of this suggests that we can consider many elements of *De Republica* to be reliable.

On the other hand, Cicero did not find it necessary to be so punctilious in every aspect in composing his dialogues. He was more than willing to attribute opinions and comments to the authority of men who likely did not express or hold them. James Zetzel, in his partial commentary, remarks flatly that "there is no reason to believe that anything said in [*De*] *Rep*[*ublica*] is an accurate reflection of anything ever said by any of the participants."[4] Cicero scandalized Marcus Junius Brutus by writing a dialogue bearing Brutus' name, with Brutus as the main character, in which Brutus expressed opinions he himself rather disagreed with. In response, Cicero tried to assure Brutus that this was not an unusual way of proceeding.[5] This haphazard approach to historicity could be disorienting if we assumed that Cicero's primary object was simply to, as he says, "recall to memory and argument among the most famous and wisest men in our city."[6] However, Cicero's mode is anything but haphazard. He is painstakingly deliberate both in terms of the facts he is faithful to and in how, and why, he departs from the facts simply.

Despite Cicero's assertion that he is recounting a historical conversation, the first moments of the dialogue are particularly likely to be ahistorical. Cicero professes to be recounting a story he heard from Publius Rutilius Rufus, a man who had participated in that conversation some thirty or forty years prior. However, as the dialogue opens and Publius Scipio Africanus is roused at dawn by the arrival of Quintus Tubero, his nephew, it is notable that our reporter, Rutilius, is conspicuously absent. Rutilius is one of the next two interlocutors to arrive, but only after Scipio tells his nephew Tubero in confidence that he does not particularly esteem purely theoretical inquiry. Given that Scipio himself becomes the great champion of theoretical inquiry in the next few pages of the dialogue, this private revelation is very significant. The necessary ahistoricity of these opening comments only serves to underscore the importance of this moment in understanding the dialogue.[7] Indeed, a number of the details we will encounter—the time of day, the location, the change in location, the order of arrival of each character and the number of them, the choices of characters to sit or stand or walk, not to mention the subject of their conversations—play a part in Cicero's literary composition.[8]

THE PROLOGUE AND THE WAYS
OF SOCRATES AND PLATO

When Scipio awakens early in the morning on the first day of the Latin holiday, he soon receives his nephew Tubero, who wastes little time in asking Scipio to reflect with him on the meaning of the appearance of the "second sun" which had reportedly been seen. The phenomenon drew the attention of the Roman Senate, and apparently much consideration was being given to its meaning. Scipio responds, but not about the second sun. Rather, he discusses the people who inquire into such things, by which Scipio sets up the problem of the two lives for us: he remarks that he wishes the wise natural philosopher Panaetius were present to illuminate the matter, but then, in confidence (Lat. *aperte*), turns and avers that the Socratic concern for "human reason" and "human life," as opposed to things divine, was "wiser" and more worthy.[9] Tubero is not initially impressed by this characterization of Socrates, noting that the old Athenian was well known for engaging in many theoretical reflections. In response, Scipio only reasserts his claim: the real, historical Socrates was concerned with practical questions relating to human action—in other words, he was convinced that the best way of life was concerned with right action—and that it was Plato, overawed by the esoteric teachings of Pythagoras, who had placed those theoretical teachings in Socrates' mouth in order to honor him.[10]

Tubero's objection and Scipio's clarification draw our attention to the significance of the distinction between a life dedicated to practical concerns in contrast with one dedicated to inquiry into the theoretical. Scipio's Socrates concerns himself with how to act well, and his interest in the nature of things and in matters divine is either non-existent or, at best, derives from his interest in human things. What ought to concern us, according to this Socrates, is simply our proper conduct in the present moment. He is concerned with what is good and bad. Scipio's Plato, however, upholds contemplation of the Good itself as a superior endeavor, thus choosing in favor of the contemplative life. Hence, Plato and Pythagoras, along with Panaetius, have charted a different course from Socrates, according to Scipio. They have not pursued human things, but divine things; they are not primarily concerned with right action and what is good and bad, but with knowledge regarding what is true and false, which may have bearing on their action, but this practical consequence is ultimately incidental to their pursuit of the truth. Whereas Socrates turns to what is primarily practical, then, the Platonic bent is primarily theoretical. (If this distinction is true and these live are irreconcilable, one might wonder how precisely Plato meant to honor Socrates by putting these teachings in his mouth, as Scipio said.) This distinction between Socrates and Plato at the beginning of *De Republica* lays the foundation for an investigation into the primacy of the active and contemplative lives which, as Leo Strauss says, "is the subject which keeps the whole book moving."[11]

THE QUESTION OF THE ACTIVE
AND CONTEMPLATIVE LIVES

Cicero believes himself to be an acolyte of the Old Academy vis-à-vis the New, and so he inherits and must grapple with their fundamental debate regarding the best way of life. Platonic and Aristotelian writings affirm the good of the life of virtue, but also indicate that some virtues involve higher goods than others. Is there a good or a virtue which the good man should pursue in particular, or a good—whether justice or the Good itself—which man should prioritize above all others? There is a difficulty in that two different goods seem to claim our total allegiance. The classical distinction comes down to whether the active life or the contemplative life is superior, the active life being characterized by the noble pursuit of justice and the contemplative life being committed to the divine pursuit of wisdom. As Leo Strauss asserts, the active life "means the life *dedicated* to action. And that is in the highest form the life of the statesman, the political life in the fullest sense,"[12] whereas the contemplative life is dedicated to something "still higher," and is embodied in "the theoretical life, or the philosophic life."[13] Necessarily, these lives depend on one another: one cannot properly pursue justice without wisdom's guidance in knowing what is just, and the pursuit of wisdom depends on the leisure and education made possible by the peace, wealth, and amity that just legislation affords. Yet, the intelligent man is necessarily confronted with the question of which way—justice or wisdom—is most choice-worthy, as there is presumably only one summum bonum by definition. Hence, we should all feel pressed to answer the question of which activity we ought most zealously embrace. Our answer to this question becomes the answer to the question of the best way of life, for Cicero as well as for us.

The theoretical (or, philosophical or contemplative) way of life recommends itself as being the best way of life in two important ways. First, the contemplative life seems best due to the value of the object of its study since it is concerned with things divine, being an investigation by the divine in man (our reason) or the divine mind which ordered the universe. Cicero writes that philosophy pursues knowledge of "the ultimate and final goal, to which all our deliberations on living well and acting rightly should be directed."[14] In the Platonic and Aristotelian traditions that greatest good is found at the height of the hierarchy of Being, which is Being itself, or "Mind," or the god. Man's participation in this divine reality and our apprehension of its order is generally called wisdom and is understandably said to be the highest and best, both in man and in itself.[15] The "good" flows from what is divinely ordered, and so contemplation is the characteristic of the truly wise man, the one who knows what is true and therefore truly good.

Second, this encounter with the true and the good recommends itself as being the object of the best way of life because it gives rise to a wonder and delight which is the rarest of pleasures, arising not from the senses or body but from the mind. Strauss draws our attention to Aristotle's discussion of *kalon* in the *Rhetoric*, in which he notes that a flower might be "beautiful" because of its sight and smell, but that there is a quality beyond this—beyond its color—that makes it delightful, something we could call the sublime.[16] As Cicero himself declares, "To tire of the search [for wisdom] is disgraceful given that its object is so beautiful [*pulcherrimum*]."[17] Even more forcefully, Cicero—or the character Cicero—notes in the *Tusculan Disputations* that "it is clear that a happy life consists in perpetual and unexhausted pleasures [*gaudiis*],"[18] a sentiment which Aristotle straightforwardly declares as well.[19] If the activity of the mind is the unique capacity of man among the animals, and thus the distinguishing part of him, then the contemplative life is that life which seems most particularly to accord with his nature. The goodness and delight of the contemplative way of life therefore recommend it as the best way of life. Of course, if this is true—if Cicero thinks it is true—then Cicero outrageously misled his audience in *De Republica*'s bold opening defense of the political life.

VARIOUS PERSPECTIVES ON THE ACTIVE
AND CONTEMPLATIVE LIVES IN CICERO

If the inquiry into how a good man should live stands at the center of *De Republica*, Cicero's preface seems assertively to side with the practical way of life. Some commentators, such as N. Wood, take this to be his obvious conclusion, setting aside a few comments "during his last, inactive years."[20] Problematically, Cicero comments in other writings, and subsequent developments in *De Republica* suggest, the possibility that his true allegiance actually lies with the superiority of the contemplative life. Strauss ultimately conceives of Cicero's writing in *De Republica* as an implicit attempt to grapple with the distinction between the two best ways of life and, for his utilitarian-minded Roman audience, to undertake "a gradual rehabilitation of theoretical philosophy."[21] Although Strauss, in his lectures on Cicero in 1959, could not reach a conclusion on Cicero's commitment to one way of life over another, Strauss himself suggests that "[t]here is no question" of the "superiority" of the contemplative life, and his readers have disagreed on Cicero's opinion on the matter.[22] It would seem that there are five logical possibilities:

a. Cicero unabashedly embraces the exclusive claim of the contemplative life
b. Cicero unabashedly embraces the exclusive claim of the practical life
c. Cicero vacillates between the superiority of one or the other life
d. Cicero believes contemplation is the best way of life but that the demands of necessity largely supersede its enjoyment
e. Cicero believes that the complete life involves a unity of contemplation and action, each exercised as appropriate in alternating modes

Of these options, the first two seem generally untenable. The fact that Cicero makes a number of statements on either side of this debate suggest he did not clearly embrace or reject either the contemplative or practical lives simply; it is why his opinion on the matter is a question at all. Even when "addressing a most sympathetic audience," Baraz notes, Cicero refuses "to wholeheartedly follow the line of thought that champions philosophy, and intellectual pursuits more generally, to the exclusion of engagement in politics,"[23] but explores the tense space between them. It is the latter three possibilities, then, that deserve further consideration.

The vacillation thesis is supported by Carlos Lévy's analysis of Cicero's varying attitudes in his writings and letters throughout his long career. Rather than coming down on one side or another, Lévy argues that "Cicero continually evolved through the ways of justifying his choice or, more exactly, his absence of choice."[24] In the course of laying out the evidence, he cites examples from Cicero's letters and his dialogues.[25] He concludes by noting that despite the inestimable attraction of the life of philosophic *otium*, or leisure, Cicero could not shake "the profound belief in the superiority of practical life over a purely theoretical life."[26] Lévy's argument supports the idea that Cicero's will, at least, vacillated between these two ways of life, and that his mind was not made up enough about the superiority of one over the other to make an exclusive commitment. Lévy's argument is plausible and creditable, though, as Schofield notes, it is more truthful to see a fundamental continuity between Cicero's political thinking and his philosophical thinking over the course of his life.[27] The matter admits of some dispute, but there is good reason to believe that Cicero's wrestling with this tension was not entirely fruitless. As Baraz suggests, "the production of the treatises . . . reflects his desire to reject the divisive view and bring the two spheres, politics and philosophy, together in a harmonious whole."[28] Although his emphasis in favor of philosophy or politics changes over the course of his life, Baraz notes that he possessed "different personae" as "a statesman, an orator, a philosopher, an *amicus*," but that one or another persona might dominate in a particular work. His vacillation is a matter of presentation, then, but not hesitation.[29] Thus, an explanation that demonstrated consistency in Cicero's thought throughout his authorial life would be more satisfying, and both of the final possibilities present such a resolution.

Walter Nicgorski ably defends the thesis that Cicero believed that the life of contemplation was best but that, according to Cicero, moral duty compels us to attend to justice and political necessity first. As a way of life, then, very few of us may rightly commit ourselves to theoretical inquiry. Nicgorski, who has made remarkable contributions to Cicero studies in the last several decades, helpfully notes that there is an extensive history of dismissing Cicero as a philosophical thinker in his own right, based in part on his zealous entrance into the political fray. Very often, these criticisms dismiss his philosophical works as derivative or hackneyed, as merely second-rate philosophy. Nicgorski rightly notes that these criticisms amount to a tacit claim that the life of the practical man and the contemplative man are incompatible: according to the critics, we are supposed to consider Cicero's life "a warning to those who would seek to bridge unbridgeable chasms."[30] Yet Cicero himself, Nicgorski writes, would have thought that his political career gave him a unique insight into things *malorum et bonorum*, things good and bad, such that "the perspective of practice and of the greatest practice, statesmanship, is an advantaged perspective, the basis for a true philosophy of life insofar as man can attain that."[31] Strauss wants to identify the theoretic Scipio with Cicero in *De Republica*, and insistently downplays Laelius' significance, but Nicgorski questions these moves.[32] Instead, he argues that "Cicero was convinced of the overall harmony of man's setting, that he took his bearings from the practical perspective and made his judgments in the speculative realm in accord with that perspective."[33] Nicgorski's arguments, thus far, support the view that Cicero believed there was a symbiotic harmony between action and contemplation.

In his tremendous latest work on Cicero, Nicgorski provides a much more analytical dissection of the relationship between theory and practice in Cicero's thought, concluding that Cicero believes that wisdom compels us to prioritize an immediate duty of justice over a life of contemplation generally.[34] In Nicgorski's estimation Cicero accepts the Platonic and Aristotelian conclusion that "wisdom is the greatest of the virtues," suggesting that Cicero agrees with them that "philosophy for its own sake—search and contemplation—was the highest human activity."[35] Nevertheless, in the course of life, wisdom persistently directs us to the priorities outlined by duty, and by justice in particular. In reaching this conclusion, Nicgorski leans heavily on Cicero's argument in *De Officiis* that the virtues may be ranked—indeed, must be ranked—to properly discern our duty in any given moment.[36] In arguing that justice and the virtues related to duty take priority over the private pursuit of wisdom, Nicgorski does not mean the "wisdom" preferred by Scipio's Socrates, who desired to know about things good and bad for men, but rather the pursuit of wisdom regarding celestial and superhuman things, the knowledge preferred by Scipio's Pythagorean Plato. This ethereal and abstract wisdom, Nicgorski writes, which is in fact the highest and most worthwhile, may be pursued *as a way of life* only "after all public tasks have been completed or in the life after death."[37] Hence, "the usual human condition" makes the theoretical way of life nearly impossible because it is impractical and would constitute an abnegation of duty, not to mention of justice, moderation, and fortitude.[38] Nicgorski clearly believes that wisdom and philosophic inquiry are a part of the complete life, but the active life claims the lion's share of one's time and attention, and duty lays claim to all of able mind and body. Thus, he goes further than Lévy's vacillation thesis, emphasizing the active life of virtue as an imposition of necessity that supersedes the activity and enjoyment of the much-preferred contemplative way of life. In making his argument, Nicgorski gestures toward the possibility of a unified way of life, but in the final analysis he determines that the practical and theoretical lives are basically incompatible. Hence, we must dutifully attend to justice until, one day, death or social irrelevance free us to live the contemplative life.

THE UNITY OF THE TWO WAYS OF LIFE

Cicero's writings, I contend, allow for another possibility, one of the unity of the active and contemplative ways of life, and that these two need not be so divorced in reality as theory might suggest. Before detailing this argument, there is an immediate objection that should be addressed. If Cicero believes that the complete life involved persevering action seasoned by the contemplative pursuit of wisdom—which is undertaken for its own sake, and not for its benefit to the republic—then why does he argue for a general subordination of wisdom to justice in *De Officiis*? E. M. Atkins is right in summarizing *De Officiis'* argument "that the wise man must never allow his interest in theoretical problems to distract him from his service to society."[39] However, we must not misconstrue this to mean that pursuing wisdom contemplatively is somehow not fitting for political man, which is to say, for all men: it is, in the end, indispensable, in proportion. In writing *De Officiis*, Cicero crafted a book of advice to young men in a pedagogically-Stoic voice, one which seeks to make exactly clear the ordering of virtues and duties. His aim is to clarify "middle duty" (*medium officium*), the "semblances of the honourable" that is attainable to "many" who will strive to attain it.[40] Cicero periodically stresses, however, that his guidance to virtuous action is not the same as genuine virtue, and he warns his readers not to presume to emulate the wise, whose "goodness" guides them into ways we are not guided.[41] Rather, the young must learn to be virtuous and wise by performing, as actors, virtuous acts they may only partly understand, and the rigid subordination of duties helps them hit the mark in most circumstances. However, the rule for the young does not prescribe right for the wise or the prudent. Nicgorski aptly identifies Cicero's emphasis on the priority of duty and of the active life, but I believe it is important to go further than this and not to downplay the persistent role of contemplation in the complete life. Cicero means it when he declares in *De Officiis* that it is "contrary to duty to be drawn by such a devotion [to wisdom] away from practical achievements," but he goes on to note that "there is often a break from [duty], and we are given many opportunities to return to our studies."[42] At such times—at the appropriate time—it is our duty to apply ourselves to the pursuit of wisdom. In alternating modes, both activity and contemplation find their regular place in the complete, and good, life.

Indeed, the Ciceronian statesman cannot afford to ignore contemplation; he must engage in theoretical inquiry as a matter of course. Throughout his writing, Cicero prioritizes the dutiful, active life, but he also persistently directs our gaze to active men with contemplative spirits, men like Scipio who will philosophize "even under the walls of Numantia."[43] Such men prove indispensable to Cicero's vision of a just republic: it turns out that the most effective men in Cicero's telling of Roman politics are often characterized by a commitment to theoretical inquiry. It is true, as Nicgorski points out, that many of our duties do not rely on philosophic or contemplative insight, because of the insights of prudence are pre-philosophic. Nature has "endowed us . . . with certain indications and instruments with which we might seek to know duties more specific than the general injunction to live according to nature."[44] Most men know what to do most of the time without the intervention of philosophy. Still, it is also true that it can be hard to know the things of nature—or anything at all—with certainty or clarity, and yet men often hold beliefs with a great deal more conviction than the facts would justify. People often opine about things in the heavens and on earth with unwarranted confidence, and sometimes this can lead to dreadful errors. In the end, indeed, it can lead to living a life in pursuit of a happiness that is not really happiness at all, or justice that is not just at all. For this reason, while living well does not require comprehensive knowledge of things beyond our ordinary experience, it does, at the very least, require that our knowledge of such things not be deeply distorted. Misunderstanding our cosmic home can readily confuse our understanding of our duty, and this means that the seriously practical man can least of all afford to forego meaningful theoretical inquiry.[45] *De Republica* thus represents a continued development of a critical line of thought in Cicero's writing, as Yelena Baraz points out: in noting that as early as 59 BC, Cicero began to frame the active and contemplative lives as each rooted in a philosophical ground: "Cicero is no longer conceived of his options as political versus the intellectual, but as a decision between two philosophical approaches."[46] The good man, in other words, may not forego a philosophically-grounded existence; the only question is whether reason counsels the exclusive pursuit of one commitment or the other.

To look to a particular incident Cicero highlights, when a band of Roman soldiers were encamped in Macedonia, they were terrified by the ominous and "sudden eclipse of the bright, full moon," not because it threatened them in any imminent sense, but because eclipses in their mind portended looming misfortune. In this instance, the consul Gaius Sulpicius Gallus was able to allay his soldiers' fears because his knowledge of heavenly and divine things—a branch of natural philosophy associated in the dialogue with the theory-minded Panaetius, Plato, and Pythagoras[47]—allowed him to explain the natural motions of heavenly spheres and the benign cause of lunar eclipses.[48] While knowledge of duty might, for some, be had without philosophy, this example suggests that it is perilous to bracket out knowledge of theoretical things from the life of duty. Indeed, the dialogue in *De Republica*, which begins with confusion surrounding the appearance of a second sun and its meaning, concludes with the memorable Dream of Scipio and its Platonic doctrine of the immortality of the soul, a dramatic piece of philosophical literature about matters highly theoretical, yet highly relevant to living well. To reiterate the point, practical men, to be effective, must be equipped with the kind of insight into the nature of things that only personal, contemplative inquiry can supply.

Ultimately, Cicero's unification of the two ways of life follows from his rather eclectic understanding of the human good and human happiness. He believed that the complete life involved both the goods of contemplation and practice as genuine goods. For the uninitiated, this claim may seem unremarkable. What it involves is the question of what happiness really is, which necessarily flows from the fact of what a man really is, since we are concerned with happiness for men. Differences of opinion in this matter led to fundamental distinctions between the philosophical schools. For the Epicurean, for example, a man is a body, and so happiness is simply the greatest pleasure of the body.[49] For the Stoic, a man is a soul regrettably enmeshed in a body, and so happiness is the perfection of the soul through virtue; virtue, for the Stoic, would involve making use of the body, but in its perfection would disentangle the soul from the body, becoming apathetic to the tickling of its sundry nubs.[50] But as we see in his cross examination in *De Finibus*, Cicero finds both of these views substantially dissatisfying and he prefers to reject the either/or.

Is human happiness a matter of body or soul in Cicero's view? A test case he sometimes appeals to in his writing is the Bull of Phalaris, a torture device contrived by Phalaris of Acragas. The unfortunate victim would be locked into the hollow, bronze bull which would then be heated by fire; the victim, beginning to cook to death inside the bull, would animate the bull with steam and screams pouring out of its nostrils and mouth.[51] On the one hand, the Epicurean would not hesitate to admit that the man being cooked must be remarkably unhappy; the Stoic, on the other hand, would hold that happiness consists in the perfection of the soul through virtue and that the happiness of any man could not actually be diminished, even a little bit, by being cruelly roasted alive. Now, while Cicero had an extraordinary respect for the Stoic teaching on virtue, as well as admiration for a man like Cato who disregarded the needs of the body on account of his virtue, his own position is more nuanced and, perhaps, more sensible.

Cicero understands happiness to involve both the goods of body and soul as actual goods. One way to unpack his perspective is to consider his peculiar emphasis on man's social nature. Society for Cicero is not merely a means to some other personal or individual end; society is not the contractual product of idiosyncratically beneficial arrangements. This is a conviction that Cicero emphasizes in a variety of ways. It is present in his preface to *De Republica*, in which he suggests that men come together naturally, and it is present in his powerful reminders in *De Officiis* that we do not belong to ourselves, but that "our country claims for itself one part of our birth, and our friends another. . . . [M]en are born for the sake of men, so that they may be able to assist one another."[52] This may seem at odds with the priority given in the Dream of Scipio to the cosmic perspective which emphatically downgrades the significance of human accomplishments. In the Dream of Scipio, Scipio's adopted grandfather tells him that "the mind of each person is each person," and that man's destiny (if he is deserving) is to be drawn back to the "home" of mind itself.[53] Scipio is also told, however, by his father Paullus, that "the god" (the mind) has seen fit to incarnate "a soul" on Earth that "they may protect that globe." This charge means that "all pious persons" should not "flee the human task assigned by the god."[54] Although the cosmic perspective is what strikes most readers about the Dream—in fact, it is meant to—Cicero did not want us to suppose that our divine pedigree in some way relieved us from our duty to terrestrial work. That would be the opposite of what he hoped to teach. The god has its purposes; piety directs our care and attention accordingly into the way of concern for the well-being of human things. Humanly speaking, bodily goods really are good; soulfully speaking (from the perspective of animus and the god), the activity of the soul requires things to be active about, and involves a seriousness about goods both human and divine, leading to Cicero's comment that "the wisdom I declare to be the foremost is the knowledge of all things human and divine."[55] Whereas Epicureans, Stoics, and the other systematizers demand the clarity of an "either/or" with respect to the exclusive priority of the goods of the body or of the soul, Cicero's Academic skepticism refuses to take a hard line: he perceives that reality stubbornly insists on the incidental or accidental good of a diverse variety of things, and although philosophy and reason help him generally clarify the right relationship of those goods, he will not discount any of them.

Cicero himself articulates this view of happiness and of man at the end of *De Finibus*. Cicero's *De Finibus* consists of a consideration and refutation of Epicurean ideas (Books 1 and 2), a consideration and refutation of Stoic teaching (Books 3 and 4), and finally a consideration and *modification* of Peripatetic teaching (Book 5). It is notable that there is no sixth book in *De Finibus*, no separate refutation of Peripatetic ideas. This is because Cicero has a substantial disagreement with both the Epicurean and Stoic philosophic systems, but his critique of the Peripatetics is essentially verbal. The Peripatetics insist that virtue is primarily responsible for happiness, such that the virtuous man is necessarily happy; they allow, however, that the "happiest" life is enabled by the good things associated with a pleasant life—friends, leisure, peace, health, and so forth—and that these things are therefore "preferable," though not actually important to happiness. The lack of them does not constitute a genuine "evil" that would compromise anyone's ability to be happy. In the dialogue, Cicero criticizes this view as irrationally dogmatic since it requires defending the rather farcical conclusion that "a wise person who is blind, disabled, suffering the gravest illness, in exile, childless, needy, and being tortured on the rack" is nevertheless happy, just not the very happiest.[56] Although Cicero credits virtue with the greatest share of man's happiness—and it is important not to understate the degree to which virtue is essential—he insists on calling "all the other things that are in accordance with nature 'goods,'" including both goods of the body and the soul.[57] Those things which the soul finds pleasant apart from the delight of intellection are also good, as well as things pleasant to the body; in some small proportion they make up a real part of the human good with which a virtuous man is concerned. The work of care for the body and the soul is a proper part of man's work, then, not on account of necessity, not because the body is useful, but because it is right. The duty counseled by reason is not *necessarily* a concession to necessity. It is, simply, proper to man to engage in work to cultivate practical goods according to nature when it is appropriate for him to do so.

It is precisely because the goods of the soul and body matter, however, that the ethical life must be characterized by continuous, meaningful contemplative activity. The care we supply to affairs in our cities and our families, and to the gods and our friends, necessarily depends on our understanding of what is good for them and what our duties are. Hence, reflection and consideration of the nature of man and his obligations are responsibilities inherent in the practical life. We discover this unification of the theoretical and the practical in the spontaneous impulse all men share that the law (a practical thing) should be directed by justice (a theoretical thing). As goods of the soul and the body both belong to happiness, contemplating to the neglect of them would be irresponsible. If one's contemplation needlessly resulted in neglect of his health or his family or estate, it would be appropriate for him to attend more diligently to practical matters than theoretical ones. If it is true that goods of the soul and body are a part of happiness, it is responsible to set aside the appropriate time for them, and not merely as a concession to necessity, but because such apt, considerate attention is the choice-worthy thing in each case.

If a complete life involves both practice and contemplation, what is the proper proportion of contemplating and acting? Whether or not contemplation provides the greatest part of happiness, it is not clear that leisured inquiry must or should be the greatest part of man's activity. Goods of the soul and body are incommensurable with the good of contemplation in the sense that one "unit" of contemplation cannot be equated, say, with ten "units" of moral virtue. It does not stand to reason that, if inquiry is the most divine use of man's faculty which produces the greatest delight, the happiest life will be divided into leisure and work according to some set ratio. The contribution of leisure to one's happiness is not measured by a quota. Presumably, for the happy man, since virtue is the greatest part of happiness and wisdom is the greatest part of virtue, contemplation will be characteristic of his life, but this does not necessitate its exclusive dominion of his time and effort. The truly wise man will also be a working man, and quite possibly a statesman. Nature dictates to Cicero that bodily and external goods make up some real part of happiness, and the sustenance of these goods requires ordinate attention, even if that attention is considerable. This effort is not inordinate so long as it does not evict the good of timely contemplation from one's life.[58]

A final indication from *De Finibus* that corroborates this idea is a claim made in defense of the Peripatetic system that Cicero tacitly endorses. Piso, the defender of the Peripatetics, in discussing which activity is best, argues that "we are born to act," but that we must not "lose sight of . . . the important ones."[59] He then goes on to identify three activities as "most important," listing but not ranking them: contemplation, through reason, of unchanging things; political theory and practice; and virtue generally, or *honestum*.[60] Each element in the list has something appropriate to man, and it is notable that each of these activities represents a component of the famous classical trifecta, the true (contemplation), the good (political theory and practice), and the beautiful or noble (*honestum*). Cicero gives no indication that a life without any one of them would be complete, good, or even sufficient for man.

If political life—and more mundane activities besides—is also the proper concern of the happy man, and these things are not merely concessions to necessity, it is nevertheless the case that necessity can and will demand inordinate attention, more in some times than others and more from some people than others. Given difficult times, the amount of attention required for the proper care of these things might obscure the possibility of leisure and contemplation. In these circumstances, Nicgorski's thesis about the practical priority of duty would be sensible: moral duty (that is, *honestum*, virtue itself) may dictate that just political action must take priority over leisurely contemplation, perhaps to its exclusion. Nevertheless, history suggests that men do enjoy reprieves from dire times, as is suggested by Cicero's own occasional writing while under intense political pressure and the alleged philosophizing Scipio undertook during his siege of Numantia.[61] Such impositions will be frustrating, and one suspects that in the ordinary course of things the vicissitudes of fortune mean that human life permanently borders on this condition. It does not mean, however, that practical activity is always a concession to necessity: it is good in itself, and the complete human life is properly engaged in practical and theoretical activity in proportionate, alternating, and overlapping modes.

SCIPIO'S FALSE DISTINCTION BETWEEN THE LIVES

In sum, the distinction between the active and contemplative lives that Scipio refers to in the prologue, and which Strauss believes propels the whole dialogue, is not ultimately as stubborn as Scipio suggests. Having had Scipio make this distinction, and using it as a lever to pry apart the two lives, it is highly doubtful that Cicero believes the distinction between Socrates and Plato to be as significant as Scipio asserts. The Scipionic distinction between Socrates and Plato has several parts: first, the claim that the historical Socrates neglected or rejected Pythagorean theorizing; second, that Plato adopted Pythagorean teaching and attributed it to Socrates; third, and most importantly, that this somehow compromised the Socratic endeavor such that Socrates and Plato are now in tension, or simply at odds. This tension ostensibly exists not only because of the Platonic turn from the active to the contemplative way of life, but because of the epistemic certainty implied in the Pythagorean way[62] in contrast to the Socratic profession of ignorance rooted in his commitment to inquiry.

With respect to the first two points, it is relatively clear that Cicero believed that Socrates rejected Pythagorean teaching and that Plato had not. That Cicero likely thought this to be the case is attested by its repetition in disconnected dialogues. The same claim is made in *De Finibus* by Piso, for example, without objection from Cicero, whose younger self is present in the conversation.[63] As Piso asserts, Socrates considered the happy life to consist of virtue, though Plato pursued the happy life through the investigation of the Pythagorean system which Socrates had "scorned."[64] The important question is whether Cicero considered this parting of ways to have driven a wedge between these two, such that any association of them in one academy would be incoherent and incorrect. The difficulty only holds if the distinction is understood to be one between Socratic skepticism and Platonic dogmatism, which Scipio implies in his initial conversation with Tubero but which is not Cicero's opinion. Rather than affirming the Scipionic assertion elsewhere, however, Cicero belies it. In the prologue, then, Scipio was simply presenting an opinion with which Cicero did not agree; at least, we are mistaken if we understand Scipio to be saying that Plato was dogmatic in adopting certain Pythagorean conclusions. As we shall see, this is an opinion which Scipio himself does not agree with either. Cicero does not relegate either the contemplative or the active life to a secondary role; indeed, he ultimately rejects the fundamental distinction.

Cicero does present us with the choice between the practical and theoretical lives, but he presents it as a false dilemma. Rather, the two ways are interdependent and both needful for the man who wishes to honor that which is good, a unified pursuit that is more choice-worthy than a life that affirms one good at the expense of the other. The practical and the theoretical mutually inform each other. The legislator needs to know what is just to make a good law, on the one hand; on the other, it is only through seeking justice in particular circumstances that one becomes able to see justice at all. Cicero affirms the classical claim that knowledge of the universal comes through an encounter with the particular, and so it is true that the legislator both does the good (a commendable thing) and is best able to know what it is when he pauses for leisured reflection (which too is commendable).

Thus, Cicero maintains an unexpected commitment to the dignity of soul and body as good, defending the conviction that the things that afflict soul and body are both genuine evils. Rather than join the Epicurean emphasis on the body, or simply embrace the Stoic emphasis on the perfection of the soul (which he does greatly appreciate), Cicero seems to affirm in works as diverse as *De Republica* and *De Finibus* that to these goods is due their proper care. Consequently, the ethical takes a necessary priority in Cicero's philosophy, since considering the good in abstract from the whole human person would necessarily neglect genuine goods. Surely there is delight in philosophy, and a delight worthy to be sought even if it means suffering "worry, anxiety, and sleeplessness";[65] nevertheless, the sublimity of this pleasure does not justify a reckless disregard for the genuine goods of soul and body. The pursuit of contemplative euphoria could not justify a life of ethical neglect or indifference.

To critics who insist that Cicero takes the two ways of life to be irreconcilable, Cicero might simply respond, as he often does, that he holds to the New Academy, and somewhat eclectically affirms what he thinks probable and refuses to affirm what is improbable. He is not systematic, but at least he is not forced by logical inference to affirm what is absurd from imperfect premises. Ever the unsystematic philosopher, Cicero holds whatever is most sensible as most probable, affirming whatever comports best with experience sifted by reason's insight. Rhetorically, this posture served as Cicero's guide in his preface to Book 1. Rather than imitate Plato, in which an abstract inquiry into "justice" leads to the proposal of a number of rather inhuman laws, Cicero appeals to the practical, emphasizing the priority of the practice of law leading to an inquiry into justice. In doing so, Cicero downgrades the philosophers and their systems, both in a rhetorical recovery of Roman nobility and virility and as part of his attempt to provide for his Roman readers a course of treatment that would properly revivify duty and illuminate how a good man should live.

NOTES

1. J. Atkins notes that both Cicero's *De Republica* and Plato's *Republic* are set during religious festivals in times past when the author was not himself present (*Politics*, 24).

2. Cicero, *Letters to Atticus,* IV.16.

3. Cp. Robert Jones: "Cicero's requests in his letters for specific factual details necessary to the dialogues he was writing (*Ad Att.*, XII, 20) and his criticism of Curio's anachronism (*Brutus*, 218–19) indicate that he was careful to avoid anachronisms in his dialogues" (Jones, "Accuracy," 307).

4. Zetzel, *Selections*, 12.

5. Jones, "Accuracy," 321–22.

6. Cicero, DRP, 1.13.

7. Going much farther than this—but reasonably so—Matthew Fox comments that Cicero's "appeal to a historical authority . . . establishes a genealogy that is obviously spurious," concluding that the dialogue is a "fictionalized past" (Fox, *History*, 89–90).

8. Matthew Fox refers to this as "evidently extraneous, but nonetheless significant, banter. . . . " highlighting its presumptive importance but making no comment about what that import might be (Fox, *History*, 91).

9. Cicero, DRP, 1.15.

10. Cicero, DRP, 1.16.

11. Strauss, "Transcript," 16–17.

12. Strauss, "Transcript," 5; *emphasis in original.*

13. Strauss, "Transcript," 6.

14. Cicero, DF, 1.11.

15. Cf. Lovejoy, *Great Chain*, 42–45.

16. Strauss, "Transcript," 241; Aristotle, *Rhetoric*, 1.6–7.

17. Cicero, DF, 1.3.

18. Cicero, TD, 5.67. *Gaudiis* might be better rendered as "joys."

19. "What was said before fits well now too, for what is proper to each is by nature most excellent and most pleasant for each. And so for a human being, this is the life that accords with the intellect, if in fact this especially *is* a human being. This life, therefore, is also the happiest" (Aristotle, *Nicomachean Ethics,* 1178a).

20. Wood, *Social*, 122.

21. Strauss, "Transcript," 20.

22. Strauss, "Transcript," 318, 285.

23. Baraz, *Republic*, 76.

24. Carlos Lévy, "versus," 59.

25. Most particularly Cicero's *Letters to Atticus* 2.5 and 2.16. In the first letter, Cicero concludes his letter about political affairs in Rome and his shortcomings in writing by saying, "I mean to forget [political strife], and devote myself heart and soul to philosophy. That, I assure you, is my intention; and I only wish I had always practised it" (2.5). It is reasonable to think that Cicero's yearning is sincere, but that his comment is tongue-in-cheek.

26. Carlos Lévy, "versus," 76.

27. Schofield, *Cicero*, 19.

28. Baraz, *Republic*, 77.

29. Baraz, *Republic*, 191.

30. Nicgorski, "Appendix," 258.

31. Nicgorski, "Appendix," 259.

32. Nicgorski, "Appendix," 271.

33. Nicgorski, "Appendix," 273.

34. Nicgorski, *Skepticism*, 115.

35. Nicgorski, *Skepticism*, 116.

36. Nicgorski, *Skepticism*, 146n.92.

37. Nicgorski, *Skepticism*, 117.

38. Nicgorski, *Skepticism*, 116–17.

39. Atkins, "Domina," 259–60.

40. Cf. Cicero, DO, 1.8, 3.13–14.

41. Cicero, DO, 1.148, 3.13–15.

42. Cicero, DO, 1.19. One is reminded of Niccolo Machiavelli's moving description of the delight he found in the habit of contemplative study: "When evening comes, I return home and go into my study. On the threshold I strip off my muddy, sweaty, workday clothes, and put on the robes of court and palace, and in this graver dress I enter the antique courts of the ancients and am welcomed by them, and there I taste the food that alone is mine, and for which I was born. And there I make bold to speak to them and ask the motives of their actions, and they, in their humanity, reply to me. And for the space of four hours I forget the world, remember no vexation, fear poverty no more, tremble no more at death: I pass indeed into their world" (qtd. in Hale, *Machiavelli*, 139).

43. Cicero, DRP, 1.17.

44. Nicgorski, *Skepticism,* 106.

45. See chapter 10 for the argument that Cicero's *rector reipublicae* is the unified embodiment of the practical and the theoretical man.

46. Baraz, *Republic*, 70.

47. Cicero, DRP, 1.15–16.

48. Cicero, DRP, 1.23.

49. See Cicero, DF, 1.29, and throughout Books 1 and 2.

50. See Cicero, DF, 3.13–14 and throughout Books 3 and 4.

51. Cicero, DF, 4.64n37.

52. Cicero, DO, 1.22.

53. Cicero, DRP, 6.30–33; Z26–29.

54. Cicero, DRP, 6.19; Z15.

55. Cicero, DO, 1.153.

56. Cicero, DF, 5.84.

57. Cicero, DF, 5.91.

58. The biblical example of the Hebraic seven day week in Genesis serves as illuminating analogy of this same point. In Genesis 1–2 and Exodus 34, God commands man to work for six days and rest on the seventh, which is set apart as the holiest day. It might be the case that man's labor on those six days addresses necessities, but it

is also, in itself, good. The holiest day is in a real sense best, but this does not mean that a good man, to live a complete life, should abandon work if he can and rest for seven days of the week; to the contrary, he should work diligently for six and rest only on the seventh, or he would be a bad man who disrespected what was right and best.

59. Cicero, DF, 5.58.

60. Cicero, DF, 5.58; Julia Annas, the editor, footnotes the ambiguity implied here and earlier in Piso's argument in the refusal to formally rank contemplation as primary.

61. Cicero, DRP, 1.17.

62. As Cicero notes in *Academica,* "I am not disposed to approve the practice traditionally ascribed to the Pythagoreans, who, when questions as to the grounds of any assertation that they advanced in debate, are said to have been accustomed to reply 'He himself said so,' 'he himself' being Pythagoras. So potent was an opinion already decided, making authority prevail unsupported by reason" (Cicero, *Academica*, 1.10).

63. Cicero, DF, 5.86–87.

64. Cicero, DF, 5.87.

65. Cicero, DF, 5.57.

Chapter 3

Socrates and Plato Come to Rome

De Republica, Book 1.13–33 and Book 6

To help us conceive of the complete human life, united in action and insight, Cicero crafted a literary model of this unity in the dramatic composition of *De Republica*. In making this model, Cicero built on the work and philosophy of his great teacher Plato, drawing on Plato's *Republic* in explicit and subtle ways, but including his own innovations. His most clever device is casting Plato and Socrates in leading roles as the Roman Scipio and Laelius. By disguising Athens' most famous philosophers in Roman dress, Cicero is not engaging in some subversive attempt to replace Roman thought with Greek philosophy. He is not, as we might assume, slyly trying to point Romans away from Rome or from the Roman emphasis on practice. Instead, Cicero ultimately means to ennoble what is best in Roman virtue and to temper Rome's destructive tendency of taking in the things of earth at the expense of things truly divine. Cicero aims to bring those goods, insofar as they are good, together.

In order to help right Roman practice, in the Dream of Scipio, Cicero devised a moving, poetic argument that counsels (at least at first blush) detachment from this world, not because our actions in this life are meaningless, but precisely because our actions mean so much more than fickle terrestrial outcomes suggest. By her earthly, imperial ambition, Cicero suggests, Rome grasps for a false glory and misleads men besides. The Dream of Scipio is meant to move Romans to govern themselves more virtuously; but, beyond this, it also turns out to be an interpretive key for understanding the relationship of the leading characters in *De Republica*, which helps us understand Cicero's argument about how to live a unified, good, and effective life. There is a direct, literary parallel between the spheres and realms in the Heavens and all nine characters who undertake this little drama on the Earth. In Cicero's literary republic, the unity of mind and act that animates the Heavens pierces the terrestrial veil to guide Scipio and Laelius in their philosophical and political leadership of their little assembly.

To see how Cicero's Heavens intersect with the Earth in *De Republica*, let me briefly recount the dialogue's proceedings. Early on the morning of the Latin holiday Scipio, already awake, greets his nephew Tubero in his bedchamber. Tubero, energetic and philosophical, quickly wends the conversation to the topic of the second sun that was troubling the Roman Senate's deliberations. Rather than launching into speculation with Tubero on the meaning of this omen, Scipio confides in Tubero that he much prefers inquiry into ethical matters to physical or metaphysical ones, and that in this way he considers himself to be like the practical Socrates rather than theoretical Plato. Before Tubero can cajole his uncle into further speculation, two more friends abruptly arrive to disrupt their close conversation. These two friends are Lucius Furius Philus and Publius Rutilius Rufus, the latter being the man who is the ostensible reporter of the dialogue. After many greetings and taking seats, the interlocutors briefly revive the strange question of the second sun until, shortly, they are interrupted once again. This time, a slave boy has arrived to announce the impending arrival of four more friends. Gaius Laelius Sapiens arrives with two sons-in-law and a close friend. Cicero, as the narrator, interjects briefly to describe the intimate and mutually admiring nature of Scipio's and Laelius' friendship. As the circle of friends assembles, Cicero is very particular to note where in Scipio's home the meetings occur, whether the characters are walking or sitting, and in what order they are seated. Greetings completed, the small group moves to an adjoining meadow, where the conversation relating to the second sun continues once more; then the group is suddenly joined by Manius Manilius, a lawyer.

Once all the characters are introduced, the conversation turns away from the second sun, in large part due to Laelius' complaint (embodying the Socrates of Scipio's description) that the sun has nothing to do with living well. They turn from discussing two suns to discussing two orbs, or orreries, which were created as models of the cosmos, one of which was impressive to the masses but the other of which was held more wonderful by the philosophical. Arising from this conversation—with some unfortunate lacunae in the manuscript—Scipio makes a stirring speech in defense of the theoretical life, not ultimately because it has practical benefit, but because he claims true happiness lies in contemplation of the unchanging things. Tubero remarks with astonishment at Scipio's utter reversal: whereas at their first meeting he had expressed a preference for ethical, Socratic studies, he has now given a euphoric peroration on the superiority of the theoretical, Platonic mode of life. Unfortunately, at this point, Scipio's response is swallowed up in an inopportune break in the text, but soon Laelius takes up the charge, defending the Socratic emphasis and asserting that he can see no meaningful happiness in knowing the movements of heavenly bodies, and that he instead believes that "better" and "happier" lives depend on orderly community and politics. The conversation thus turns to the question of what the best form of a political community is.

SCIPIO ON THE PRACTICAL AND THEORETICAL LIVES

As was said, the dialogue proper begins with Scipio making a significant distinction between Socrates and Plato. Socrates, in Scipio's telling, is a model of the active life committed to doing the good and embodying the noble, and Plato is a model of the contemplative life, committed to knowing the good and apprehending the true.[1] Cicero's preface to the dialogue in *De Republica* seems to take a strong stance in favor of Socrates, as does Scipio, who identifies himself exclusively with Socrates at first. Yet, within a span of pages, Scipio has summarily reversed himself: it appears that he was routinely engaged in discussions about astronomy with Rutilius, even in the thick of military campaigns,[2] and when the conversation of the assembled circle pursues an astronomical vein, he proves to be an ardent defender of the knowledge of the heavenly things.[3] Scipio's nephew Tubero seems to point out this apparent pivot in Scipio's argument, but Scipio's response is swallowed in an inopportune lacuna: "Do you see, Africanus, what a little while ago seemed otherwise to you—," Tubero declares before the text breaks off, suggesting that he perceives the change in Scipio's argument.[4] Scipio continues speaking extensively after the gap, however, which gives us some sense of his thinking.

Scipio's response not only differs from the Socratic preference he set down in the prologue, but seems in fact to repudiate it entirely, a fact which must be accounted for. In a series of observations that anticipate the revelation of his dream at the end of *De Republica*, Scipio dismisses the worth of attainment in human life when compared to eternity along with the infinitesimal splash of glorious actions on Earth given the scale of the cosmos. The man who truly has a right to all things is the one who, in his wisdom, renounces the worth of those things, "refusing to call them 'goods.'"[5] This man considers political service "necessary" and "not something to be desired";[6] this man considers the height of activity the exertion of contemplative pursuits.[7] He concludes by declaring that "only those who are refined in the arts appropriate to humanity are [truly] human beings,"[8] for which reason Scipio states finally that "learning, erudite men, and those studies of yours, Tubero, have always pleased me."[9] In other words, Scipio seems quite emphatically to state his approval of theoretical study, and only secondarily because it gives man some perspective and guidance on his situation on Earth. It is preeminently worthwhile for its own sake. The contemplative life, not the ethical life, is superior. As Leo Strauss says, it seems that Scipio unambiguously sets forth "the supremacy of the theoretical life."[10], [11]

This reversal on Scipio's part begs the question of what his true opinion is, or whether he has one. However, before concluding that we must choose one or the other as Scipio's true opinion, it is reasonable to ask whether it is not Scipio's mind that has changed, but his rhetoric that has changed to suit the setting. Scipio may, in public, be inclined to defend the value of theoretical inquiry but, privately—as he confessed in the intimacy of his bedchamber— prefer inquiry into ethical matters. Now, this would reverse our expectations somewhat dramatically: we might expect someone to be "practical" publicly and reserve philosophical discourse for solitary enjoyment. Still, taking Scipio's statements seriously and also trying to preserve the dramatic integrity of the dialogue, this is the simplest resolution, and there is good reason to suppose it is correct. Cicero takes some pains to set the conversation in the prologue off from the rest of the dialogue, drawing our attention both to the fact that Scipio and his nephew Tubero are still alone[12] and to the fact that it occurred before the ostensible reporter of the conversation, Publius Rutilius, has even arrived.[13] This suggests that Scipio's early revelation of his Socratic preference is one he holds personally but does not defend publicly. Indeed, Tubero presumes that his uncle will be interested in discussions of astronomy—likely based on previous expressions of interest—but Scipio's declines and takes Tubero into his confidence: "But, Tubero—now I will speak to you openly what I feel—I do not agree much with our close friend [Panaetius] on this entire kind of thing."[14] Only in the privacy of his bedchamber will Scipio "now" speak "openly" about his practical bent. Scipio clearly seems to prefer practically-minded discourse personally, even though he defends theoretical inquiry publicly. Why must he hold this opinion close, however? Most simply, it is possible that Scipio does not want to disappoint his learned circle of friends, most of whom seem intrigued by the mystery of the second sun, by eschewing theoretical discussion. However, would they not be as provoked by a staunch defense of the preference he stated in his bedchamber for the Socratic, ethical emphasis? Why this difference?

The best explanation of the difference is that Scipio undertakes his public defense of the theoretical to protect and serve the practical sphere. He believes he must concern himself with theoretical matters in public life, even "under the walls of Numantia itself,"[15] for much the same reason that his father's friend did in the incident with the lunar eclipse (see chapter 2): even if one can fulfill his duty in life, and so live well, without comprehensive theoretical knowledge or study, one will certainly be misled in understanding his duty if his knowledge of the real and true is fundamentally distorted. As Strauss notes, prudent counsel and command are regularly contradicted by

competing theoretical claims (e.g., ideological absolutism or simple supersti-
tions), which means that "there is always therefore necessary a theoretical
defense of the prudential sphere."[16] The responsible public man can never
merely be practically or ethically concerned because, in the final analysis,
right action is dictated by the nature of things, and right action is often
misunderstood or prevented by the wrong understandings of these things.[17]
Hence, it would seem likely that Scipio boldly asserts the priority of *theoria*
as a way of defending good *praxis*. This, however, does not entirely resolve
the difficulty. Even if this is true, the contemplative goods that Scipio pivots
to defend seem incompatible with considering practical goods to be "good"
at all, which raises the question of how, precisely, he is making a defense of
the practical life of virtue. The persistence of this puzzle leads us further in.

LAELIUS AND SCIPIO AS CICERO'S ROMAN SOCRATES AND PLATO

The provocative distinction Scipio makes between Socrates and Plato draws
our attention to the distinction between the two lives, but his abrupt reversal
of preference—rejecting the Socratic for the Platonic—puts the reader on
notice, especially when the mantle of Socrates is immediately, seamlessly
taken up by Laelius. Following his defense of the knowledge of astronomy,
Scipio gives a lengthy apology for theoretical study, asking ultimately,
"what position of command, what magistracy, what kingdom can be more
preeminent than a man who looks down on all human things and regards
them as inferior to wisdom and never turns over anything in his mind unless
it is everlasting and divine?"[18] Laelius follows Scipio's statement in defense
of the theoretical life by seeming to object, though again an inopportune
lacuna obscures the bulk of the text. Nevertheless, after the gap he is quot-
ing Ennius' *Iphigenia*: "What's the point of observing astronomers' signs in
the heavens"?[19] Scipio had professed to Tubero in the prologue that he was
"still inclined to judge Socrates wiser, who put aside all care of this kind and
said that either things sought about nature are greater than human reason can
achieve or they hold no concern at all for human life."[20] Laelius, directing the
discussion from the heavens to the city in response to Scipio's statements,
paraphrases the Socratic objection, which had at that point also been Scipio's,
from the prologue: if there is a second sun, Laelius says, "we can know nothing of these things; or even if we know a great deal, we cannot be better or
happier because of this knowledge."[21] Laelius, in other words, now articulates
and defends the point of view ostensibly held by Scipio and Socrates in the
earlier prologue.

Indeed, in the remainder of the dialogue, Scipio takes up the role of the Scipionic Plato and Laelius that of the Scipionic Socrates. These analogies between Scipio and Plato and Laelius and Socrates are intimated in a large variety of other ways. Most basically, Cicero's book is called *De Republica,* after all, and intended as an homage to the Platonic *Republic.* Beyond emulating Plato in his seeming-embrace of the theoretical life, Scipio makes use of the Platonic similes of the helmsman and the physician,[22] and translates Plato, ostensibly verbatim, extensively on the cycle of regimes,[23] a translation which Laelius knowingly affirms—one can imagine with a wink and a nod—by declaring, "You have expressed precisely what he said."[24] It is Scipio who, in Book 2, proceeds to unfold the development of Rome's mixed regime, the best form of government according to Scipio, which is analogous to the "city in speech" in the Plato's *Republic.*[25] Finally, it is the Dream of Scipio which serves as the *pièce de résistance* in Cicero's Platonic emulation, a capstone that corresponds not only to the Myth of Er in Book 10 of Plato's *Republic,* but also to the famous Allegory of the Cave, as William H. F. Altman has pointed out.[26] As the Myth of Er makes a mythological argument for the just life on the basis of rewards in the next life, so the Dream of Scipio counsels noble, dedicated service to country now for the joy that will follow in the life to come. And as the Allegory of the Cave imaginatively describes the ascent from ignorance about the good into the sunlit realm of knowing, Scipio in his dream (and the reader with him) ascends from terrestrial obscurity into the bright heavenly realms which illumine his understanding of the good. In summary, Cicero seems to associate Scipio with Plato in several important ways.

The correspondence between Laelius and Socrates (as Scipio describes the Greek philosopher in the prologue)[27] also runs through the dialogue, but it is worth noting that the association of Laelius and Socrates runs through Cicero's writings more generally. In *Cato Maior de Senectute,* a dialogue about attaining a peaceful old age, the literary frame of the dialogue is a clear imitation of the opening dialogue of Book 1 of Plato's *Republic,* with the elderly Cato standing in for the old man Cephalus and Laelius standing in for Socrates. In the dialogue, Laelius-as-Socrates asks Cato a series of questions highly reminiscent of the probing inquiries that Socrates put to Cephalus. Likewise, in *Laelius de Amicitia,* a dialogue on friendship in which Laelius recalls his friendship with Scipio, Gaius Fannius emphasizes his estimation of Laelius' wisdom by setting him alongside Socrates in being considered wise.[28] Cicero furthermore explicitly compares Socrates and Laelius with respect to their characteristics, such as their *hilaritas,* or good humor,[29] and "equanimity [*aequabilitatis*]."[30]

Cicero, it seems, held Laelius to be a particularly Socratic person in general, but we see the parallels in greater detail in *De Republica.* Socrates, Scipio says, was characterized by "wit and subtlety of conversation,"[31] and

Laelius makes the first joke of the dialogue soon after he arrives. The joke, made at Manilius' expense, also displays Laelius' Socratic irony, as it mocks the legislative art in which he himself "greatly excel[s]."[32] Cicero declares in his *Tusculan Disputations* that "Socrates first called philosophy down from heaven, and gave it a place in cities, and introduced it even into men's homes, and forced it to make inquiry into life and morals, and things good and evil."[33] Likewise, Laelius urges the conversation to pivot from a discussion of the two suns to "matters relevant to our homes and to the republic."[34] When inquiry into the value of astronomical theory for political life is pursued further, it is Laelius again who turns the conversation, this time to the discussion of the best regime.[35] Indeed, as Socrates' maieutic guidance steered conversations in the Platonic dialogues, Laelius' guiding questions are present at almost every pivot in the dialogue, directing the conversation to "things good and evil." It is Laelius who wends the conversation from astronomy to the best regime and compels Scipio to address the matter,[36] and when Scipio wishes only to address the mixed regime, Laelius turns him back to the simple forms;[37] it is Laelius who presents the argument, reminiscent of the practical beginning of Plato's *Republic*, for why men should prefer justice to injustice.[38] Finally, it is Laelius whose question about "stable and more robust kinds of rewards" than glory lead Scipio to reveal his dream to the other interlocutors. What is Socratic about this character—again, following the Scipionic characterization—is the ever-present concern for human things and the continual push to inquiry. Certainly, Cicero does not reduce Scipio and Laelius to ham-fisted character types, being careful to maintain the dramatic integrity of his work, and so we should not expect a flattened transposition of Plato and Socrates into *De Republica*. Yet, Cicero intends Scipio to stand in for Plato and Laelius to stand in for Socrates.[39]

THE SECOND SUN AND THE UNITY
OF THE TWO WAYS OF LIFE

Having established this parallel, the question remains whether we are meant to see Socrates and Plato, and the lives they represent, in competition for ascendancy in *De Republica*, or whether Cicero intends to winnow the choice to one best life, or whether he means to embrace them both in a unity. Some readers of *De Republica* have settled this question by assuming, quite understandably, that Scipio is the main character of the dialogue, and that since Scipio, in the bulk of the dialogue defends the theoretical life, this must be what Cicero thinks is best, even though he grants that one must be practical because of duty and necessity. J. Atkins and others point out the inadequacy of presuming Scipio to speak for Cicero, a point of view which has increasingly fallen out of favor.[40] This assumption does not adequately take into account Scipio's reversal of his stated opinion in the prologue, however, or adequately grasp the importance of Laelius to the dialogue. It also runs roughshod over Cicero's avowed practicality in his prologue. Just as the claim about the choice-worthy way of life switches centers, so Cicero continually switches the center between Scipio and Laelius, a means by which he ultimately directs us to a unity of these ways of life and of these two men.

The alternation between Scipio and Laelius does not simply begin with Scipio switching allegiances between Socrates and Plato, but in other details of great and small significance in the dialogue. Cicero seems to make something of a game of switching centers, in fact; one thing, then another is continually being presented as being superior or supreme. Scipio first identifies himself with the practical Socrates, then argues like the theoretical Plato. Scipio at one point explicitly identifies Jupiter as "the one king of all gods and human beings"[41] but later in his dream downplays Jupiter with scant mention and honors the Sun as "the leader, chief, and director of the other lights, the mind and balance of the universe."[42] Scipio is the first character to be introduced in *De Republica*, but then Laelius is the character whose introduction is characterized by the most pomp, and he is literally central, being the fifth of nine interlocutors to be introduced. Scipio then highlights Laelius' centrality when he honors him by literally placing him in the center of the group of interlocutors. Furthermore, upon Laelius' arrival, it is explained that Scipio considers Laelius a father when they are in Rome due to his age, but that Laelius considers Scipio to be nearly a god when abroad on account of his triumphs.[43] Scipio is the character who does the bulk of the speaking throughout the book, but (in the text we have) Laelius is most frequently the character who decides the course of conversation, as has been noted. Indeed, the primacy of Scipio, which seems memorably confirmed in his retelling of the Dream of Scipio, is turned on its head at precisely the moment of its unfolding when a puzzle from the beginning of the book—the meaning of the second sun—is resolved by a final clue, a turnabout which once again places Laelius at the center. This important point will require some significant explanation.

One of the persistent questions raised by Cicero's *De Republica* is the meaning of the second sun which Tubero brings up in conversation with Scipio Africanus in their meeting at the beginning of the dialogue. Tubero raises it because he wants Scipio to comment on its meaning, and every set of characters that arrives in the following moments is told the topic of conversation is the "second sun," raising its profile for the reader, but the interlocutors themselves never agree on its significance, at least not in the text we have. For the characters it serves as a speculative conversational appetizer before they turn to the main course of the dialogue; to the reader it comes as a provoking challenge.

There are several reasons we should suppose Cicero means for us to look for a deeper meaning in the second sun, firstly because of its profile in early conversation in the dialogue. Although Cicero asserts that he is reporting a conversation that occurred decades earlier, basing his writing on a report by Publius Rutilius, no academic critic or casual reader would suppose that Cicero would have felt a need to report the interlocutor's chit-chat before they turned to the serious discussion of the Roman and ideal republics. Nevertheless, Cicero does, and he dwells on it. Furthermore, the conversation does not begin when its ostensible source, Publius Rutilius, arrives, but several minutes before.[44] Cicero need not have claimed an authorial source for his dialogue at all, and yet he does so immediately after having reported dialogue which Rutilius would not have heard. This can reasonably be construed as Cicero's way of underscoring that Scipio and Tubero's "chit chat" is part of Cicero's own framing of the dialogue. Finally, the other points Cicero brings out in that framing conversation—Tubero's question about the second sun and Scipio's assertion that Plato, as an act of piety, placed his own wisdom in Socrates' mouth—also strongly suggest themselves to be important framing devices for the dialogue. Hence, an attentive reader might reasonably suppose that the second sun must have some significance for the dialogue generally.

The second set of details begging for explanation is Cicero's somewhat detailed stage-setting and introduction of the characters. It is necessary to explore this scene in detail to draw out its significance. The pretext for the meeting of these figures is the Latin holiday. It is apparently dawn and Scipio is still in his bedchamber when Tubero arrives by himself, and this is where the conversation about the second sun is initiated.[45] When the next two interlocutors arrive in a pair, one each is seated with Scipio and Tubero, and the newcomers, asking to know the subject of conversation, are told it is the second sun, but the conversation is interrupted once again before they can continue, which will require the subject to be introduced for a third time.[46] Cicero, in introducing the next interlocutors, takes the trouble of telling us that Laelius and company are preceded and announced by a slave boy. This results in Scipio dressing and then moving, along with his friends, from Scipio's inner sanctum to the porch to await Laelius. The four newest interlocutors soon arrive: Laelius, two sons-in-law, and a fourth individual.

Here, a strange ritual commences: Scipio, after greeting his guests, turns and sets Laelius in the center of the group, and Cicero explains that this was "a certain law" [*ius*] in their friendship, that Laelius honored him like a god when abroad, and Scipio honored Laelius as a parent, due to his age, when at home (*domi*, adverbial, denoting "place where"; "Rome" is the implied home and is interpolated in both Fott's and Zetzel's translations, but the word literally denotes a home, such as the one they are in).[47] Appropriately, Scipio arranges them so that Laelius sits in the middle, giving him honor. Problematically, however, there are eight interlocutors, and so there is no true center. Then, after emphasizing the importance of place in the relationship of the two men, the conversation is moved from that place out of the home and to a sunny spot in a nearby meadow.[48] (Now they both are and are not *domi*, "at home.") Unannounced, they are joined by Manius Manilius, a "*vir prudens*," who assumes for himself the seat next to Laelius.[49] Depending on who is in the center, Manilius has either placed himself at the head of the group or beneath Laelius in honor, which seems to be an intentional ambiguity. Given that Manilius is closely tied to civil law in *De Republica*[50] and Laelius to justice (given his defense of justice in Book 3), it is appropriate and provocative that it is ambiguous which one now sits in the center. (This is, of course, another example of "alternating centers" in the dialogue.) Due to the new arrival, there are now nine interlocutors and three have been distinguished by Cicero in some way: Scipio in terms of glory, Laelius in terms of age, and Manilius in terms of prudence. Cicero's detailed arrangement of characters provokes questions that are not immediately answered and whose relevance is not immediately evident.[51]

The third relevant set of details to note is the Dream of Scipio, which came to fame in its own right and is often referenced apart from *De Republica* itself. It includes an elaborate, detailed account of the heavens, but reading Scipio's account with the previous details in mind suggests some striking parallels to the characters introduced at the beginning of the dialogue.[52] To explain these things we must carefully review the content of the dream. In Scipio's account, after a long night of discussion about republics and monarchies with King Masinissa, Scipio finally falls asleep in the early morning. (Notably, by way of comparison, the action in *De Republica* begins early in the morning.) In his dream, Scipio's grandfather reveals to him a vision of the heavens and gives him an account of the relative size and orbits of the planets and stars, counseling him to "look always at these heavenly things, scorn those human things," although Scipio's gaze continually falls back on Earth.[53] Every sphere has unique characteristics and is discussed individually or in a set.

The descriptions of the nine spheres harmonize substantially with the nine characters as they arrive, albeit in reverse order. The Earth, at the center of the cosmos and also in the middle due to the orbit of the other spheres around it ("middle and ninth"), remains stationary and draws all other bodies toward it.[54] Scipio, likewise, is the center weight that has drawn all the other interlocutors to himself, and is both the mean and the extreme: he is placed at the center by Laelius, but is first in line of interlocutors to be introduced to the reader. Next is the Moon, the first of the moving spheres, a pale light which has a partial kinship to the terrestrial, changing sphere. Appropriately,

Quintus Tubero is Scipio's nephew, and just as the moon reports the sun's light to earth, Tubero, the first of the "moving" interlocutors, brings to Scipio's attention the light of the suns which had appeared over the Senate.[55] The next two planets are Venus and Mercury, introduced together as twin "attendants" of the Sun;[56] the next two interlocutors, arriving together "suddenly," are Lucius Furius Philus and Publius Rutilius. Publius Rutilius, who corresponds to Mercury, the messenger of the gods, is noted as the "authorial source" for the conversation,[57] the messenger who carried that conversation to Cicero and thereby ostensibly eternalizes it for us. Lucius Furius Philus, who is very displeased to make the case for injustice in the dialogue, and whose surname is presumably rooted in the Greek φίλος ("friend" or "love") corresponds to Venus and is greeted "with the greatest friendliness" by Scipio.[58]

It is only appropriate that the next light receive its due pomp and circumstance: the Sun, "roughly" in the center, the "mind and balance of the universe" which is the "leader, chief, and director of the other lights."[59] In its relative pomp it corresponds to the next interlocutor, Laelius, whose arrival is announced by a slave (a body ruled by another's mind), and who arrives as the head of a small entourage, a group which he governs as father-in-law (Gaius Fannius and Quintus Scaevola) and mentor (Spurius Mummius).[60] Laelius, in relation to the others, is characterized by all four Aristotelian types of rule: kingly (by age over Mummius and Scipio), mastery (by mind over the slave boy), parental (by position over his sons-in-law), and political (ruling with Scipio in turns). Just as the sun lies "roughly" in the center, so Laelius is the central character to arrive (fifth of nine) and is subsequently explicitly placed at the center by Scipio. In a clever subtlety, Cicero makes exactly nine references to the sun in this prologue, and Laelius is introduced in the sentence immediately following the fifth reference, counting each reference to twin suns as two.[61] Furthermore, once the connection between the opening and closing scenes of the dialogues is established, and the connection between the Dream and the Platonic analogy of the cave, we see a similar analogy to the initial arrival of the characters. Scipio, in his bedroom very early in the morning, receives word from Tubero about the apparent second sun. The interior space and darkness, and the *report* of the *apparent* second sun are highly reminiscent of the man who finds himself in Plato's cave. When his guests arrive, Scipio is joined by each of them in his bedroom—it is hard to say whether or not we should think this strange—but they only move out of the bedroom when the report of another "sun" arrives in the form of the slave boy reporting the coming of Laelius. Then the small party moves from the bedroom to the porch to greet Laelius, and finally to the "sunniest place of a small meadow."[62] There are thus multiple converging lines which attach Laelius to the Sun, both in terms of position and common characteristic.

The next three planets—Mars, Jupiter, and Saturn—correspond as a set to Spurius Mummius, Gaius Fannius, and Quintus Scaevola, his sons-in-law. Given that these characters have so little dialogue in the manuscript of *De Republica* that is handed down to us, it is unclear how precisely they should be associated with the remaining planets. It is possible that Spurius Mummius is connected to Mars as he has a particular hatred of rhetoricians,[63] and it is reasonable that Cicero's statesmanly beneficence to mankind—and every philosopher's and statesman's gift to man—is accomplished, and must be accomplished, through right speech, or true oratory. To war against good word and speeches, or *logoi*, is thus to war against mankind; indeed, as Schofield notes, "Cicero believed that both philosophy and statesmanship needed eloquence if they were to be at their best."[64] Nevertheless, it is difficult to discern clear attachments between these planets and interlocutors, and this is in no small part due to the fragmentary nature of the text. However, it is doubtful that Cicero considered them very significant. Cicero states in a letter to Atticus that he intended Scipio, Laelius, Philus, and Manilius to carry the weight of the dialogue ("I have put the discussion in the mouths of" those four, he declares), but goes on to say that he merely "added" the others; this was quite possibly done merely to help round out the number of interlocutors.[65] Hence, if the connections are less emphatic, this is to be expected.

The final sphere, the Heaven, revolves in a different direction than all the rest of the moving spheres, "forwards" instead of backwards.[66] This is the perspective from which Scipio is looking on, it seems. It is also the sphere which readers might intuitively want to associate with Scipio. This is a reasonable instinct and it raises an important question. After all, is Scipio not the Platonist? However, in the midst of Scipio's dream it is emphasized that Scipio himself is continually drawn back to Earth and must have his gaze redirected to higher things by Africanus, and Scipio ultimately, of course, does return to Earth. While we are reasonable to associate Scipio with the Heavens in his dream, then, it is also reasonable to conclude the opposite— but given Cicero's persistence in alternating poles, it is most reasonable to associate him with both. The ninth interlocutor, the *vir prudens*, Manius Manilius, is also appropriately associated with both the Heaven and the Earth: it is to the diligent and prudent man that dominion on Earth and a home in the Heaven belongs. As Africanus unfolds the matter, the Heaven is "the highest god," and is similar to the Earth in that it is not one of the "lights" which is governed by Sun, though it "embraces" all of them.[67] This highest god does not move or direct the planets, but simply encloses them, giving definition to the space within which they move. As an expert in law, Manilius comments at one point that without law (presumably civil law) "no one can know what is his and what is another's,"[68] an apt analogy to definition provided by the Heaven. The law that delineates possessions does not also guide men in knowing what their possessions are for: that requires the guidance of a mind, or the Sun in the economy of Scipio's dream. Cicero's treatment on Manilius in *De Oratore* likewise helps us understand this association, as he paints of picture of a man who was "representative of the broad education required of the orator, and of old-fashioned generosity in helping others with his legal knowledge."[69] Nevertheless, given the dearth of dialogue by Manilius in *De Republica* as it has been received, it is difficult to say much more than this.

To emphasize the point, there is an appropriate ambiguity or unity in the dual identification of Scipio and Manilius and Earth and Heaven, just as there is an ambiguous unity between wisdom and prudence in the cardinal virtues. This ambiguity is in fact in keeping with Cicero's Academic skepticism, which believes that there are better and worse opinions, but that "truth" cannot be stated simply or finally. Rather, as J. Atkins says, Cicero "[prompts the reader] to exercise his or her critical faculties to discover [his] message."[70] This alternation of centers—the prudent man and the wise man could be associated with either the Heavens or the Earth—is not confusion or indetermination, but simply another instance of Cicero's insistent overlapping of the active and contemplative spheres.

To return to the argument regarding the two ways of life, this analogy between the speakers and the spheres demonstrates that at precisely the point when Scipio's highly Platonic unfolding of the nature of man and his relation to the cosmos is given to us in the Dream of Scipio—so very memorably— the attentive reader notes that Cicero is directing us (and the theoretic Scipio) to return to the beginning, to the Socratic Laelius, who has been placed in the center as the guide of all the rest. It is important to note that we are not directed back to Laelius because Cicero wishes us to suppose that Laelius is greater than Scipio. There is no doubt that Scipio drives the lion's share of commentary in *De Republica*, and it is provoking that in *On the Nature of the Gods* Cicero, recalling the twin suns, laments the death of Scipio as the extinguishing of "another sun."[71] Both Scipio and Laelius serve as our guides in living well. Cicero's teaching is that the complete life—a life of theory and practice—consists of duly alternating or overlapping centers. Those on the Earth look to the Heavens to orient themselves and their actions; even from its far remove, the Sun is a beneficent guide. Scipio's Dream seems to teach that this is not accidentally true, but actually true. The navigator can learn where he is on the globe because the stars tell him so, but that is a measure of his own clever devising. The stars meant to tell him nothing. On the other hand, the Dream emphasizes that the guidance of the Heavens—including the ensouling of men on Earth—is genuinely accomplished by the guidance of the Sun for the sake of those on Earth.[72]

In sum, the significance of this discourse between Cicero's Plato and Socrates is not to make it evident that one or the other is superior, but to reveal the superiority of their interplay. This interplay does not establish a doctrine, but models an approach, a method, a commitment to contemplative inquiry which overflows in committed, involved action that refers again to theory to calibrate its course. It is a poetic image of the unity of the Socratic and Platonic modes, and ultimately a unity of the two ways of life. This unity is apparent not only in the interplay between Laelius and Scipio, but also in each man. Throughout the dialogue, they each seem to be aware of what the other is thinking already; they both evince the practical and theoretical wisdom that characterizes unified lives. They assume different modes, however, for the sake of guiding the assembled community in what could be said to be something of a conspiracy on their parts. The men themselves do not embrace fundamentally different ways of life, but deeply sympathetic, overlapping ways of life.

THE UNITY OF SOCRATES AND PLATO
AND OF THE TWO WAYS OF LIFE

It is impossible, then, that Scipio's distinction between Socrates and Plato is in fact Cicero's own. We can find confirmation of this in Cicero's oft-stated commitment to the New Academy. Skepticism and dogmatism make poor bedfellows. It would be impossible for Cicero to commit to the wisdom of the Socratic method of skeptical inquiry, rooted in the Socratic profession of ignorance, while simultaneously praising as divine Plato's ostensibly-dogmatic conclusions and arguments. In fact, Cicero's works are riddled with references to Socrates and Plato, and at times he conflates them. He makes reference to both as being "divine,"[73] and will at times simultaneously credit Socrates and Plato for the same writing or argument,[74] undermining the notion that he considers them fundamentally at odds. The bulk of Cicero's laudatory references, especially in his private correspondence, are to Plato, whom he considers most worthy of consideration and praise,[75] while a reference in *De Finibus* to Plato's "intention . . . to combine Pythagorean doctrines with his portrayal of Socrates and take on board subjects that Socrates had scorned" is a rare example corroborating the historical basis of the Scipionic distinction, showing that he has it in view in his writing beyond *De Republica*, but he does not belabor it elsewhere.[76]

Ultimately, Cicero asserts vociferously that neither Plato nor Socrates established any doctrines at all. He advances this claim despite the fact that Plato certainly put forward a variety of teachings, such as the immortality of the soul, reincarnation, *anamnesis*, and the theory of the Forms, to name a few. Yet Cicero asserts that Plato ultimately shared Socrates' skepticism. Cicero has Varro declare in *Academica*, "The method of discussion pursued by Socrates in almost all the dialogues . . . is to affirm nothing himself but to refute others, to assert that he knows nothing except the fact of his own ignorance."[77] Confirming this opinion is Cicero the character, who affirms what Varro declared: "They call this school the New Academy—to me it seems old, at all events if we count Plato a member of the Old Academy, in whose books nothing is stated positively and there is much arguing both pro and contra, all things are inquired into and no certain statement is made."[78] Cicero likewise declares in a famous passage in the *Tusculan Disputations* that Plato's "manifold [Lat. *multiplex;* concealed or layered] method of discussion" has given rise to many schools of thought, but that the New Academy is the true Socratic one.[79] Socrates, Cicero writes, had taught by "concealing [his] own opinion, relieving others of their errors, and on every question seeking to ascertain what is most probable."[80] In sum, Cicero believed that neither Socrates nor Plato intended to teach any doctrines, but engaged in a mode of inquiry which "Socrates thought . . . the best way of determining what has the nearest semblance to truth [*veri simillimum*]."[81] Hence, although Cicero credits the notion that Socrates' concern was more ethical and Plato's more theoretical, Cicero believes that their shared commitment to inquiry and the skeptical way meant they were not divided by dogmatism. Rather, Socrates and Plato and their ways of life are united by a mode or method.

If Cicero does not think the two ways of life are fundamentally at odds, it is eminently reasonable to ask why he suggests at the beginning of *De Republica* that they are. Certainly, even though the lives are not fundamentally at odds, the modes of practical and theoretical inquiry do exist in a dynamic tension. This fact is regularly on display in a variety of settings. In classrooms, to give a practical example, the tension is evident when students ask their teacher what the "answer" is and gets a five-minute response concluding that "it depends," which rarely clarifies what *precisely* the student should be writing down. Similarly, a legislator might wonder what the law should be and consult a philosopher on the meaning of justice, and be frustrated by the encounter because, once again, "it depends." The problem is not that the teacher and the philosopher know too much or do not really know at all, but that what is fitting is highly circumstantial, reminiscent of Aristotle's Golden Mean.

The dynamic tension between Scipio and Laelius helps to reveal important things about the republic, but it also reveals *how* to pursue answers to important questions about the republic. Just as Cicero lauds Plato as a *multiplex* author, Cicero has two primary purposes in demonstrating the tension between Scipio and Laelius. First, Cicero's Academic mode is modeled in the interplay between Scipio and Laelius, with questions guiding conversation toward truth. Cicero inquires in order to uncover the real, and so the better arguments are advanced through dialogue and inquiry. Laelius, by and large, provides the questions, and Scipio provides many of the answers, but their tug-and-pull is more productive than a monologue by either one would be.

The second reason Cicero emphasizes the tension is that he is sensitive to the need to balance the demands of being a genuine philosopher and being a philosophic statesman. A genuine philosopher seeks after the truth, perhaps recklessly indifferent to received opinion if it does not conform to the truth as he uncovers it; yet, a philosophic statesman must inquire responsibly, not simply because he is concerned for the security of his position (vis-à-vis accusations of impiety or injustice) but because he is engaged in genuine work of care for his fellow citizens, and to recklessly challenge custom and law is not an act of care if it leads to disorder. Hence, the statesman's activity in the political sphere imitates the maieutic engagement of Socrates in his personal encounters, attempting to bring reason that is merely latent in a city or a soul into being more particular and effective. Scipio and Laelius together play the part of the philosophic statesman, providing an image of the good, but embodying tensions that emphasize that their teachings are not the final word. On this score, it is notable that Philus, a member of the New Academy, is given the distasteful task of defending injustice, which he does. Cicero sees the importance of philosophizing daringly (in keeping with his allegiance to the New Academy), but always responsibly.

Cicero, in the end, is not content simply to report what the Greeks thought; he does not bring "the philosophers" or "their philosophies" to Rome, but philosophy itself. Martial Romans, mindful both of practicality and of glory, offer a unique challenge and opportunity: Can the good and the honorable be reconciled? Cicero's philosophical insight and sustained argument is that truth does not brook division, and he weaves this vision of a unified life into the words and the very structure of the dialogue, particularly in the analogy between our nine interlocutors and the nine heavenly spheres.

Cicero's "both-and" approach to theory and practice not only provides a unified way, but provides salutary encouragement where his individual readers may be deficient. For the careful reader, Cicero does not look to leave a simple conclusion or argument. For the theoretically-minded man, Cicero looks to persuade to politics, and he demonstrates the role of theory in countering bad theory (e.g., the superstition of the masses). For the politically-minded, popular glory is diminished in light of the knowledge of its cosmic insignificance, and a hale, republican notion of glory is established in its place. No reader can be content to leave the dialogue rejecting theory or abandoning practice, a point that will be underscored in chapters 4 and 5. Cicero's bias is toward the unity of these things as the preferable choice for man more so than to one or the other. The choice-worthy human endeavor lies in a unity of leisured thought and noble deed.

NOTES

1. Cicero, DRP, 1.15.
2. Cicero, DRP, 1.17.
3. Cicero, DRP, 1.23.
4. Cicero, DRP, 1.26.
5. Cicero, DRP, 1.27.
6. Cicero, DRP, 1.27.
7. Cicero, DRP, 1.27.
8. Cicero, DRP, 1.28.
9. Cicero, DRP, 1.29.

10. Strauss, "Transcript," 23. Not all commentators take Scipio at his word here that the theoretical life is best, but assume that he is simply providing a one-sided view (see J. Atkins, *Politics*, 53, for example). This desire to preserve consistency in Scipio's statements on the subject are understandable. However, his earlier and later statements are not consistent, and this becomes an important point in interpreting the dialogue.

11. J. Atkins states that Laelius is "the defender of the city" and that Scipio is the defender of "the mixed life" (*Politics*, 39). Certainly, taking various stretches of dialogue at face value, this is a reasonable opinion. However, it is also true that Scipio seems, sometimes, the practical defender of the city, but also at other points the absolute defender of the theoretical life. These shifts in representation are not accidental and shouldn't be overlooked. As characters, Laelius and Scipio are above all pedagogues working in a conspiracy designed by Cicero to show us a complete life.

12. Cicero, DRP, 1.15, "before the others come."

13. Cicero, DRP, 1.17.

14. Cicero, DRP, 1.15. A speculative hint that Cicero means his readers to pay close attention is found here, in Scipio's profession that he will tell Tubero "openly" [*aperte*] what he thinks. The root of the Latin *aperte* is *aperio*, "I uncover," which is nearly a homonym of the philosophically significant Greek word ἀπορία (puzzle, mystery), but meaning precisely the opposite: Scipio is revealing something, but Cicero means for his well-educated reader to be alert for something being concealed. Hence, what Scipio tells us is not clarifying, but an introduction to a puzzle. Whether or not this subtlety is intended by Cicero, there is no doubt that Scipio's profession does not clarify, but only puzzles.

15. Cicero, DRP, 1.17.

16. Strauss, "Transcript," 19.

17. One implication of the argument regarding Scipio's esoteric practicality is that the "theoretical" Scipio and the "practical" Laelius are more intellectually complicit than it seems on the surface of the conversation. They are, to some extent, in cahoots. This will become more clear as the meaning of the second sun unfolds.

18. Cicero, DRP, 1.28. It is notable that, directly after this ode to the contemplative life, Scipio quotes "Plato, or someone else" on how geometrical markings in the sand are a clear sign of men nearby, being signs of intelligence. However, the saying he references actually belongs to Aristippus, another student of Socrates who spurned his

master's teaching and indulged himself in a life of pleasure and gain. In other words, Scipio, who has become our Plato in the dialogue, misquotes "himself," directing our attention to someone who apparently found *both* the contemplative and active ways of life to be utter foolishness, preferring sophistry and pleasure. Vitruius, a younger contemporary of Cicero, tells that when Aristippus was cast up on the coast of the Rhodians, seeing the drawings in the sand, he went into the city and so impressed the citizens with his philosophizing that they bestowed him with many gifts, in keeping with his practice of philosophizing not for the sake of truth but for gain (*De Architectura* 6.1).

19. Cicero, DRP, 1.30.
20. Cicero, DRP, 1.16.
21. Cicero, DRP, 1.32.
22. Cicero, DRP, 1.62.
23. Cicero, DRP, 1.66–67. J. Atkins comments that "Scipio seems to have a respect for Plato's political philosophy that Laelius lacks" (*Politics*, 60).
24. Cicero, DRP, 1.68.
25. Cicero, DRP, 1.45. Since I am arguing that Socrates corresponds to Laelius, and since it is Socrates who presents us with the City in Speech in Plato's *Republic*, it might seem as though this undermines the distinction I am trying to make. However, as a vehicle for teachings of a "theoretical" orientation, if we follow the classification Scipio makes in *De Republica* 1.15, these teachings are rightly credited to Plato, not Socrates.
26. Plato, *Republic*, 514a–520a; Altman, "Altruism," 85.
27. Cicero, DRP, 1.15
28. Cicero, DA, 7.
29. Cicero, DO, 1.108.
30. Cicero, DRP, 1.90.
31. Cicero, DRP, 1.15–16.
32. Cicero, DRP, 1.20.
33. Cicero, TD, 5.11.
34. Cicero, DRP, 1.19.
35. Cicero, DRP, 1.30.
36. Cicero, DRP, 1.33–34.
37. Cicero, DRP, 1.46.
38. Cicero, DRP, 3.
39. It must be of interest, too, that Cicero attached himself to Laelius twice in his personal letters. In writing a disappointed letter to Pompesus Magnus, Cicero declares that, "[L]et me tell you that what I did for the salvation of the country is approved by the judgment and testimony of the whole world. You are a much greater man than Africanus, but I am not much inferior to Laelius either; and when you come home you will recognize that I have acted with such prudence and spirit, that you will not be ashamed of being coupled with me in politics as well as in private friendship" (*Letters to Friends* 5.7). This letter, written in 62 BC, which came roughly ten years before Cicero wrote his *De Republica*, strongly suggests that he understood his own life and work in the same terms as those of Laelius. Reinforcing this association,

Cicero wrote to Atticus in 59 BC that he would in the future write to him using the pseudonym Laelius, a precaution required by perilous times, something he reiterated in a follow-up letter (*Letters to Atticus* 2.19–20).

40. J. Atkins, *Politics*, 34–5ff.

41. Cicero, DRP, 1.56.

42. Cicero, DRP, 6.21.

43. Cicero, DRP, 1.18.

44. Cicero, DRP, 1.17.

45. Cicero, DRP, 1.14–16.

46. Cicero, DRP, 1.17.

47. Cicero, DRP, 1.18.

48. The Latin word for "sunny" (*aprico*) is not related to the word for sun that has been used to describe the two suns (*sol*). Hence, it might seem that connecting them is improper. However, *aprico* is a form of *aperio*, which came up in an adverbial form just a little earlier, at a critical moment. When Tubero has raised the question of the second sun, Scipio tells him in a moment of intimate revelation (*aperte*) that he considered Socrates' ethical emphasis to be wiser than Plato's theoretical turn. Based on what Scipio says here, he seems to be exposing a closely-held opinion that things such as the second sun do not matter. However, by settling *in aprico maxime pratuli loco* ("in the part of the meadow most exposed to the sun"), Cicero cleverly unites the significance of the sun (investigation into which is theoretical in nature) and the Scipio's Socratic preference (which is practical in orientation). In Cicero's mind, the New Academy is uniquely able to unite these two concerns.

49. Cicero, DRP, 1.18.

50. Cicero, DRP, 1.20.

51. It is appropriate to note some other significant details here. Nine characters are introduced in all; based on both historical detail and presentation in the dialogue, we can deduce that a number of them are Stoics and a number are not. There are no Epicureans. Curiously, in order of introduction, all the Stoic characters are even-numbered (2, Tubero; 4, Rutilius; 6, Mummius; 8, Scaevola) and all the non-Stoic characters are odd-numbered (1, Scipio; 3, Philus; 5, Laelius; 7, Fannius; 9, Manilius). Some commentators consider Philus and Laelius to be Stoics, but I would argue that Cicero's characterization of them in this dialogue belies that description. They are as Stoic as Cicero himself—admirers, even expositors, but not zealous acolytes. Schofield likewise registers his doubts that we should understand Laelius to be a dyed-in-the-wool skeptic (*Cicero*, 137n.15).

Charles Kesler, in his dissertation, describes what he calls "a running joke on the philosophical schools" in the introduction of characters. He notes that the assembled group, centered around Laelius, meets on the portico, the Roman version of a *stoa*, or covered walkway, in which Zeno of Citium laid down the teachings of Stoicism. Then they walk hither and thither, recalling the Peripatetics, before settling in a sunny meadow, which Kesler associates with the New Academy (Kesler, *Natural Law*, 141). I would affirm and extend, with slight modification, Kesler's observations.

The joke actually begins with the Old Academy, highlighting Plato's esotericism, as Scipio and Tubero meet in his bedchamber and play out a collision between practical and theoretical concerns, including a private revelation of a fundamental orientation toward the ethical. The conversation then moves to the portico and lingers in the Stoic mode *before* Laelius arrives. After he arrives, Laelius is placed in the center by Scipio—again, an elevation of the practical—and the group wanders about in the Peripatetic fashion at that point. Finally, the group settles in the sunny meadow to seek understanding, now representing the New Academy, bringing the earlier question about the sun and its meaning full circle.

52. This is a hypothesis of a parallel between one or two characters in *De Republica* and the spheres in the Dream of Scipio briefly entertained by Strauss in his 1959 course on Cicero, but not developed, and his identification of Laelius with Earth disagrees with my conclusion detailed below (Strauss, "Transcript," 96). Joshua Stein, professor of history at Roger Williams University, delivered a paper on "Cicero's Cosmos: The Universe as Metaphor" in December 2000 which hypothesized the possibility of an analogy between the planets and the interlocutors, but he observed no parallels between them.

53. Cicero, DRP, 6.19, 24.

54. Cicero, DRP, 6.21.

55. Cicero, DRP, 6.21.

56. Cicero, DRP, 6.21.

57. Cicero, DRP, 1.17.

58. Cicero, DRP, 1.17.

59. Cicero, DRP, 6.21. Cicero's ordering of the planets, which places the Sun at the center, follows the Chaldean ordering of the planets rather than the Egyptian ordering favored by Plato in the Myth of Er and the *Timaeus*. The Egyptian order was Saturn, Jupiter, Mars, Venus, Mercury, Sun, Moon, and Earth. See P. R. Coleman-Norton, "Cicero and the Music of the Spheres," 237n.9.

60. Cicero, DRP, 1.18.

61. Cicero, DRP, 1.15, "other sun," "two suns"; 1.17, "two suns"; 1.18, Laelius arrives; 1.19, "two suns"; 1.20, "two suns." That Cicero is, indeed, playing number games is also suggested by the fact that, in order of introduction, all the odd numbered characters are non-Stoics (or not clearly Stoics) whereas all the even numbered characters are (see note 51).

62. Cicero, DRP, 1.17–18.

63. Cicero, DRP, 5.6.

64. Schofield, *Cicero*, 16.

65. Cicero, *Letters to Atticus,* CXLII.

66. Cicero, DRP, 6.21.

67. Cicero, DRP.

68. Cicero, DRP, 1.20.

69. Hariman, *Prudence*, 54.

70. J. Atkins, *Politics*, 43.

71. Cicero, DND 2.14.

72. Cicero, DRP, 6.19; Z15.

73. Cf. the reference to Socrates' "divine goodness" in *De Officiis* 1.148 and references to Plato's divinity in a letter to Atticus ("[o]ur god Plato"; Cicero, *Letters*

to Friends, 1.4.16), to his divine words (*scripta divinitus*) in a letter to P. Lentulus (Cicero, *Letters to Friends*, 1.9.12), to "that divine man" by Marcus in *De Legibus* (Cicero, *De Legibus*, 3.1).

74. For example, in *De Senectute*, Cato introduces the argument of Socrates, "the wisest of men," regarding the immortality of the soul, concluding the same by noting that, "This, in substance, is Plato's teaching" (Cicero, *De Senectute*, 21). In *De Divinatione* he notes what "Socrates" has said about going to sleep in the proper state to avoid bad dreams, concluding that "I have reproduced Plato's very words" (Cicero, *De Divinatione*, 1.29).

75. Cf. the letter to P. Lentulus in which he declares that Plato is the one "whose teaching I earnestly endeavor to follow [*vehementer auctorem sequor*]" (Cicero, *Letters to Friends*, 1.9.18), and the letter to Quintus in which he declares Plato "the foremost of men in genius and learning" (Cicero, *Letters to Friends, Letters to His Brother Quintus*, 1.1.28). See also a multitude of references particularly in *De Legibus* (Cicero, *De Legibus*, 1.15, 2.14, 3.1), *Tusculanae Disputationes*, and *Academica* which restate Plato's teachings or praise them.

76. Cicero, DF, 5.87.

77. Cicero, *Academica*, 1.16.

78. Cicero, *Academica*, *1.46.*

79. Cicero, TD, 5.11; note the conflation of Platonic and Socratic teaching.

80. Cicero, TD, 5.11.

81. Cicero, TD, 5.11.

Chapter 4

Political Philosophy and the Unity of the Two Ways

De Republica, 1.20–64

The beginning of *De Republica*—both Cicero's preface and the initial dialogue between Scipio, Tubero, and Laelius—centered on the question of whether the active or contemplative way of life was best. Being on holiday as they are, unfettered by necessity, should they concern themselves with the things above or the things below, with the eternal or the changing? Chapters 1, 2, and 3 advanced the argument that, despite Cicero's pedagogical stand against the contemplative life in his preface, he is advancing a subtle argument for the unity of these two ways. It turns out that no sort of inquiry more capably represents this unity than political philosophy, which turns it gaze now to first things, now to present things, now to things to come, aiming continually to understand how men can best live.

The arrival of the venerable Laelius, his attendants, and Manilius to the conversation prompts Philus to comment that they need not abandon their philosophical discussion regarding the second sun, but that they should now "discuss more carefully" (Lat. *accuratius*).[1] Philus' diligence here parallels a similar comment near the end of Book 1 when, after the extended discussion of the simple regimes, Scipio comments that he will need to speak carefully (*accuratius*) about the *commutationibus rerum publicarum*, the change or alteration of republics from one to another.[2] What is meant by "careful" speech is not what we might expect, because what follows Philus' comment is a course of conversation that wanders from anecdote to anecdote and finally to a somewhat repetitive discussion of the simple forms of republics; what follows Scipio's comment is the suspect, even haphazard, histories of the Roman kingship and republic in Book 2. In truth, both of these speeches are "careful," but they are not careful in the way we expect. Cicero's writing is first and foremost pedagogical, meaning that he emphasizes corrective

69

opinions, not simply the account he believes is correct. In *De Finibus*, for example, to the Epicurean he defends the Stoic, to the Stoic the Peripatetic, and to the Peripatetic the view he (or his persona) finds more probable. It is in careful reading, however, that we can discern the golden thread of Cicero's own insight running through his argument.

In the previous chapters, I suggested that the productive interplay and tension between the modes of life forges the path toward a unified way of life. Now, Philus' commentary on the spheres of Gallus develops the astronomical analogy to show us how to take hold of politics and civic life as another nexus of unity between theory and practice, the unchanging and the changing. Although Philus is not widely held to be Cicero's mouthpiece in the dialogue, he is in this case, which becomes clear in the course of the argument and also in the play-within-a-play acted out by Scipio and Laelius in which the unified relationship of active and contemplative is put on display. Unpacking the cycle of regimes, finally, will help demonstrate how philosophic statesmanship is a prerequisite of a sustainable political order.

The second part of Book 1, which is the focus of this chapter, is simultaneously a discourse and a play, one which reveals that the life of the citizen, rightly understood, is the nexus that joins the active and contemplative ways of life into the fully human life. Cicero believes that politics has a great deal to do with philosophy, and philosophy with politics, much more so than abstract consideration might suggest. Indeed, politics in Cicero's understanding is not the closing of a philosophic horizon, but the vehicle for a whole people's openness to being.

THE CONFLICT BETWEEN THE
CIVIL AND NATURAL LAW

The conflict between the active and contemplative lives exists because the chief activity and end of each resides in distinct realms, and where they touch they seem to do so destructively, not constructively. A civil society maintains order based on a shared understanding of justice expressed in law, but philosophy questions our assumptions about justice; on the other hand, a life truly devoted to contemplation demands a rigor and commitment that is frustrated by the thousand daily impositions of civic duty and the active life. This tension is evident as Cicero's interlocutors, all assembled at Scipio's home, commence their conversation. When Philus tells Laelius that they had been about to discuss the second sun, Laelius gives his Socratic objection: the matter is irrelevant to man. Philus responds with a poetic reminder that "this whole universe" is a home which men share with the gods, and so these inquiries are not simply irrelevant—and they are also wonderfully delightful at that.[3,4] Laelius, somewhat surprisingly, readily concedes to this argument and makes a joke that they should proceed unless Manilius wishes to make an interdict simply banishing each sun to its proper place. Manilius responds with exasperation that Laelius is mocking civil law, commenting that without it, "no one can know what is his and what is another's."[5] This light exchange, which seems at first glance to constitute mere banter, directs our attention to some significant problems on closer inspection.

Specifically, this brief exchange between Laelius and Manilius raises two issues, one epistemological and the other ontological. The epistemological issue has to do with property and law. How do we know what belongs to us and to another? Manilius' specific claim about civil law is significant in what it says about the limit of human knowing. Is it true that no one can know what he owns unless the civil law has spoken? On the one hand, generally speaking, this claim is manifestly untrue. In practice, among neighbors or among nations throughout history, there is little ambiguity about possessions except on the margins. Most property, whether private or communal, does not become a matter of dispute because custom and reason readily clarify ownership in most cases, whether codified civil law has spoken on the matter or not. People know what is their own and what is not; a thief knows that he is stealing. On the other hand, when legitimate disputes about ownership arise, they can be extremely difficult to adjudicate. In these disputes it would be easy to resolve the conflict at random (by flipping a coin, for example), but such a random method doesn't even pretend to look to what is just and what is right, and is understandably unsatisfactory. How can matters be settled by right and with the requisite certainty? Manilius claims this task for the law-maker.[6] The civil law affords a *quasi* clarity, a practical clarification of what is yours and mine that can address most disputes to public satisfaction. Yet, the law can be poorly executed or wrong in itself, and even when the law is formally right, there are claims to right that can transcend legal right. The civil law significantly helps in addressing disputes about right, but at best it often only approximates justice rather than perfectly guaranteeing it.

It is no accident—to broaden our gaze—that this little aside between Laelius and Manilius hints at a similar, critical issue in Socrates' question to Cephalus at the beginning of Plato's *Republic*. In both dialogues, the issue is raised almost right from the start. In Plato's case, the question of property, of "mine" and "yours," is seen in the first attempt by the interlocutors to establish a definition of justice. If a man deposits a sword with a friend and then comes back to claim it when he's become insane, should his friend give him his property or deny it to him?[7] The point of this dilemma is to reveal the tension between law and right, since to deny the insane man his sword would be a *pro forma* violation of law, but to give a dangerous weapon to a madman would seem to be wrong, even though it is his property. Manilius, if we take him at his word, would be inclined to resolve such conflicts on the basis of law, but it is obviously problematic to be handing swords out to madmen, which is Socrates' response. Reasonable men recognize that what the law commands is not always right. Problematically, however, if claims of "right" are given preeminence to the law, then law would in effect be irrelevant.

Scipio expresses the claim of the supremacy of right over law only a little later in *De Republica* when he declares that the "wise man" is justified in taking and using, regardless of civil law, on the basis of the right of wisdom, which truly knows the proper use of each thing. The "wise man," Scipio asserts, may "truly claim all things as his own by right not of the Quirites but of the wise, not by a civil obligation but by the common law of nature."[8] Whether or not this is true, it would be deeply problematic in practice. Sometimes the law is wrong, but nearly all men believe themselves wise and would be delighted to be laws unto themselves. It is perhaps questionable, furthermore, whether a truly wise man exists;[9] regardless, the rule for the wise man can hardly be the rule for all. As we will see shortly, Laelius enters to mediate between Manilius and Scipio with his Socratic, ethically-oriented insight.

Beyond the epistemological difficulty, there is an ontological difficulty in the conflict between law and right. Is there, in fact, an underlying principle of order, or a metaphysics, in human things? Is there a *ratio* for reason to grasp? The second sun is a disruption of the ordinary appearance of heavenly things, but not one of the characters seems to assume that something is wrong or out of order in the celestial realm as a result. They assume that this appearance merely signifies a problem or disorder in earthly affairs, which the heavens in their perfection are nevertheless wont to signify. When Tubero first comes to Scipio, he asks whether they should discuss the "meaning" (Lat. *ratio*) of the second sun because he presumes that it appears according to reason or nature such that a proper account can be given of it. According to his presumption—and, as far as we know, the assumption of all the characters in the dialogue—the heavens seem to change because the sun, planets, and stars *seem* to move errantly in the sky, though in actual fact they follow a sublime celestial order. Even the staggering motions of the planets—sometimes following an arc of movement, sometimes holding still, sometimes darting backwards, from an earthly perspective—are said to follow some law. Hence, the change in the heavens suggested by a second sun is merely apparent; it does not indicate a deviation from the proper ordering of things above. In his initial conversation with Tubero, Scipio confesses his preference for inquiring into a question that is more relevant, but also more difficult: What principle of order or right governs terrestrial, human affairs? The earthly realm is mutable not only because things move—things also move in the heavens—but because they do not readily or agreeably conform to a principle of order or reason.

They are free; they can will to do otherwise. Reason does not inhere in the affairs of men. If this is true, is it proper to speak of "right" in the context of human affairs at all? Thus, Manilius' simple declaration that only civil law tells a man what is his and what is not his—that only civil law orders human community, because there is no other tangible ordering principle—brings to our attention the problem that reason is severely lacking in human affairs. Perhaps it is lacking altogether.

The epistemological and ontological problems posed by the conflict between civil law and natural right seem, superficially, irreconcilable. If there is no nexus between them, then law is necessarily a convenient lie which maintains peace but not right, and politics is merely a struggle between and among the wills of the strong. This problem sets the stage for the discussion to follow. Just as Tubero had wanted to inquire into the "meaning" (Lat. *ratio*) of the second sun, so Cicero had stated in his preface his intention to express the *ratio* of political things.[10] Laelius is not keen to discuss the second sun, but he embraces the notion that right is a proper concern for human beings and that there is an order in things which points the way for the flourishing of men and republics. Scipio, likewise, affirms that there is a principle of right by which the wise may lay claim to all things, but his high assertion offers no relief to the practical problem of ordering human affairs. It is Laelius who brings the ethical question to the fore, asking for a discussion that will clarify the touch point between the effectiveness of the civil law praised by Manilius and the true ordering of the natural law praised by Scipio.

THE TWO GLOBES OF GALLUS

After the arrival of the interlocutors, and after Philus' call for careful discussion and the raising of the problem of law, Philus continues the conversation with his account of the globes, or orreries, seen by Gaius Sulpicius Gallus. These models of the cosmos had been carried off from Syracuse by Marcus Marcellus' grandfather. One of them was placed in the Temple of Virtue and was "lovelier and more renowned by the crowd," apparently being open to public view at least to some extent.[11] In contrast, of all the rewards he could have gained by right of conquest from "that most opulent and ornate city," Marcellus' grandfather only claimed for himself a second orrery.[12] Philus reports that this globe seemed unimpressive, certainly compared to the one in the Temple of Virtue, which was "solid and full," and had not only been "fashioned" by Thales of Miletus, but was inscribed (Lat. *descriptionem*) with the heavenly wanderers by Eudoxus of Cnidus, "a student of Plato," and its wondrous design "commemorated in verse" by Aratus the poet.[13] Marcellus' orrery, on the other hand, seemed rather plain. However, unlike the more ornate globe, it was capable of movement, "contain[ing] the motions of the sun, the moon, and the five planets that are called wanderers and, so to speak, roamers, [which] could not be drawn on the solid globe."[14] It was a cosmic clock of sorts, a wondrous construction which would not be imitated for more than 1,500 years. There are a number of observations to be made about this comparison.

First, on the one hand, the discussion of the two globes is meant to make a *distinction* between two modes of knowing or making known, the popular way and the way of the wise. In the dialogue, the importance of this distinction follows directly from the mystery regarding the nature of the second sun, but more directly it parallels the problem of the apparent tension between civil and natural law.

Second, on the other hand, the discussion of the globes is meant to show a *unity* between the two globes. Both of them offer models of the heavens, but one is merely a static approximation whereas the other is a dynamic apprehension of the true motions of the spheres. Likewise, the civil law is a static approximation of right which makes evident, even in an imperfect way, a reality which is otherwise obscure. The civil law is right for the most part, which is better than letting obscurity in matters of law remain unaddressed. Yet, he who grasps "right" in itself is uniquely able to see in obscure matters, especially in cases where the law is wrong. This distinction between the two globes is likewise akin to the distinction between middle and complete knowledge that Cicero spells out in *De Officiis*. The action of the ordinary man on the basis of middle knowledge (or, decorum or appropriateness) may look much the same as the action of the wise man based on complete knowledge (or, wisdom) in most cases, but the reason "why" for the ordinary man is simple and for the wise man very deep. Middle and complete knowledge in action may act the same (as the two globes describe the same astronomical reality) but they are not quite the same (one based on a static approximation of the truth and the other one a dynamic apprehension of the truth in itself). Both of these first two points, the distinction and unity of the globes, must be discussed further in the following section.

Third, the discussion of the orrery is meant to help us understand—or help us understand how to understand—the nature of political things themselves. In other words, the cosmological analogy offers a *ratio*. As Robert Gallagher notes, the astronomical language used to discuss the motions of the sun, moon, and planets is very intentionally carried over by Cicero into his discussion of the cycle of regimes.[15] Cicero's intention is to show how the motions of regimes may be regulated by the guide who understands the natures of things. This point will be most productively addressed after the discussion of the simple regimes and the cycle of regimes.

THE DISTINCTION AND UNIFICATION
OF TWO MODES OF KNOWING

The comparison between the two globes continues the conversation intro-duced earlier in the prologue between practical and theoretical concerns. Most superficially, the two globes serve as reflections of the real, but they are reflections that allow insight into different truths. The truths, or goods, of practice—courage and justice most particularly—are, like the orb of Thales in the Temple of Virtue, "lovelier and more renowned by the crowd." The orb of Archimedes, however, is entirely opaque to the many, and only wonderful to the one who, in privacy and contemplation, seeks insight.[16] Marcellus, who plundered it from Syracuse, was so taken by its worth that he forsook all other treasure and took only this globe to his home.[17] As Strauss sees a fundamental antithesis between the two ways of life, we could draw a distinction between these two globes, the orientation of the person who delights in them, and the relative quality of their delight. But, I would suggest, this emphasis would be mistaken. The significance of the globes lies in the degree to which they do, in fact, overlap in their revelation, albeit in different modes, and this becomes clear in the subsequent discussion.

Of the unifying connections between these globes, two stand out: first, that the two globes do in fact describe the same reality, but in different ways; second, that Marcellus brought them both (not one or the other) to Rome. With respect to their similarity, it is important to emphasize that the globe popular with the crowd is hardly ordinary or vulgar. Not only is its construc-tion a work of art, but the artist who embellished it with the planets, Eudoxus of Cnidus, is noted to have been "a student of Plato."[18] Furthermore, Aratus translated this accomplishment into poetry in his *Phaenomena*, a poem which Cicero himself translated into Latin in roughly 90 BC. Both Aratus and his poem are referenced several times in Cicero's work.[19] For Cicero, Aratus' poetry—or at least his own translation of Aratus' poetry—is not merely amusement, but education, and political education at that. At the beginning of Book 2 of Cicero's *De Legibus*, the companion book to *De Republica*, the character Marcus declares that they must begin the work of legislation from Jupiter.[20] Scipio makes a similar comment in making his case, a little later in Book 1 of *De Republica*, that kingship is the best of the simple regimes.[21] The value of beginning with Jupiter, as Scipio says, is that "all educated and uneducated men agree" that he is "the one king of all gods and human beings."[22] As Timothy Caspar has noted, to begin with Jupiter, then, is to begin with the presumption of a governing authority or principle made evident through images to the eyes of all, but understood phenomenally by the ignorant and noumenally by the educated (as Scipio goes on to say, the "common teachers . . . of accomplished men. . . . have felt that this entire universe [is ruled] by a mind").[23] The globe that Marcellus donated to the Temple of Virtue was a fitting gift because, like the poem or argument that "begin[s] with Jupiter," it is a way of illuminating the order and truth of things in a way that is accessible to those who would not otherwise understand. This is likewise the distinction that unifies the two globes: one reveals, simplistically, the reality of celestial order to the many, preparing them for wisdom, while the other, wondrously, reveals the complexity of celestial order to the wise, or to those already seeking wisdom.

A longer lacuna interrupts Gallus' description of the motions of the orrery. Scipio is speaking after it. On his way to giving his unexpected and astonishing praise of the theoretical life, Scipio makes an argument that recollects Plato's analogy of the helmsman.[24] In that analogy, Plato imagined a ship (an analogy to the polis) with a shipowner who was very great but rather dull (the *demos*, or people), in which the sailors (the *politeuma*, or governing class) quarrel and compete over who should be in charge of the ship. In their competition, the sailors continually denounce the relevance of knowledge of sailing or navigation and declare that it is unteachable in order to protect their own opportunity for ruling. In addition, they abuse and dismiss the man who has studied the sea, wind, and sky as being useless, when he is in fact the "true pilot" (488a-e). In Plato's story, this pessimistic account of political affairs simply serves as an indictment of the disunity of wisdom and rule. In Scipio's story, however, the "true pilot" is vindicated. Speaking of the same Gallus whom Philus had brought up in connection with the orbs, Scipio recounts how, while on campaign, there was a terrifying lunar eclipse. The soldiers, as a result, were deeply "disturbed by superstition and fear,"[25] but Gallus pacified them, not by some pretense that the event was a good omen, but by arguing that it was no omen at all: "he did not hesitate to teach openly in camp that this . . . had happened then and at certain times would always happen when the sun was so located that it could not reach the moon with its own light."[26] Whereas in Plato's analogy the show of learning was dismissed with derision, the authoritative show of wisdom finds much greater success in Cicero's rendering, as Scipio notes that "he [Gallus] . . . banished the empty superstition and fear from the disturbed men."[27]

Scipio's argument is a rejuvenation of the idea that wisdom is relevant and salutary to political life. The understanding of things that theoretical inquiry brings about should govern over men but it does not, as Plato argues, whereas Scipio suggests that wise understanding does not always rule, but can. This Scipionic optimism is further emphasized in a second anecdote regarding Pericles, which demonstrates both the relevance and the practical influence of celestial knowledge. In this second instance, Pericles assuaged Athenian fears following a solar eclipse, overcoming superstition with reason.[28] Scipio's description of Pericles' success ties this argument back into Cicero's larger scheme to provide an account of the meaning [*ratio*] of political things: "When [Pericles] taught this by arguing and by [giving] reasons [*rationibus*], he freed the people from fear" (DRP 1.25). Cicero's ambition to present a teaching on the *ratio* of political things is hopeful not only because it means there really is a *ratio* of political things (as Plato would agree), but more so because that reason truly can be brought to bear on human affairs, because human beings will embrace it if it is properly revealed to them. Reason can even overcome fear and unreason. Cicero is bold enough to believe that his rhetoric can accomplish this great deed.

Yet, Cicero is not so carried away by his own capacities that he does not recognize the limits of the possible. Lest we become too confident in the teaching of unalloyed *theoria* suggested by Scipio, Cicero gives us immediate reason to pause. Both Gallus and Pericles successfully alleviated the people's fear through their teachings about the movement of astronomical bodies, but Scipio then offers a third example which makes a different point. Appealing to the authority of Ennius and the *pontifices*, Scipio undergirds the claims of Romulus' divinity by pointing out intersections between historical records and calculations of previous eclipses. Scipio notes, "Although in fact nature snatched away Romulus during the darkness to a human exit, it is said that his virtue carried him off to heaven."[29] Problematically, as Fott notes, not only was there not an eclipse during that time, but other historians do not even record that there was said to have been one during Romulus' death.[30] As far as we can tell Cicero has fabricated both of these details out of whole cloth, a fact which would have been apparent to his contemporary readers. Cicero has dressed up truth in his own Noble Lie. This fabrication does not undermine the effectiveness of theory in politics, but it suggests that theory may need the help of poets, leading us back to the value of Gallus' popular, static sphere, which is a Noble Lie in its own way. For the many to properly understand the significance of Romulus, the intrinsic must be made extrinsic by being made visible with poetic adornment.[31] It is good to think of one's founder as a god; it points men to the heavens, law to justice, and thought to unchanging right.

Notwithstanding Cicero's concession that darkness clouds the minds of men to some extent, which poets must pierce with pleasing and bright fictions, Cicero departs to an astonishing degree from Plato's skepticism about the possibility of infusing and ordering the body politic according to the *ratio* of things. His optimism underscores the degree to which he sees amity between the two modes of growing wise: through the beautiful and honorable, which spontaneously evokes admiration from all, and through the true, which beckons the subtle with its profound depth.

At this point in the dialogue Tubero points out that Scipio seems to have changed what he said at the beginning when he had expressed a preference

for Socratic inquiry into the ethical. Now, instead, Scipio seems to a significant degree to be defending the utility of theoretical study. Unfortunately, a
lacuna obscures Scipio's response, but one wonders how Scipio could have
offered a response that aligned these two perspectives. Scipio's new view is
hardly moderate or interested in theory for the sake of practice. Rather, Scipio
offers an unabashed defense of the contemplative life which prioritizes the
pursuit of philosophy and concedes nothing other than the truth as good,
and only engages in practical matters as a concession to necessity. He would
consider nothing that constitutes the goods of an ordinary human life—"our
fields, buildings, cattle, and enormous amounts of silver and gold"—to be
genuine goods.[32] Rather, the wise man "looks down on all human things," and
so such a man, we must infer, looks down on family, friends, and country as
well.[33] Scipio's words are a clear echo of the words of his adoptive grandfather, Scipio Africanus, who declares in the Dream of Scipio at the end of the
book, "look always at these heavenly things, scorn those human things."[34]

Scipio's astonishing dismissal does not go unremarked: Laelius responds
to Scipio with precisely the opposite point of view, emphasizing the value of
"other studies of a freer character" which are useful "in life or even to the
republic itself."[35] Contra Scipio, Laelius insists that speculation regarding the
heavens is not very worthwhile, but that our concern with safeguarding human
things is. The complexity and contradiction—already evident in Scipio's
reversal of his earlier statement—is deepened when we note, somewhat unexpectedly, that Laelius' opinion is also affirmed in the Dream of Scipio, with
Scipio's father Paullus declaring that Scipio should not "flee the human task
assigned by the god" but rather "cultivate piety and justice," particularly with
"respect to your parents and relatives, but most important[ly] with respect to
your fatherland."[36] Scipio's grandfather likewise exhorts his adoptive grand-
son, "You should employ [your eternal soul] in the best matters! And the best
cares [*optimae curae*] are for the safety [*salute*] of the fatherland."[37]

These comments by Scipio and Laelius—with Scipio unexpectedly reversing himself from the Socratic (and Laelian) position he had professed in the
prologue—establish two poles within an apparent unity: nothing is good
except eternal things and yet the most worthwhile concern is care for human
things. These twain, one would think, ne'er can meet—and yet they must, or
Cicero's project has failed. The apparent inconsistency between these two
perspectives is ultimately resolved in Cicero's explication of the soul in the
very last paragraph of *De Republica* (see chapter 5), but the remainder of
Book 1 offers us Cicero's illustration of the unity of the two lives in conversation and relationship between Laelius and Scipio.

NOTES

1. Cicero, DRP, 1.19.

2. Cicero, DRP, 1.65.

3. Cicero, DRP, 1.19. This comment by Philus, which is reminiscent of Stoic teaching about man's home in the cosmopolis, is one reason why Philus is sometimes considered a Stoic. Cicero himself, taking his writing as a whole, would doubtlessly affirm Philus' statement as well, however, and he is an avowed Academic Skeptic. One can responsibly speculate that *if* there is any character in *De Republica* who speaks or acts for Cicero, it may well be Philus.

4. The consequence of the cosmos being our home is that Scipio and Laelius are therefore always at home (and, in some sense, always abroad). One should likely not place too much stress on this detail, but it is notable given the stated relationship between Scipio and Laelius, that Laelius honored Scipio as a god when abroad and that Scipio honored Laelius as a father when at home (Cicero, DRP, 1.19). Philus' comment adds an interesting twist. This same ambiguity was already implied in the group's settling into the sunny meadow, which meant they were both home and not at home.

5. Cicero, DRP, 1.20.

6. Cicero, DRP, 1.20.

7. Plato, *Republic*, 331e.

8. Cicero, DRP, 1.27. Amusingly, and perhaps importantly, Scipio ends this extended praise of wisdom with a "saying" by "Plato, or someone else" about a man who saw geometrical drawings in the sand on a shoreline and knew thereby that other human beings must be nearby. This saying belongs to Aristippus, in fact, who was likewise a disciple of Socrates but seems to have chosen the enjoyment of temporal goods over the sempiternal good. Scipio has "stolen" this quotation; either he is not wise (or, at least, knowledgeable enough to know whose quotations are whose) or, being wise, he has a right to steal it and, presumably, misattribute it to Plato.

9. Only two such men are identified by Cicero: Socrates and Aristippus, of all people: "No one should be led into the error of thinking that because Socrates or Aristippus did or said something contrary to custom and civic practice, that is something he may do himself. For those men acquired such freedom on account of great, indeed divine, goodness" (Cicero, DO, 1.148).

10. Cicero, DRP, 1.15, 1.13.

11. Cicero, DRP, 1.22.

12. Although Polybius discusses the siege of Syracuse, no other extant source confirms the story that Cicero tells of how Marcellus took the two orbs, donating the magnificent one to the Temple of Virtue and keeping the smaller one for himself.

13. Cicero, DRP, 1.21–22.

14. Cicero, DRP, 1.22.

15. Gallagher, "Metaphor."

16. Cicero, DRP, 1.22.

17. Cicero, DRP, 1.21.

18. Cicero, DRP, 1.22.

19. Obliquely in *De Republica* but explicitly in *De Legibus* and *De Natura Deorum*, for example.

20. Cicero, DL, 2.7.

21. Cicero, DRP, 1.56.

22. Cicero, DRP, 1.56.

23. Cicero, DRP, 1.56. I am indebted to Timothy Caspar, *Recovering the Ancient View of Founding*, for these insights regarding Aratus' poetry in Cicero (Caspar, "Recovering," 169–73).

24. Plato, *Republic*, 488a-e.

25. Cicero, DRP, 1.23.

26. Cicero, DRP, 1.23.

27. Cicero, DRP, 1.24.

28. Cicero, DRP, 1.25.

29. Cicero, DRP, 1.25.

30. Cicero, DRP, 1.25n.56, 57.

31. Cicero will engage in his own poetic history to make the implicit explicit in his history of Rome in *De Republica,* Book 2, which seems to distort Roman history but in fact strives to bring out the *ius* threading faintly through the Roman order.

32. Cicero, DRP, 1.27.

33. Cicero, DRP, 1.28.

34. Cicero, DRP, 6.24; Z20.

35. Cicero, DRP, 1.31.

36. Cicero, DRP, 6.19–20; Z15–16.

37. Cicero, DRP, 6.33; Z29.

Chapter 5

How to Go to the Heavens

De Republica, Book 6, redux

Chapter 1 began by suggesting that Cicero's *De Republica* was an attempt to answer the question, "How should a good man live?" As a Roman, as a powerful man in his own right, Cicero was necessarily himself interested in knowing how a good man should rule and what his actions had to do with the ever after. The elder Africanus declares in the Dream of Scipio—asserting a point that Cicero would affirm in general—"[f]or all those who have preserved, assisted, increased their fatherland, there is a certain place marked out in heaven where happy persons enjoy everlasting life."[1] For Scipio and for Cicero, there is an ineluctable parallel between the things above and the things below; an eternal soul inhabits every human being; principles of right known to the wise and the prudent pervade human affairs. Taking this broad, cosmic view, indeed, the narrow calculations of simplistic utilitarians show themselves to be foolhardy. What is good and what is truly useful are one and the same, in the final analysis, an argument that Cicero develops extensively in his *De Officiis*. Thus, Cicero's political teaching turns out to be concerned not only with the politically salutary, but with the salvific. Cicero is concerned with political statesmanship and the best constitution because he is concerned with things beyond the political; he is concerned with this given city in light of man's universal and eternal home. Living well does not involve following a narrow prescription or formula, however; rather, it involves prudently navigating the way between various poles.

Cicero grapples with the tension and connection between the particular and the universal throughout *De Republica*. A central way he does this is through illuminating several instructive binaries, such as the first and second suns, the active and contemplative lives, the eternal Heavens and the temporal Earth, the concern over foreign influence in domestic affairs, and a related theme of adoption and natural parentage. Cicero uses these tropes continually throughout *De Republica*, consistently highlighting the tensions they create while

81

persisting in the conclusion that they are productive tensions. The question for us should not be, for example, how to insulate the domestic scene from foreign influence: Cicero is not interested in driving the Greeks out of Rome. The question, rather, is how to mediate between foreign influence and domestic order to derive the best outcome. Indeed, Cicero's whole political scheme rests on the reality and reconciliation of these various tensions, a mode in keeping with his Academic skepticism more than with any sort of dogmatism.

THE DREAM OF SCIPIO: THE ACTIVE AND CONTEMPLATIVE LIVES REVISITED

The tension between the active and contemplative lives is paralleled in the tension between other pairs, such as between the Heavens and the Earth and natural or adopted parents. These analogies help illuminate fresh dimensions of the tension and its proper resolution. When Scipio begins his dream, which offers the clearest example of this approach, he encounters his adoptive grandfather, Publius Cornelius Scipio Africanus. Africanus reveals to Scipio the glory he will earn in overcoming Carthage and foretells of his service to the republic that will prove so central to the salvation of Rome.[2] His grandfather notes, finally, that "there is a certain place marked out in heaven where happy persons enjoy everlasting life," specifying that "guides and preservers of [cities], having departed from here, return here."[3] In sum, Scipio's adopted parent discusses Scipio's earthly glory with him, but with eyes raised to heaven. Now Scipio encounters his deceased natural father, Lucius Aemilius Paullus, in an emotional reunion. In tears, Scipio begs to know why he should not hasten to shuffle off his mortal coil to come join his father in the Heavens, but Paullus cautions him with a word about the divine charge that men have to abide by their earthly callings: "Human beings have been begotten under this law: that they may protect that globe you see in the middle of this sacred zone, which is called Earth."[4] Paullus emphasizes the importance of his son fulfilling his earthly duty, since "[t]hat life [of pious service to family and fatherland] is [a/the] way to heaven."[5] Then the adoptive Africanus returns to guide Scipio through the secrets of the heavenly spheres and their music.[6] In an implicit rebuke of Paullus' emphasis on human duty, when Scipio's eyes "repeatedly" fall back to Earth, his elderly grandfather remonstrates that he should "look always at these heavenly things, scorn those human things."[7] There is a tension between the earthly and heavenly orientations, one which is paralleled both in the tension between the active and contemplative lives and in the emphases of Scipio's natural and adoptive parents.

Paullus' advice to Scipio suggests that political duty is the only way a man may deserve to enter the heavenly realms, but Cicero, likely intentionally, leaves the finality of this assumption unclear. This ambiguity is present in the division among translators on how to render the article in Paullus' declaration that a life of pious service is "a" or "the" "way to heaven."[8] The translation of this small word pivots on a very great question in *De Republica*: is the active life, which is essentially concerned with executing political duties, the best way of life?[9] Rudd (1998) and Zetzel (1999), for example, prefer the definite article, suggesting that the active mode of life is the only relevant mode of life for human beings who ultimately wish to transcend the earthly sphere. Fott (2014) prefers the indefinite article, however, suggesting that there may be another route. The primary support for Fott's translation is the fact that, mere paragraphs later, Africanus notes that "educated men, having imitated this [heavenly] place with strings of musical instruments and songs, have opened for themselves a return to it, just like others who have cultivated divine studies in human life with preeminent talents."[10] In his commentary, Zetzel (1995) also notes the significance of this sentence and helpfully notes that the phrase "divine studies" is also used in *De Senectute* 24 to refer to poetry and philosophy.

Who, then, can be saved? Speculative philosophers such as Pythagoras might possibly pave their way to the Heavens on the strength of their contemplative insight, but this reference is Cicero's nod of appreciation to such men, not an esoteric repudiation of the political virtue he has been championing all along. Preceding his observation that "educated men [*docti homines*] . . . have opened for themselves a return to Heaven," Africanus states that of the "eight courses" of the heavenly spheres, two of which share an identical "pitch," "cause seven sounds distinguished by intervals," then concluding somewhat mysteriously that "that number is the knot of almost everything."[11] Zetzel astutely connects both of these comments to Cicero's preface where he says that those who still find themselves persuaded by the philosophers (despite his critiques) should "listen to those whose authority and glory are highest among highly educated men [*doctissimos homines*]." He goes on to identify, specifically, "those seven men the Greeks called wise," noting that "almost all were engaged at the center of public affairs."[12] Within the economy of Scipio's Dream, we should take the elder Africanus at his word that theoretical inquiry "opens up" a way to the Heavens, but we should not overestimate the significance of this observation. Six of the seven men to whom Cicero directs us are either noted for their political philosophy or involvement in political affairs.[13] As has been said, action and contemplation, like beautiful acts and beauty itself, are overlapping, reinforcing pursuits. Action that is not oriented by contemplative insight hits the mark only accidentally at best, with little credit to the actor; and contemplation not crowned by accomplishment is an incomplete thought. Thus, in the Dream, as Schofield says, "Politics is not . . . devalued, but placed firmly in a broader context."[14] All throughout

De Republica Cicero maintains that virtuous action is the means by which man is good and does good and that the virtuous action that fulfills man's god-ordained duty is largely political, because it has to do with living together well and in accordance with right.

The apparent contradiction between Paullus' earthly emphasis and the elder Africanus' heavenly emphasis is ultimately the fit medicine for the moment. In the Dream, when Scipio pleads with his natural father to be allowed to escape earthly bonds and aspire to the heavens—hinting at suicide[15]—Paullus moderates his son's desires by emphasizing duty to family and fatherland; but when Scipio's gaze afterward persistently steals back to Earth, Africanus responds by emphasizing the divine and sublime existence in the Heavens as an explicit counterpoint. In other words, though Paullus and Africanus seem to be offering competing perspectives at first glance, in truth their counsels are complementary medicines for souls drawn either too much to Heaven or too much to Earth. Both counsels should be heeded, neither neglected. This same prudent alternation explains Scipio's surprising reversal in Book 1: first he professes privately to Tubero (who eagerly wishes to discuss the second sun) that he is wary of impractical contemplation but, when shepherding a conversation about political life, he publicly valorizes apolitical wisdom as the most worthwhile thing to help orient politics by universal right.[16] Different rhetorical emphases are meet for different men and different moments. This modulated approach of Cicero's, by the by, would seem to help explain his habit of alternating between referring to Scipio as "Scipio" or as "Africanus," at least early in the dialogue. "Scipio," the natural man, echoes the earthly perspective championed by his father Paullus when Tubero wants to fritter away valuable leisure discussing the apparent second sun; "Africanus," the glorious man, expresses the heavenly point of view preached by the elder Africanus to the citizens of his little republic lest they confuse Roman law for genuine justice, Roman custom for genuine wisdom, or Roman splendor for genuine glory. For example, Cicero refers to "Africanus" when noting how he philosophized "even under the walls of Numantia";[17] when Scipio is describing and defending the man who despises earthly things in comparison to heavenly ones;[18] and when Scipio "return[s] to first principles" to discuss the republic.[19] In the ordinary course of conversation, Scipio is always, otherwise, merely "Scipio."

To accept this idea that there is no straightforward "answer" to the best way of life, but that every person must prudently navigate the poles of action and contemplation, one need not be an Academic skeptic as Cicero was, although it would help. Cicero, in keeping with the Academic approach, does not ultimately attempt to fabricate a theory that systematizes all reality and formulates ready-made answers to every question about how to live (even if he is willing to provide general guidelines, as he does in *De Officiis*). Throughout his writings he criticizes the Epicureans, the Stoics, and even the Peripatetics for the way they eviscerate common sense in a brutalist or Procrustean fashion, sifting out the elements of human experience or wisdom's counsel that do not fit within their frameworks. In *De Finibus,* in particular, Cicero spurns the Epicureans because they deny the soul (Books 1 and 2), chides the Stoics for spurning the body (Books 3 and 4), and quibbles with the Peripatetics for discounting the place of pleasure in happiness (Book 5). Cicero accepts all reasonable experience and conclusions as meaningful and real in some way. If a given theory cannot make sense of the full scope of human experience, so much the worse for the theory: Cicero stands with the facts. Cicero does, of course, seek to reconcile difficulties. However, when tensions arise—such as between the call to the Heavens and to the Earth, between contemplation and the active life—Cicero's preference is for the productive tension. In such cases, Cicero suggests that alternatives serve as tonics to the opposite's excess. Cicero's somewhat eclectic approach to theory does not mean he rejects theory entirely, only that he holds any given theory loosely. He takes his guidance from what prudence tells him is fitting.

THE KEYSTONE: PLATO'S THEORY OF THE SOUL

The Dream of Scipio is a powerful attempt at mythmaking—serving as an analogy to Plato's Cave and the Myth of Er simultaneously—but Cicero, who had spurned the philosophers in the first pages of *De Republica*, shows his hand by concluding with a dense philosophical argument. That argument is a presentation by Africanus of Plato's theory of the soul, an example of a theory Cicero advanced more generally.[20] Africanus exhorts Scipio to remember that his true self is not his apparent form, but that "the mind of each person is each person," and that this divine element means that man is "a god" who governs the "fragile body" just as "the eternal god himself moves the partly mortal universe."[21] In the argument that proceeds, Africanus unfolds the argument that all life—everything which contains the spring of motion within itself—must originate from an unmoved mover, from a beginning that had no beginning and which exists eternally, since otherwise "the entire heaven and all nature necessarily would collapse and stop."[22] This same element that governs the cosmos—the soul—is embodied in man, establishing not only an analogy but an interconnection between earthly conduct and heavenly order. Just as universal mind is concerned with the perfect order of the heavenly spheres, so the incarnate soul should "employ itself in the best matters," the order of earthly communities. Thus concerned, Africanus asserts, a soul "will fly more swiftly to its own seat and home here"—and all the more so if, while on Earth, it "contemplat[es] those things that are beyond" rather than engrossing itself in bodily concerns, which shackle the soul to Earth.[23] This theoretical account, presented at the pinnacle of both *De Republica* and the Dream of Scipio, acts as a keystone in Cicero's argument in establishing a nexus between the things above and the things below.

This argument resolves an early concern in the dialogue that "law" and "right" have nothing to do with each other—indeed, that right is inscrutable and that law, in consequence, is only the will of the stronger. This concern arises when Manilius states that "no one can know what is his and what is another's" without civil law, a claim that parallels the discussion in Book 1 of Plato's *Republic* about property (i.e., swords belonging to madmen) and right (i.e., whether madmen have an absolute right to their swords).[24] When Africanus downplays the significance of human affairs by showing how miniscule human accomplishment is relative to the cosmos, readers might mistakenly draw the conclusion that the actions of antlike men scurrying for short whiles on their pitiful hills can hardly matter, or perhaps that it is foolish to think that justice or injustice on such a small scale could have any significance. From the point of view of truth and goodness, however, justice is as important on the small scale as it is on the large scale. The law really does have to do with "right," and "right" is a pivotal concern for human beings regardless of scale.

The idea of the soul is a keystone in *De Republica*, binding together Heaven and Earth, but Cicero's argument does not depend on this account being true. Cicero, as an Academic skeptic, trusts the intuition that the right he perceives is genuine "right" and not merely custom, but also recognizes the value of providing an account to help explain that this is so. Plato's argument for a principle of mind that governs both the macrocosm of the universe and the microcosm of human society is the link that dignifies human endeavor and elevates the significance of our actions out of this moment and into eternity. As a skeptic, Cicero would not ultimately assert that Plato's explanation must be the final, comprehensive answer to the question of right in human affairs. Regardless of Plato's theory, although we may find it somewhat puzzling to know why reasoning minds find themselves enmeshed in mortal bodies, and that their bodies are so small compared to the heavenly ones, this does not mean our minds do not reason or that our souls do not matter: they do, and therefore they must live according to reason in their context, a context which Cicero believes includes both Earth and the cosmos. The doctrine of the immortality of the soul is a theoretical explanation that offers one good way to intellectually reconcile the disjunction between the eternal and the temporal into a unity of alternating, but reinforcing centers.

Ultimately, the reconciliation of the active and contemplative lives does not mean there is no tension between them, but this tension draws the very best out of us. In the second book of Cicero's *De Legibus*, the character Marcus declares that all men have two fatherlands, "one of nature, the other of citizenship." He confesses, furthermore, that his greatest delight is the natural home of his youth, but that he is often compelled by duty to attend to the greater concerns of the city.[25] Though he longs to linger in the home where his own father "spent most of his life . . . in literary studies," he commits himself to the greater land which "encompass[es]" the first.[26] Similarly, from our point of view we are adopted, in a sense, into the heavenly spheres, but our primary affection belongs to our natural parent.[27] It is this devotion that spurred Scipio to his virtuous endeavor on Rome's behalf, and it is this virtue which "opens an entrance to the heaven for those who have deserved well of their fatherland."[28]

NOTES

1. Cicero, DRP, 6.17; Z13.
2. Cicero, DRP, 6.15; Z11.
3. Cicero, DRP, 6.17; Z17.
4. Cicero, DRP, 6.19; Z15.
5. Cicero, DRP, 6.20; Z16.
6. Cicero, DRP, 6.21–23; Z17–19.
7. Cicero, DRP, 6.24; Z20.
8. Cicero, DRP, 6.20; Z16.
9. The question could be complicated further: Is it possible that the way of life that is "best" on Earth is not the way of life that leads to the Heavens? For example, is it possible that the contemplative life's *imitatio dei* engages in the highest activity and rouses the rarest delight, but that it is the virtuous laborer who will win a place in the Heavens? This could be the case if contemplation is "best," but justice is what is required. If this is so, human existence is tragically riven between duty and the good. However, Cicero does not seem to believe there is a disjunction between the good life and the life deserving of the Heaven's reward. One of Cicero's claims in *De Republica*, and in his writings generally, is that the good and the useful are fundamentally aligned. This difficulty and its resolution—that a man who has his eyes set on the Heavens will put his hand to the plow and persevere, come what may, on Earth—strikingly anticipate the mystery Christianity will bring to Rome within a century, that the life in imitation of God means embodying the suffering servant.
10. Cicero, DRP, 6.22; Z18.
11. Cicero, DRP, 6.23; Z19.
12. Cicero, DRP, 1.12; Zetzel, *Selections*, 241.

13. The list varies, but Fott renders it as including Bias, Chilon, Cleobulus, Myson, Pittacus, Solon, and Thales, with Thales being the notable exception to political involvement (Fott 34fn.28).

14. Schofield, *Cicero*, 108.

15. Cf. Zetzel, *Selections*, 232.

16. Cicero, DRP, 1.15, 26–29.

17. Cicero, DRP, 1.17.

18. Cicero, DRP, 1.26–29 ("Do you see, Africanus").

19. Cicero, DRP, 1.38.

20. In addition to paraphrases of Plato's *Phaedrus* in DRP 6.26–28 (cf. Zetzel, *Selections,* 249–253), which relate directly to the soul, Cicero translated Plato's *Timaeus* into Latin, a dialogue related to explaining the origin of soul (Annas, *On Moral Ends*, xxii).

21. Cicero, DRP, 6.31; Z27.

22. Cicero, DRP, 6.32; Z28.

23. Cicero, DRP, 6.33; Z29.

24. Cicero, DRP, 1.20.

25. Cicero, DL, 2.3.

26. Cicero, DL, 2.3, 2.5; cf. DRP 1.14, 19.

27. Cf. Cicero's comment vis-à-vis Tusculum and Rome in the beginning of DL 2.5.

28. Cicero, DRP, 6.30; Z26.

PART 2

Cicero's Political Teaching

Chapter 6

On the Regime

De Republica, 1.20–64

Cicero's apparent optimism regarding the philosophic education of the many is the striking claim undergirding the discussion of regimes that proceeds from this point in the dialogue. Laelius and company prevail on Scipio to speak to them out of his learning regarding "the best form of a city," which Laelius sees as the proper introduction to a series of politically-oriented inquiries.[1] Despite his extraordinary praise of the contemplative life, Scipio now explains that these considerations are what he is most often concerned with, since "this one task—the management and administration of the republic" was a charge laid upon him by his "parents and ancestors."[2]

Before Scipio begins his explanation of the types of regimes, he undertakes an explanation of what a regime is. Scipio begins his speech by promising not to begin as the Greeks did. He will not "begin with the first meeting of male and female" (as Aristotle did), and he will not "give frequent verbal definitions of what each thing is" (as Plato did).[3] So he states, but he then proceeds to do just the opposite, a subtle and amusing way for Cicero to concede to the Greeks that they did, in fact, know how to engage in inquiry well. He begins with a definition of a republic (a "'thing' of a people," based on the literal translation of *res publica*) and then goes on to explain what a "people" is.[4] Cicero gestures to Aristotle with his commentary on the "natural herding together" of men, denoting our natural sociability.[5] Were all of our needs provided for we would still gather together, Cicero asserts, a comment which he strikingly reiterates in *De Officiis* about both man, generally, and the wise man himself.[6]

As a minor point of distinction, Scipio's genetic argument for the origin of society here departs rhetorically from Aristotle's in emphasizing the whole more than the parts. Aristotle's genetic argument in *The Politics*, Book 1, begins with the parts and works up to the whole: man comes together for procreation (male and female) and survival (the natural ruler and ruled), the

91

household forms for daily needs, the village forms for non-daily needs, and the polis may possibly then emerge as a flourishing of the concern for justice and living well.[7] Cicero's discussion is not so granular, either in detail or in its serious recognition of a pre-social existence.

HOW PERSONS BECOME A PEOPLE

Cicero would consider it crucial for us to understand that man's good, man's place, is found in and through community. To put it somewhat emphatically (and somewhat anachronistically), Cicero's "state of nature" is man in political society. "The first cause" of this assembling of a people, Cicero declares, "is not so much weakness as a certain natural herding together, so to speak, of human beings."[8] Society is not woven on a loom formed by the imposition of external necessity and primal urges, in his telling, but on account of an original sociability. In emphasizing natural sociability rather than convention or necessity, Cicero is siding with Plato, Aristotle, and the Stoics against Protagoras and Epicurus.[9] This hearkens back to the claim Cicero made in the preface[10] that men come together because it is good and out of an ingrained desire to seek the good of one another, rather than due to the compulsions of fear, scarcity, or need. This "herding together," a given of man's nature, is informed and infused by man's innate reason and spontaneously generates a people through a "multitude being joined in agreement in right and allied in a community of mutual benefit."[11]

The important question to ask is what Cicero means by *"coetus multitudinis iuris consensu."*[12] Schofield rightly notes that Cicero's formulation is "original" to him and has "far-reaching theoretical implications," and needs to be carefully considered. What is the nature of the agreement that forms a people? Is *"consensu"* best rendered as explicit "consent" (a strong reading) or "concord" (a weaker reading) or "consensus" (a moderate reading)? And does *"iuris"* refer to agreement "about right," as David Fott avers, implying an agreement conditioned on the shared understanding of justice;[13] an agreement to justice based upon specified, concomitant "rights," as argued by J. W. Atkins;[14] "on law," implying an agreement tied to a specific legal expression of justice, as James Zetzel argues;[15] the "consensus of justice," as Schofield argues, meaning substantial enjoyment both of the exercise, and the result of the exercise, of rights;[16] or more generally "in right," as Walter Nicgorski says, implying the broad commitment of one people to submit to justice or right together in general?[17] The differences between and among these possibilities are crucial. If a "people" is based on an agreement about the meaning of right, then an Epicurean and a Stoic (for instance) cannot be part of the same people; changes in opinions about justice would fracture the social bond, and hence philosophy would inherently be an anti-political act, an act of parricide. Although *ius* could quite possibly be understood to imply "rights" due to the Roman emphasis on property in civil law, Atkins' argument for this translation is made by inference and, though right, should go farther. He captures an aspect of Cicero's meaning, but not yet the whole, and broader interpretations will prove more satisfying. Likewise, if a "people" is based only on agreement regarding a particular expression of law, as Zetzel suggests, then a people would potentially be dissolved with a change in the law. In any of these cases, any long-lived people would only be a people nominally, but due to changes in law and conceptions of justice over time would never truly be participating in the same republic as their ancestors. They would not be a "people" in the full sense that Cicero has in mind. (Cicero's usage of *lex* and *ius* also belies the attempt to reduce *iuris* to "law.")[18] None of these definitions is sufficient to capture Cicero's meaning. Much more satisfying is Schofield's argument that a "people" are one insofar as they experience a "consensus in justice," or a substantial enjoyment of rights and the beneficial outcome of their exercise. He helpfully illuminates the practical aspect of political life that finds unity in unanimity, and elsewhere makes the important point that liberty and the enjoyment of rights was, for Cicero, something enjoyed by a people rather than by individuals.[19] The common experience of justice itself creates the consensus that forms a people.[20] Agreeing with Schofield, then, in terms of the practical meaning of *iuris consensu*, there is nevertheless another dimension to the kind of consensus or agreement that knits a people together, one that precedes political practice and resides in cult and culture, that is more essential to Cicero's understanding.

A most Ciceronian understanding of civic unity is found in the suggestion that a "people" is fundamentally formed by an agreement "in right" or to right generally, much as Nicgorski suggests. In forming partnerships we assume a shared rationality which makes it possible to deliberate meaningfully about right in particular instances whether or not we have thought about them much beforehand. Human society is constituted by people who are allied together, but not necessarily all in agreement. Whereas modern theorists such as Thomas Hobbes and John Locke, eschewing teleological formulations, drive man into society by fear or scarcity and bind him to that covenant by an alleged act of his will, Cicero emphasizes that beneficent nature and circumstance conspire to draw man into a common endeavor with his fellow men for the sake of right and common benefit, even if the assembled multitude does not quite know or claim to know what justice is. Man does not need necessity to orient him to society; nature, orienting man to his good, inhabits him with society.

That men could enter into society agreeing "in right" without per se knowing what it is both describes social realities very well and is the position most consistent with Cicero's philosophical commitment to Academic skepticism. Who, indeed, knows what is true with the degree of certainty and with the requisite scope that he does not need to improve his understanding? This is a task to which man, invested with reason, is perennially called. It would be strange if nature brought man into society under such conditions that to inquire into a deeper understanding of right would violate his social bond.[21] That Cicero's emphasis here is the shared orientation to right and not an express agreement regarding right is confirmed by the repetition of the definition of a "people" in the Dream of Scipio when the Elder Africanus states that "assemblies and assemblages of human beings" are those which are "united in right," a formulation that retains the emphasis on "right" but leaves out the *consensu* which was part of the first definition.[22] It is reasonable to conclude that the "agreement" is more tacit than explicit.[23]

If a multitude can become a people by together embracing a commitment to right without knowing exactly what it is, this does not mean that every cluster of persons is a people. A soldier surrounded by enemies is not joined with them in a community of mutual benefit; a foreigner in a marketplace is subject to laws regarding theft but does not participate in ordaining them or in punishing offenders, and so is not truly joined (*coetus*) "in right"; a man in a bowling league does participate in community based on a certain sort of order and a certain sort of benefit, and is thus a "people" of its own, but only in a very thin sense. A man in civil society proper, however, when confronted by some violation of right—whether of the express law, ordained customs, or principles of equity—will join with his fellow citizens in deliberation and binding judgment in a community formed as much by nature as by men. The foundation of this union is the agreement "in right" suggested by Nicgorski; its outlet in practice is the enjoyment of rights and their beneficial practice outlined by Schofield.

There are greater and lesser skeptics of the notion that Cicero actually agrees with Scipio's argument about man's sociability. In particular, Charles Kesler is deeply skeptical of the idea that Cicero truly believes man's sociability is a more fundamental cause of society than necessity. Rather, he states that Cicero (in writing Scipio's account of the origin of peoples) "observes a gentlemanly decorum by refusing to lift the veil that covers the origins of the people."[24] Kesler goes on to comment that Cicero obscures the "artificiality of the city," though he does not explain why he thinks that Cicero would have thought the city artificial and not natural.[25] To support his opinion, he cites a comment in Cicero's youthful *De Inventione* that suggests that pre-communal man was also pre-social, simply "wandering dispersed in the fields like animals."[26] However, Scipio explicitly declares in his discussion that "this species is not solitary, nor does it wander alone," suggesting a repudiation of this earlier view.[27] Cicero's account of pre-social man and society's origins in *De Officiis* is likewise more dignified, suggesting a change in his thinking.[28]

Scipio's stated conclusion follows from an anthropology confirmed throughout Cicero's writing, especially in the preface to *De Republica* and in the passages mentioned in *De Officiis*. In *De Legibus*, the character Marcus references the arguments "Scipio expressed" in *De Republica*, noting man's distinction from the grazing animals rather than his similarity to them, and attributing this not to the act of a divine man raising them up into society (as in *De Inventione*) but due to divine "planting" of the "human race."[29] Marcus concludes, "Now since god [thus] begot and adorned the human being . . . it is clear . . . that nature itself proceeds further by itself: even with no one teaching it . . . it alone strengthens and fully develops reason."[30] Once again, Cicero substantially de-emphasizes the role of necessity or any special intervention in the development of human beings in community. They are not individuated in a pre-social setting where couplings of male-female and master-slave form and persevere because of daily and non-daily needs. As William Frank notes, "Cicero has no sympathy for the common misperception that social life is somehow derivative of ends and purposes more fundamentally individual."[31] In originating society, Cicero emphasizes the natural desire human beings have to dwell with one another.[32]

THE ROLE OF DELIBERATION IN POLITICAL LIFE

When a people have come together in a community, Scipio goes on to note that they undertake three tasks: finding a place for themselves, making it a dwelling place, and adorning that place—now become a "town or a city"—with "shrines and common spaces" (Lat. *delubris distinctam spatiisque communibus*).[33] Implied in this coming together is what Cicero assumes distinguishes a "people" from an "assemblage of human beings," specifically in their being "united in agreement about right [*iuris*]" and in their "sharing of advantage [*utilitas*]."[34] The question then is whether this order will remain or will collapse, and deliberation (Lat. *consilio*) must therefore rule in order to sustain it.[35]

This deliberation must take its orientation from man's sociable nature first of all. The task of deliberation is not to discover and apply right in the abstract but rather to safeguard the agreement, the social bond, of a people.[36] This is a critical point for Cicero, and unfortunately one which suffers from some confusion. Cicero declares, *Id autem consilium primum semper ad eam causam referendum est, quae causa genuit civitatem* ("this deliberation, foremost of all, should always look back on the cause that gave birth to the city").[37] But what is the "cause" of the city? David Fott notes that Sabine and Smith (1929) understood the "causes" to be the choosing of the place and the characteristics of the multitude, and so forth, but Fott rightly criticizes this interpretation for wrongly ascribing multiple factors where Cicero refers to one "cause."[38] However, Fott somewhat misses the mark as well, going on to point to two causes himself, based on Scipio's earlier clarification that a people is "an assemblage of a multitude united in agreement about right [*iuris*] and in the sharing of advantage [*utilitatis*]."[39] Schofield, alternately, suggests that the first cause is "the binding together of human beings effected by justice," in the sense that they become one people by virtue of sharing in the enjoyment of justice.[40] Neither Fott nor Schofield fully uncover the Ciceronian meaning, though they help to flesh it out. Scipio's reference to the "foremost . . . cause"[41] refers to what Scipio had explicitly stated was the "foremost cause" (Lat. *prima causa*) of the city only a few lines earlier, the "certain natural herding together, so to speak, of human beings."[42] Men's sociability is the seed of society, and advantage and right are its root and flower. (In a fragment from Book 4, an unknown speaker uses the same terminology to make the same point: "the citizens' fellowship of living happily and honorably . . . is indeed the first cause of assembling.")[42][43] Agreement and justice are not preconditions of society, or necessarily our conscious intention. Rather, men seek society and friendship spontaneously: agreement, justice, and common benefit are the confirming bonds of our societies, the fruits of amity, but not the origin of community.[44] This is a key distinction: if this is true, then the primary task of deliberation is to preserve the social friendship, the felt sense of being a people, that is the prerequisite of political life. This certainly involves respecting agreements, justice, and common benefit, but it reaches much more profoundly to cult and culture and to the soul of a city.

In wanting to emphasize the agreement made about right, some commentators perhaps succumb to the temptation to over-theorize or over-rationalize Scipio's account. However, the cause of man's coming together is not an agreement about what, in particular, is right, but the spur of nature which invigorates men to live together according to right, whatever precisely it may be.[45] As was said earlier, in Cicero's conception of man's nature, this spontaneously involves a shared commitment to right and to mutual benefit. That Cicero believes that deliberation should be primarily concerned with the bond of fellowship is confirmed only a few sentences later when Scipio declares that any of the three forms of rule is "tolerable" so long as it "maintains the bond that first bound human beings among themselves in the fellowship of a republic."[46] Legislators, then, should seek the justice that maintains peace through right rather than a zealous pursuit of right that exacts penalties at the expense of peace.

THE *STATUS* AND THE SOUL

Having established the need for deliberation in maintaining a people and its "thing," the republic, the question of who will undertake that deliberation on behalf of the republic arises. Through whose guidance can a people best be preserved in right? In keeping with the classical tradition, Scipio identifies the possibility of the rule of the one, the few, or the many, identifying them with kingly, aristocratic, or popular rule.[47] The object of the inquiry is to identify the best regime, but Scipio proves unwilling to state a conclusion in this regard until forced into doing so by Laelius, though he discusses his dissatisfaction with the popular city extensively.

The inquiry that began the discussion regarding republics and regimes concerned knowing the "best form" (*optimum statum*) of the republic. This begs the question of what a "form" is. Sorting out its meaning is complicated by the fact that Cicero frequently employs three words that overlap with *status*,[48] his primary term for "form," and sometimes alternates their uses. These three words are *genus*,[49] *modus*,[50] and *forma*.[51] *Genus* and *forma* seem more specifically to refer to the formal, defining characteristics of a given regime: one, few, many, or mixed. This distinction is suggested by a fragment from *De Republica* preserved by Nonnius, the exact placement of which is uncertain: "the republic was established in its best form [*statu optimo*], which is a moderate blend of those three types [*tribus generibus*], the regal, the aristocratic, and the popular."[52] This same distinction is evident in another fragmented line in Book 2, in which Scipio says, "if you are inquiring about the type [*genus*] of the best form [*optimi status*] without the model [*exemplo*] of a particular people, we must use the image of nature."[53] Every type of regime can be denoted by its *genus,* but *status* is a broader concept which also refers to the character of a regime and thus to the character of the people it forms. However, why does Cicero sometimes refer to the *status* as a *modus*, a "measure" or "manner"? Answering this question requires unpacking more explicitly what Cicero means by *status*.

Cicero gives us a very explicit suggestion of what he means by *status* in a passage in *De Legibus* when the character Marcus declares: "[Plato] says that the forms [*status*] of cities are changed along with changes in musicians' songs; but I think that the customs [*mores*] of cities change along with changes in the nobles' lives and ways."[54] The ineluctable parallel Marcus draws here between *status* and *mores* suggests that Cicero is thinking of a definition which is not simply formal (as with *genus*) nor is it simply institutional. The essence of a *status* is distinctly moral, having to do with a way of life. As Schofield aptly comments, "For Cicero . . . it appears that what contributes mots to the curability of a *res publica* is a people's way of life, given shape by its established practices and laws, and the sorts of human being that it fosters, rather than its political system."[55] Related to the reference Marcus made to Plato, music, and the soul, there is a parallel passage in which Cicero discusses the order of the mixed regime, a passage in which Scipio draws the same parallel between music and civic order:

> As with lyres or flutes, so also with song itself and voices, a certain harmony must be maintained from distinct sounds, and trained ears cannot bear for it to be changed or discordant; yet this harmony is made concordant and congruent by the moderation of very similar voices. So a city harmonizes in the agreement of very dissimilar persons through reason moderated by the intermingling of the highest, lowest, and middle orders, as with sounds. What musicians call harmony in song is concord in a city, the closest and best bond of safety in every republic.[56]

Although Scipio does not explicitly mention the *status* here (the text is cut off at this point, leaving a significant, 22-page gap), it is clearly what he has in view, showing how Cicero's overarching concern is to elucidate how the parts of a city may be harmonized to produce the "agreement [*consensu*] of dissimilar persons."[57] The mixed regime does not primarily exist to separate, check, and balance powers, as in the modern sense of a constitution, but rather to beget a balanced *status*, a moral constitution, which will serve as a stable foundation for the commonwealth. It is clear that the constitution of a people and the organization of their regime are intimately linked, which is further confirmed in Scipio's explication of Rome's republican history: "Hold on to what I said at the beginning: unless there is in the city an evenhanded balancing of [right], duty, and service, so that there is enough power in the magistrates, enough authority in the deliberation of the leading men, and enough freedom in the people, this form [*status*] of the republic cannot be preserved safe from change."[58] If Cicero's formal concern is the republic, his substantial concern is the *status*.

Given the significance of the *status* to Cicero's work, one might wonder why his book is not called *De Statu*. Indeed, given the acknowledged fact that *De Republica* is Cicero's emulation of Plato's famous work—entitled the *Politeia*—this is more puzzling, given that the Greek *politeia* is more specifically parallel in meaning to Cicero's use of *status* than *republica*.[59] They refer to the "constitution" of a people, both in terms of a moral constitution and a political or legal constitution, and at the heart of the endeavor to explain the meaning of political things in both thinkers is the claim that there is a critical nexus between the moral and political dimensions of a body politic. But there are a few reasons to suppose why Cicero titled his work as he did. First, the term "re publica" would be more familiar to his Roman audience; second, it would seem more obviously relevant to his Roman audience; and third, the "'thing' of the people" is most precisely the *status*, meaning that *re publica* is an apt placeholder for that term. As Nicgorski argues, Cicero's main disagreement with Plato, "if it be much of a quarrel, has to do with the utility of a detailed depiction of the city in speech."[60] There is little reason to think that Cicero differs fundamentally from Plato in his understanding of the meaning of political things, but in bringing political philosophy to Rome, Cicero is keen that it be salutary both to Rome and to the reputation of philosophy. He accomplishes this by formally engaging in an authorial task "on the republic" which, in effect, is really a book "on the form" or "on the constitution."

The idea of a "constitution" is clearly relevant to a discourse on political things, but Cicero goes further in pointing to the regime as a nexus that binds the political and philosophic together. In several instances, Cicero uses the word *modus* as a synonym for *status*, a curious alternation which helps unveil the deeper significance of the inquiry into regimes. Hearkening back to other usages of *modus*, in the prologue Scipio and Tubero discuss the difference between two other *modi* in the way of Plato and the way of Socrates. Just as Cicero means to unite these two strands, a "constitution" binds together theory and practice by ensconcing precepts of universal justice in particular laws. One of the difficulties discussed by scholars such as Leo Strauss is that the "way," customs, or laws of a people simultaneously reveal and obscure justice. The tendency of critical thought has been to suggest that the particularity of a people is ultimately not only unphilosophic because of its attachment to particular expressions of law instead of justice simply, but even anti-philosophic because to question the grounding of the law in justice is to undermine the law. (Hence they killed Socrates.) However, Cicero persistently maintains the possibility of a politics, and thus of an entire people, open to philosophy's reorientation.

An inextricable issue in the discussion of Scipio's definition of a "people" is the question of their relationship to right, and particularly their openness to right, and thus to the ground of right. As a matter of course, it is true that a people come to feel themselves a people through being united in a common attachment to right. Scipio's definition of a people does not require them to cling to that particular, common understanding in order to remain a people, as was argued earlier; they can remain a people so long as they maintain a shared commitment to right in practice, even if their understanding changes.[61] The notion that *ius* is true but not summed up in "truth statements" is very much in accord with Cicero's avowed skepticism. We can approach truth, we can be right or wrong about it, but it can never be reduced to a simple and comprehensive statement. It is not merely that political slogans cannot capture truth in itself, but that the most subtle writing can only approach it and never fully comprehend or encompass it. Given these things, Cicero would

understandably define a people so as to maintain that *even a people* could live
with an openness to being. Such an openness, especially for a people, would
require prudent guidance, of course. As Walter Nicgorski argues in *Cicero's
Skepticism and His Recovery of Political Philosophy*, Cicero turns from
emphasizing the regime to emphasizing the guide. It is important to recognize
that in doing so Cicero does not downgrade the significance of the regime;
if anything, he has an elevated conception of its possibility. The discussion
of simple regimes is ultimately also a discussion about the government and
education of souls.

THE SIMPLE REGIMES

With the concept of the *status* clarified, we may return to the discussion of
the simple regimes. Cicero's identification of the simple regimes is in keeping
with the classical tradition's division of the rule of the one, few, and many.
Each of these has a good and bad form: the rule of the one may be kingly
or tyrannical, the rule of few may be aristocratic or factious, the rule of the
many may be popular or a disordered multitude or mob (*turba*). Kingship
is characterized by the rule of a "fair-minded, wise" man, whereas aristocracy is characterized by the governance of the "leading, select" men—even
the "best" men if we take the word *optimas* (aristocrat) at face value.[62] The
many (the people) are not characterized by any particular virtue other than
a non-grasping love of freedom. The only advantage of popular rule (if the
many are just) is the stability that comes from their all having a share in
deliberation. Rather than emphasizing strengths, Scipio's discussion of the
simple regimes very quickly tips into a discussion of their defects, since
Scipio's dominant perception of the simple regimes is that they are unreliable
compared to the mixed regime. The fundamental problem for the simple types
of regimes is that they do not sufficiently allow for sharing in right or for
right to be realized in such a way as to maintain concord. In kingship and in
aristocracy the multitude do not sufficiently share in deliberation, and so the
people do not have "a share in freedom," a state of affairs which offends and
concerns them.[63] Problematically for the popular regime, insufficient respect
is paid to the leading citizens and to the wise because there are no distinctions
of rank, and so the best do not carry any more weight than the worst.[64] Each
of these forms can be "tolerable," Scipio says, but they are not particularly
stable and are prone to slipping into defects.[65]

To keep the simple regimes in their proper courses requires "some great
citizen and almost divine man, while governing the republic, to foresee those
that threaten and to direct its course and keep it in his power."[66] Although this

reference foreshadows the introduction of the guide, Scipio's reference to this "wise" and "divine" figure is meant to underscore the difficulty of maintaining the simple regimes in their best condition, and not to suggest that it is either preferable or plausible to do so. To the contrary, Scipio recommends that they turn the conversation to the mixed regime because of this difficulty: it would be foolish to embrace a political order premised on the existence and office-holding of a wonderfully great man. Scipio has expressed significant reservations about the people because of who they are and, now, of kingship because of who a king would need to be. On this basis, if we stopped here, it would be altogether reasonable to presume that Scipio had concluded his argument regarding the best regime in favor of aristocracy and meant to move on to a discussion of the mixed regime because of its practicability.

In a surprising turn, however, Laelius interjects to ask for further discourse on the simple regimes, wishing Scipio to finish the discussion of the best simple regime properly "unless it is troublesome" (*nisi molestum est*).[67] Given Scipio's suggestion that the mixed regime is of much more practical concern to men interested in good government, this is an unexpected turn on Laelius' part. Earlier in the dialogue, notably, Laelius had defended his indifference to the second sun with a similar turn of phrase: "let it really be as it appeared, provided it is not troublesome" (*modo ne sit molestum*).[68] Laelius' interest in the simple regimes appears to be more than idle curiosity, since he reiterates this request not once, but twice (again in 1.54). But more unexpected than Laelius' new-found theoretical interest is Scipio's reticence to answer his question. Ultimately, it takes three requests by Laelius to compel his answer. What is it that Laelius is so determined to accomplish in pressing the matter of the simple regimes forward if the mixed regime is the true *optimum statum*? And why does Scipio not wish to indulge him? Something of a puzzle has sprung to the fore in the midst of the discussion.

The resolution to this puzzle is found in recalling that Cicero did not write a treatise, but a dialogue, and that the characters are each playing a part. In this case, furthermore, not only is each character a member in the dialogue, but a participant in a play-within-a-play that models for us the harmonizing rule of prudence in the republic and the regime. It is this play which helps us understand the dance that takes place between Scipio and Laelius.

THE PLAY WITHIN A PLAY: THE
ILLUSTRATION OF THE MIXED REGIME

The characters that gathered at Scipio's estate during the Latin holiday form a community that looks, on close inspection, less like a mere multitude and more like its own little republic. The group, free from compulsion due to the holiday, assemble of their own volition due to their sociable natures. As they trickle in, the friends cast about for a proper topic of conversation, mediating and moderating their discussion to satisfy the interests and opinions of the whole, thus naturally coming to a *consensus in iure* (agreement in right) and settling on a topic suited to common benefit, and thereby satisfying Scipio's definition of a people. The literal arrangement of individuals around Laelius, recognizing proper distinctions of age and glory, along with the eventual movement to the sunny meadow, establishes the community in a place and signifies the final development of this little republic.[69] With a society established on the basis of friendship and a common endeavor, they take up the shared work of deliberation. Then, as the discussion gets underway, each of the regimes is represented in a curious way, as each of the interlocutors provides his assent or approval to turns in the conversation, either personally or via proxy. The interlocutors arrive freely, as individuals or in groups, and each individual or group assents to pursuing the conversation regarding the second sun. Then, as the conversation turns—because of Laelius' objection to celestial contemplation—Laelius proposes that they have Scipio explain the *optimum statum*, the best form of the city. Only three characters now give their explicit approval, but seem to speak for all the rest, in an aristocratic turn: Philus, Manilius, and Mummius.[70] Finally, when Scipio proposes to begin the conversation with a discussion of the republic simply—what it is—the only character whose approval is relevant now is Laelius.[71] He gives it and the conversation begins, as well as a sort of play-within-a-play. But who are the leading players?

Through all this, we see that Laelius has shaped the regime by insisting on making practical the discussion of the second sun; by nominating Scipio for the tutor of the company and presiding over the vote and installation; by representing the opinions and interests of the group to and against Scipio; and ultimately by submitting to the wisdom of Scipio through a process of dialogue and inquiry. Notably, from this point on for the rest of Book 1, only Laelius and Scipio speak. Scipio provides the guidance, but in this little republic Laelius is the kingly governor and guide, in more ways than one. The regime that exists is made up of the mixed elements of the various simple regimes, but highlighted for us in this critical discussion of the meaning of political things is the interplay between the kingly guide and his teacher. They are like two suns.

This particular emphasis on the relationship between Laelius and Scipio recalls the earlier distinction made between them at their first meeting. Laelius "worshiped Scipio as a god" due to Scipio's glory when on campaign outside the city and Scipio submitting to Laelius' age in filial respect when *in domo*, at home (presumably in Rome).[72] The specific setting of the dialogue in Book 1 is intentionally ambiguous in this respect. On the one hand, the little gathering is outside of Rome, their home proper; on the other hand, they are at Scipio's home, which becomes the "cosmion" of this conversation. Yet, the conversation intentionally moved from the inner chamber to the porch (the threshold of home and field), and then to a meadow outside the home. Our little band is a community in its own right, with Laelius at its center, but it has migrated *ex domo*. With this movement, both the conditions of the friendship are met: Laelius, in his authority, commands the order of affairs and Scipio, in his glory, divines the nature of things.[73] The conversation proceeds to take place between Scipio and Laelius nearly exclusively because it is a conversation between law and justice, or practice and theory, with theory striving to convince practice of its relevance, and succeeding.

With the characters in the play revealed, we should return to the question of why Laelius wishes to discuss the best of the simple regimes and why Scipio does not. Laelius already seems to be intimately familiar with Scipio's thoughts regarding the mixed regime and its superiority. He has commented, after all, that he "remembered very often you would discuss with Panaetius in the presence of Polybius . . . and assemble many [arguments] and teach that the best form of the city, by far, is the one our ancestors left us."[74] Perhaps Laelius does not know Scipio's mind regarding the best of the simple regimes specifically, however; or it is possible that Laelius knows Scipio's answer quite well but wishes him to state and defend it for the benefit of the others. Once again, given that Scipio suggests that the mixed regime is of more practical interest, this theoretical interest on Laelius' part is somewhat unexpected and may seem somewhat pedantic. What Laelius hopes to learn by uncovering Scipio's opinion on this matter is not altogether clear, but we can discern several possible reasons for this development.

The first possibility is that Laelius, being concerned with matters regarding the republic, is invested in fully and adequately addressing matters of political theory. This would be reasonable and, if true, it would mean there would be no actual inconsistency with his earlier skepticism regarding inquiry. Earlier he was merely expressing frustration with what passed at the time for natural philosophy and relatively abstract considerations. Political theory has practical implications, but every theoretical discussion is to some extent undertaken for its own sake; besides which, one cannot always know what is practically relevant in theory until it has been properly explicated. Laelius' interest here is simultaneously properly practical and theoretical.

Second, in the contest of regimes, Scipio's silence may be appropriately politic. His discussion of the popular element makes it obvious that he believes freedom is important but that it readily veers into licentiousness. Kingship is the regime which, in theory, most fully unites wisdom and rule.[75] His ultimate opinion in favor of monarchy is one that Scipio believes may be offensive or problematic, and it seems outmoded to Romans, and so he wants to rush past it. In making his defense of the regime to the assembled group, Scipio must appeal to the poets and philosophers to justify his conclusion as reasonable because their republican practice must otherwise repudiate his conclusion.[76] Scipio would simply prefer to explain the mixed regime, in the context of which explaining the role of the one would be less offensive. After all, Scipio is not expressing theory simply but political theory, and doing so in a politic fashion. Theory, unvarnished, can easily offend, and Scipio—who defended the utility of theory in politics earlier by explaining how Gallus' explanation of eclipses removed the people's fear—is now choosing to shield theory from the harm of an indelicate revelation.

Third, this insistence on knowing which element is best and ought to rule is a perennial political reality. Each element feels its distinction and roots for it, even in the mixed regime—"yes, a mixed regime, but we must have the upper hand"! The regime requires a guide to harmonize these demands. Insofar as Laelius rules the little assembly, he simultaneously gives voice to this demand for clarity regarding rule and subsequently moderates the squabble by appropriately resisting Scipio's eventual assertion in favor of kingship. Laelius himself—although he serves as the kingly element in the group— never expresses a preference for one part or form, civilly resisting Scipio's argument for kingship until he is "almost to the point of agreeing," but not quite.[77] Laelius, who is Scipio's only interlocutor in the entire discussion of regimes, rules in the little assembly due to the concession of the other parts, not due to his own assertion. Although some commentators seem comfortable claiming a preference on Laelius' part for aristocracy,[78] there is no clear indication in the text we have that this is actually Laelius' preference. The only pertinent comment is made by Scipio in response to Laelius: "Then why do you doubt what you should feel about the republic? If the thing has been transferred to [*plures*] persons, one may understand that there will be no ruling command, which cannot exist unless it is united."[79] Both Zetzel and Fott somewhat presumptuously choose to translate *plures* as "several," suggesting that Laelius has expressed a preference for a republic governed by the few. Problematically, *plures* could very reasonably be translated as simply "more" or even "many more." The same issue arises when Laelius declares, "What, I beseech [you], is the difference between the one and the several [*plures*], if justice is in the several [*pluribus*]?"[80] In each of these cases, these translations have assumed that Laelius is defending aristocracy against kingship, when in fact he is simply representing the claims of the other elements of the regime against kingship. (Schofield rightly prefers to translate *plures* as "plurality.")[81] A subsequent comment by Scipio helps to confirm this, even suggesting that Laelius has made some comment in favor of the right of the many to rule: "Then you will agree more, Laelius, if I omit the similarities between one helmsman and one physician—that it is more correct to entrust a ship to the former, an ill man to the latter (provided they are worthy in these arts), than to many [Lat. *multis*] men."[82] Laelius seems to be resisting the claim of kings on behalf of both the many and the few.[83]

Laelius persistently requested Scipio to reveal his preference, and when he revealed his preference, he argued with him about it extensively; notably, Laelius had argued with Scipio about nothing else until this point. In taking up this argument, however, Laelius seemed more interested in embodying and moderating this dispute between regimes than in advancing any claim of his own. In doing so, Laelius helped maintain amity and balance in the mixed regime of the little assembly. The kingly element, Laelius, tentatively defends the claims of the aristocratic and popular elements while the divine element, Scipio, vindicates Laelius' kingly rule. Friendship and right have been preserved simultaneously. It is the interplay between Laelius and Scipio that leads to the politic result. Laelius, by pushing the discussion to the point of the identification of the best simple regime participates in an unfolding which ultimately allows Scipio to make a reluctant argument in favor of the rule of the wise man—reluctant because he does so at Laelius' insistence. Laelius, as the authority, represents the claims of the popular and aristocratic elements of the regime, maintaining harmony in their little community. Laelius, the model of the guide, thus establishes the conditions in which Scipio can make or explicate this theoretical claim without causing the degree of offense which might otherwise arise. This defense, and Laelius' sensitive resistance to it, ultimately vindicates the rule of reason in the regime. Early in this chapter we saw how Manilius' defense of the civil law raised the question of the relationship between natural and civil law; in this conspiracy of sorts between Scipio and Laelius we are given an illustration of how the philosopher and the statesman can indeed be friends, each honoring the other in their respective spheres for the betterment of all human affairs.

The eventual revelation of the guide in Cicero is a development that easily lends itself to downplaying the significance of the regime in Cicero's thought. In a sense, this is true: no static republican order can maintain the harmony of parts in any given society, but the balancing of these parts requires prudent guidance, and so the prudent guide comes to the fore. However, the guide is important precisely because the regime matters. The constitutional order represents an orientation of the whole to a better or worse conception of *ius*, and even though "right" can never be fully circumscribed, it can be distorted through the license of a corrupt people or corrupt governors. What is astonishing in this teaching is Cicero's optimism with respect to the philosophic reorientation of whole peoples. Although the many and the few will not perceive truth with the same ready depth, they behold and admire the same reality: the two globes of Gallus remind us of the two modes of revelation and two audiences, but also of the one reality they represent. In Book 1 of *De*

Republica, Cicero gives us an illustration of this teaching in the play dramatically enacted by the characters forming their own regime.

NOTES

1. Cicero, DRP, 1.33.
2. Cicero, DRP, 1.35.
3. Cicero, DRP, 1.38. Cf. J. Atkins, *Politics*, 56–57.
4. Cicero, DRP, 1.39.
5. Reminiscent in particular of Aristotle's *Politics* 1.1253a.
6. Cicero, DO, 1.12 and especially 1.153: "In my view those duties that have their roots in sociability conform more to nature than those drawn from learning . . . suppose a wise man were granted a life plentifully supplied with everything he needed so that he could, by himself and completely at leisure, reflect and meditate upon everything worth learning. But suppose also that he were so alone that he never saw another man: would he not then depart from life?"
7. Aristotle, *Politics*, 1251a25–1253a15.
8. Cicero, DRP, 1.39.
9. Brouwer, "Richer," 35.
10. Cf. Cicero, DRP, 1.3.
11. Cicero, DRP, 1.39; my translation. R. Brouwer helpfully explicates this definition in light of contemporary Roman law, suggesting that this definition accounts for the tripartite concern of civil law with property, persons, and obligations: "A *res publica* can be understood as the property (*res*) of a distinct group of persons (*personae*) that form a partnership (*obligatio*)" (Brouwer, "Richer," 36).
12. One of the notable reasons for interest in Cicero by relatively modern thinkers is his articulation of a social contract theory in emphasizing the agreement of the multitude. This has been understated and overstated.
13. Cf. Cicero, DRP, 1.39; Fott, "Introduction," 4.
14. Atkins, J. W., *Politics*, 130–37. He is careful to caution readers not to understand him in too Lockean of a sense (148–49).
15. Zetzel, DRP, 1.39a. Wood argues, not dissimilarly, that the phrase is best translated, "a union of a large number of men in agreement in respect to what is right and just and associated in the common interest" (*Social*, 126). As is argued further down the page, both of these translations over-specify what Cicero has in mind.
16. Schofield, *Cicero*, 49 and 58n.79–80.
17. Nicgorski, *Skepticism*, 169.
18. Schofield, *Cicero*, 66–67.
19. Schofield, *Cicero*, 30.
20. Schofield, *Cicero*, 67.
21. This highlights an important distinction between modern skepticism (such as that expressed by John Locke) and Cicero's Academic skepticism. Whereas Locke refuses to articulate a *summum bonum* (see *Essay Concerning Human Understanding*, Book 2, chapter 21, §55) because of stubborn differences in human opinion on the

matter, Cicero maintained that one could, through conscientious inquiry, grasp what was probably true of man and his good with sufficient clarity to base one's life on his conclusions. Cicero's optimism in this regard allows him to claim that the human partnership is rooted on the assumption of reason broadly rather than a shared conception of right, rights, or laws.

There are defenders of the idea that Cicero was in fact himself a radical skeptic (see Charles Brittain, "Cicero's Skeptical Method" in *Cicero's "De Finibus": Philosophical Approaches*, 12–40), but the argument most consistent with Cicero's own consistent testimony is the one most thoroughly advanced by Harald Thorsrud that Cicero was a moderate or mitigated skeptic (see especially "Radical and Mitigated Skepticism in Cicero's *Academica*" in *Cicero's Practical Philosophy*, 133–51).

22. Cicero, DRP, 6.17; Z13.

23. This interpretation is plausible on its own, but it gets some tentative confirmation from the *Institutes* of Gaius, a formalization of Roman law and legal terminology in the 2nd century AD Of course, Gaius' writing post-dates Cicero by more than a century and usages may have changed in the intervening time. Nevertheless, Gaius writes that a "contract is concluded by delivery of a thing, by words [*verbis*], by writing [*litteris*], or by consent [*consensu*]" (3.89). The distinction between these (signaled by *aut . . . aut* in the Latin) suggests that "consent" is an expectation or agreement *not* accompanied by either "words" or "writing," but a shared assumption of a common work. As Edward Poste, the translator and commentator of Gaius' *Institutes* writes, consensus consists "of two dissimilar elements, an intention signified by a promisor, and a corresponding expectation signified by a promisee. . . . The consensus of the parties is the chiming or going together of this intention with this expectation" (Poste, "Commentary," 3.89).

24. Kesler, *Natural Law*, 159.

25. Kesler, *Natural Law*, 160.

26. Kesler, *Natural Law*, 159.

27. Cicero, DRP, 1.39.

28. Cf. Cicero, DRP, 2.15.

29. Cicero, DL, 1.24.

30. Cicero, DL, 1.27.

31. Frank, "Retrieving," 9.

32. Walter Nicgorski undertakes an extensive discussion of the same points in his book *Cicero's Skepticism and His Recovery of Political Philosophy* (see 168–75). My analysis concurs with his in most details and in his conclusion. Nicgorski also agrees that "*consensu iuris*" is best translated as "agreement in right," though he does not discuss the significance of what it means to agree in right as opposed to "about right" or "about law."

33. Cicero, DRP, 1.41.

34. Cicero, DRP, 1.39. Aristotle also distinguishes between a city and a mere assemblage, noting that walls do not make a city, but citizens. Citizens are those who share in office, and office is concerned with the well-being of the city. Cicero's criteria are implied in Aristotle's, though Cicero has "de-politicized" his account by

not mentioning the citizen. All the members of the multitude (generally speaking, to be sure) agree on *ius* and *utilitas*, though not all exercise authority.

35. Cicero, DRP, 1.41.

36. Given Cicero's argument that the useful (*utilitas*) and the good (*bonum*) are one when rightly understood, and given that society, citizenship, and the political life are constituent parts of man's good, it is entirely sensible that deliberation should be concerned not with justice in the abstract but with what is to the people's true benefit, which must begin with the preservation of their social bond, the foundation of their community.

37. Cicero, DRP, 1.41; my translation.

38. Cicero, DRP, 1.41n.86.

39. Cicero, DRP, 1.41n.86; DRP, 1.39 (Fott's translation).

40. Schofield, *Cicero*, 68. See also 76–77.

41. Cicero, DRP, 1.41.

42. Cicero, DRP, 1.39.

43. DRP, 4.1; Z3.

44. Cicero frames this point in a somewhat different way in *De Officiis*, though the implication is fundamentally the same. In that work, Cicero identifies four categories of fellowship (Lat., *societas*) among men, including the community of mankind, the bond of tribe and tongue, the colleagues in law, camaraderie, and commerce, and the blood ties that yoke immediate relations (DO 1.54). Cicero resists prioritizing these in a clear way, stating that the most "serious" and "dearest" fellowship is with the republic, yet immediately adding that our first duty is to our country and our parents, thus giving both priority, while still further qualifying this ordering by noting that the sociability and rationality which characterize man are best satisfied in friendship, giving it a priority of its own (DO 1.57–58). The biological, the political, and the amicable (universal and particular) are each primary in their own way.

45. Or, at least, to seem to live according to right. The nature of man is inveterately oriented to the good; all men want to be, or at least seem, good. The fundamental difficulty is that men readily assume that the useful and the good are different things. As Marcus states in *De Legibus*, "Socrates correctly used to curse the person who first separated advantage from right, for he used to complain that this was the source of all disasters" (Cicero, DL, 1.33).

46. Cicero, DRP, 1.42.

47. Cicero, DRP, 1.42.

48. Cf. DRP, 1.33, 42, 44, 49, 51, 65, 68, 70–71; 2.2, 30, 33, 40–41, 43, 47, 56–57, 60, 62, 65–66; 6.2.

49. Cf. DRP, 1.42, 1.44–45, 64–65, 68–69; 2.22, 41–43, 47, 65–66; 3.17 (Z23), 35 (Z45), 36 (Z46–47).

50. Cf. DRP, 1.46, 67–69; 2.43.

51. Cf. DRP, 1.53; 2.22, 43.

52. Cicero, DRP, 87; Fragment 5.

53. Cicero, DRP, 2.66.

54. Cicero, DL, 3.32.

55. Schofield, *Cicero*, 84.

56. Cicero, DRP, 2.69.

57. Cicero, DRP, 2.69.

58. Cicero, DRP, 2.57.

59. This identification of *status* with *politeia* is affirmed by Elizabeth Asmis in her article "A New Kind of Model: Cicero's Roman Constitution in *De Republica*" (377n.1). Neither Asmis nor David Fott nor James Zetzel in their respective translations or notes give any particular attention to the term *status* in Cicero, though they discuss issues related to the form and character of the regime. This is a puzzling ellipsis in Cicero scholarship.

60. Nicgorski, "Cicero's Focus," 245.

61. By "right in practice" I mean the work of deliberation and judgment in assemblies and courts in particular.

62. Cicero, DRP, 1.42.

63. Cicero, DRP, 1.43.

64. Cicero, DRP, 1.43.

65. Cicero, DRP, 1.42–43.

66. Cicero, DRP, 1.45.

67. Cicero, DRP, 1.46.

68. Cicero, DRP, 1.32.

69. Cicero, DRP, 1.17–20. Literally, of course, Cicero would never say that a group of nine people talking shop at a friend's house could actually constitute a republic. Literarily, however, Cicero has created a "cosmion" in which these nine men form a quasi-people and a quasi-republic.

70. Cicero, DRP, 1.34. It is unclear why these three would be singled out at this point. In a fragmented sentence preceding a lacuna we see that Philus and Manilius were singled out in a comment by Laelius as well (Cicero, DRP, 1.30). Their selection may be related to the fact that Philus represents the philosophers in Book 3 and that Manilius seems to represent civil law. In a comment in Book 3, Mummius indicates his decided preference for aristocracy over a kingly or popular republic, though he prefers a king to popular rule (Cicero, DRP, 3.36; Z46). Perhaps he is a representative of nobility or *honestum*, so that *honestum*, the *iuris civile*, and the *iuris naturale* are represented.

71. Cicero, DRP, 1.38.

72. Cicero, DRP, 1.18.

73. It is significant, of course, that the character who embodies civil law arrives only when the little band has moved into the meadow, in the condition in which both Laelius and Scipio rule in their own ways. Manilius, the *vir prudens*, represents the nexus of justice and law, every city and this city, the meeting point of the perennial and the present. It is appropriate that he goes to sit next to Laelius. He is closely allied to his rule, but under the wing of his authority.

74. Cicero, DRP, 1.34.

75. Schofield cites Nicgorski in discussing Cicero's approach of presenting us with "the perfected condition" of things so that we can better understand how to approximate or approach them (*Cicero*, 73). As Schofield notes, Scipio does not (in the text we have) express this principle, and we might go farther and say that he

seems to repudiate it by preferring to rush over the simple forms in order to reach the mixed regime.

76. Cicero, DRP, 1.54–63. In recounting the history of Rome in Book 2, Scipio's generous gloss on the kingship could serve to bolster the theoretical defense of kingship. Rome's kingship begins and ends in tyranny, however, which would make it a poor example to the assembled group. History is less persuasive than poetry or philosophy because it furnishes ample examples of both the successes and failures of all regimes. History, furthermore, can only make a persuasive case about a regime's being good or bad by appealing to poetry and philosophy.

77. Cicero, DRP, 1.61.

78. Cf. Kesler, *Natural Law*, 161, 164.

79. Cicero, DRP, 1.60.

80. Cicero, DRP, 1.61; Fott's translation; only a few lines later Fott translates *plures* as "many."

81. Schofield, *Cicero*, 72.

82. Cicero, DRP, 1.62. *Multis* is the simple adjective; *plures* is the comparative form of *multis*.

83. J. Atkins notes that scholars are mistaken to think that Cicero himself, moreover, is quite as dedicated to defending aristocracy in *De Republica* as is sometimes assumed. There is reason to believe that his staunch defense of the optimates in *Pro Sestio* was more rhetorical and circumstantial than absolute (*Politics* 111n.110).

Chapter 7

The Cycle of Regimes

De Republica, Book 2

Now we come to the figurative midday of the first day of conversation. Book 2 commences the second half of the conversation and of the day, and it turns from a discussion of cosmology and of the simple regimes to Scipio's retelling of Rome's history. What Scipio and the others aim to discern is the best regime, in practice and in theory. At the conclusion of Book 1, Scipio had noted that, "When our own republic has been explained as a model, I will tailor to it, if I can, the entire speech that I must give about the best form of the city."[1] Given that so much of the remainder of *De Republica* is missing, Cicero fortunately wastes no time in beginning to fulfill this promise. Besides making use of Rome as a model of the best regime, Cicero subtly wove significant aspects of his teaching about the "meaning of political things" into the structure of his Roman history. Although Scipio begins his speech by claiming that his explanation of the best regime is not like that of Socrates, who "fashioned" a city in speech instead of relying on a historical example, Scipio's history turns out to be at least as artful as it is historical.[2] Scipio notes that Plato in his *Republic* devised a city "in which the meaning [*ratio*] of political things could be examined," but though he will deviate from Plato in describing a historical city, he will nevertheless reveal "the same meaning" that Plato saw.[3] Predictably, as a result, Scipio's narrative turns out to be deeply pedagogical and not merely expositional.

This pedagogical undercurrent suggests that Cicero's purposes in writing his own history of Rome are manifold: he writes as a historian, but more so as a teacher and as a statesman. However historical many aspects of Cicero's history are, it bears the artful, tell-tale marks of a city in speech. As a pedagogue Cicero weaves a sweeping scene through which he has threaded the winding "*ratio* of political things." This golden thread reveals the paradigm for understanding the courses of cities and of men in cities. That Scipio's history is more than a history is wryly observed by Laelius early in the narrative as he interjects "you [Scipio], ascribe to reason [Lat. *ratio*] those things concerning the site of the city that Romulus established by chance or necessity."[4] A *ratio*—a meaning, an account, an explanation, a glimpse within—is grasped by the intellect and offers a perspective on the real that unveils its underlying unity. Cicero is striving to communicate the true sense of the story of political society generally as revealed in the Roman story specifically.

This insight into the nature of things is hard to express and hard to comprehend, and so Cicero makes use of the pedagogical potency of testimony and story. Explaining the *ratio*, or meaning, of things involves engaging in a mode of revealing, a certain clarifying approach to truth, which can be perceived but never reduced to a blunt statement of fact. The imagination, here, can help—by means of history or poetry, for example—by taking reason by the hand and drawing it from point to point to clarify the very nature of things. When done well and when perceived by the prepared mind, reason thus comes to know certain essential things in human life, things we can recognize in all times and places. Experience sifted by *ratio* into an *oratio* is thus a form of revelation, and, unsurprisingly, Laelius goes on to remark, "As you follow the remaining kings to the end, I seem already to foresee the republic fully developed, so to speak."[5] Given Cicero's revelatory aim, whether we learn the meaning of political things by studying a fictional or historical city is ultimately beside the point. The point is to reveal the *ratio* in political things, or what in Greek might be referred to as its *logos* (reason, speech). This observation, combined with the fact that the history of Rome Scipio outlines is factually suspect, collapses the alleged distance between Socrates' "city in speech" and Scipio's "city in deed."

As a statesman, Cicero engages in this revelatory project because he believes that Rome needs reason to root her virtue, since the ambitious virility which has been the touchstone of Roman greatness has also resulted in continual turmoil through her years. For reason to be Roman, however, it must be—or must seem to be—native born. The Roman spirit is too proud to adopt any but her native sons. Hence, Cicero brings philosophy into the Latin tongue and the Roman polity through his writings, but Cicero goes much further than this: in the course of *De Republica* he makes the sustained argument that the well-being of Roman order depends essentially on philosophy and reason and not only on Roman virility and spiritedness. The good and the useful find their coincidence in the true. Scipio's recounting of the history of the kings of Rome ultimately reveals the contrast between Cicero's openly- and closely-held teachings in *De Republica*. Cicero's open implication, simply, is that Rome sprung up from her native soil through the virtue and insight of her sons, and that virtue and reason—what is best in Rome—is truly Roman. As Manilius interjects enthusiastically at one point, "I am content with the fact that we are accomplished not in arts that have been imported from overseas but in native, domestic virtues."[6] Yet, Cicero persistently highlights the beneficent influence of foreign learning throughout the history in Book 2. Although as a statesman Scipio attempts to make reason Roman, Scipio's history of Rome strongly suggests that the love of wisdom, in Rome's case, comes from the foreigner and the Greek.

Cicero's teaching regarding the meaning of political things is found in part through reading carefully his account of the founding, decline, and recovery of the Roman political order. To lay the ground for understanding his account it is important, first, to study his teaching regarding the cycle of regimes; second, to study his teaching on the Roman kingship, with its emphasis on statesmanship; third, to study his teaching on the republic, with its emphasis on the regime; and finally to explain how Cicero illustrates his teaching on the "meaning of political things" throughout these writings.

THE CYCLE OF REGIMES

The notion that regimes sometimes collapse is a matter of common sense, but that there is a pattern to the change and demise of regimes is an important claim. It supposes there are fixed realities in human nature and political society that persistently channel the course of human communities. If there are, in fact, fixed realities that dictate a cycle of regimes—if there is some such thing as a nature in human things, to a lesser or greater degree—then reason might be able to apprehend the pattern and, in theory, predictably influence the course of development or decline in a regime. "Good government," as Publius remarks in *Federalist* 1, may be preserved by "reflection and choice" rather than mere "accident and force." The idea of a regular cycle of regimes, which is at least as old as Plato, is the framework around which Cicero tells his story of Rome. Although it is more than this, Cicero's history of the Roman kingship and the Roman republic is a pedagogical device for illustrating his teaching on the cycle of regime. This illustration is prefaced in Book 1 by a general explanation of Cicero's understanding of the idea.[7]

THE DECLINE AND RECOVERY OF REGIMES

Robert Gallagher helpfully and importantly explains the importance of Cicero's cosmological metaphors and imagery to his work as a whole, and especially in highlighting Cicero's attempt to explicate the *cursus mutationem*, the course of change in regimes. The study of the heavens yields a knowledge of the regular courses of the planets—despite their apparent, even reckless, wandering—and so Gallagher notes that "Scipio urges his interlocutors to master the political wisdom required to recognize and foresee such motion when it begins, so that they can intervene in the commonwealth, and regulate its motion, or even counteract it."[8] In support of Gallagher's argument, it is notable that Philus, in introducing the anecdote about the sphere of Marcellus, declares that he "will report nothing new [*novi*] to you, nor have I thought or discovered [*inventum*] anything," going on to recall the *memoria* of a "highly educated man [*doctissimum*]."[9] These words are strikingly reminiscent of Cicero's own words in concluding his preface, that "The kind of reasoning [*ratio*] that I must introduce is neither new [*nova*] nor discovered [*inventa*] by me," concluding that he will "recall to memory [*memoria*]" what was said by the most renowned and wise men (*clarissimorum ac sapentissimorum*).[10] Gallagher's excellent analysis rightly draws our attention to the connection between heavenly and earthly things in Cicero, but I differ with him identifying what constitutes the *cursus mutationem*, however. Gallagher points to Scipio's exhortation to maintain a balance between the "rights, duties, and functions" in the magistrates, aristocrats, and the people, but this wise reminder is a principle, not a pathway.[11] We must look for the *cursus mutationem* elsewhere.

The discussion of this course of changes in regimes begins at *De Republica* 1.62, immediately following the argument about simple regimes. Scipio demarcates the pivot in the conversation by noting that he will now "come to greater things," a phrase used by Laelius and Scipio earlier to mean the art of political practice, or statesmanship.[12] Scipio then gives a rapid-fire summation of the fall of the Roman kingship under Tarquinius Superbus, a brief discourse marked by seven *tum* statements. These seven developments outline a specific pattern of decline which Scipio then generalizes in his formal discussion of the *cursus mutationem* from 1.64–68, indicating that it is a pattern with universal applicability. Scipio proceeds to outline this pattern of the cycle of regimes in two distinct but overlapping ways, one involving the formal movement from regime to regime and the other involving the informal constitutional struggle in every regime.

THE FORMAL CYCLE OF REGIMES

The fundamental kinds of regimes, according to Scipio, are six in number: "out of this [most offensive city of the mob] [arises] the aristocratic one or the factious one, [or from] that [city] [there arises] a tyrannical one or kingly one or even often the popular one."[13] After a brief interruption, this discussion continues and Scipio more specifically describes the likely courses of devolution and rejuvenation in regimes. His description is summarized in this chart:

GENERAL ACCOUNT

KINGS -> TYRANTS -> "LEADING MEN OR PEOPLES" -> FACTIONS OR TYRANTS (1.68)

SPECIFIC ACCOUNT

IF THE PEOPLE ARE JUST ("SENSIBLE AND WISE," 1.65):

KING ⟶ TYRANT

ARISTOCRATS (USUALLY HAPPENS; GOVERNS "AS IF IT WERE KINGLY" [1.65])

THE PEOPLE (IF JUST) — . . . ⟶ THE PEOPLE (UNJUST) (SEE BELOW)

IF THE PEOPLE ARE UNJUST (LICENTIOUS, 1.66-7):

KING/ARISTOCRATS ⟶ THE PEOPLE (UNJUST) ⟶ TYRANT

"RESPECTABLE MEN" ("OFTEN") (QUASI-ARISTOCRATS)

"DARING MEN" (FACTION)

Scipio begins by saying that the "first, most certain change" in the cycle of regimes is the fall of the kingly regime into a tyrannical one due to injustice in a given king. He does not clarify whether he begins with kingship because kingship tends to come first chronologically or because it comes first logically.[14] What follows from the corruption of a just king is tyranny, a terrible regime which is most commonly overcome by aristocrats, though sometimes by the people. Scipio's extensive discussion of the popular regime has suggested its instability, and it is therefore not surprising that he supposes that the people—whether they are ruling or being ruled—can easily grow in their passion for not being ruled, an indulgent limitlessness which they call freedom.[15] Scipio articulates the principle that excess breeds excess, such that an unruly multitude collapses into tyranny, but as the regimes cycle on, Scipio states that this tyranny either falls due to the action of "good men" [*boni*] (which is most common, and in which case "the city is remade") or "daring men" [*audaces*], which produces a factious city governed by some small part for its own benefit.[16] As Scipio summarizes, "So the form [*status*] of the republic, as if it were a ball, is seized from kings by tyrants, then from them by leading men or peoples, then from them by either factions[17] or tyrants."[18]

OBSERVATIONS ON THE FORMAL CYCLE OF REGIMES

There are several points to be made about Scipio's articulation of the cycle of regimes:

First, it is worth noting that none of the good regimes ever replace other good regimes—kingship, aristocracy, and just popular rule never replace each other, but only bad forms of regimes. Kingship devolves into tyranny (in the same reign, Scipio says), and is likely overcome in this instance by aristocrats or perhaps by a just people. A just people is unstable and may all too easily decline into an unjust people, and, if they do not already rule, an unjust people may readily tear down a kingship or an aristocracy. An unjust people devolves into a tyranny, and they subsequently have no power to overcome their self-inflicted slavery. Rather, a tyranny over an unjust people is overcome by the "*boni*" (a good development) or by the "*audaces*" (a questionable development). The unjust would not be likely to accept rulers from the aristocratic class proper on account of fear, suspicion, and envy.

Second, a critical factor in the cycle of regimes is the moral condition of the people. Indeed, the cycles that Scipio outlines take rather different courses depending on whether the people are corrupt or not. If the people are "good," then tyranny may be overcome by the people themselves. However, if the people are bad, it is a matter of inevitability that their regime will quickly collapse into tyranny. A corrupt people inexorably corrupts the regime, but is powerless to improve it: in the cycle described, they never manage to overcome any of the other forms of government.[19]

Third, it has been noted that Scipio suggests that once kingship is undone, it can likely not be recovered, and the same appears to be true of the rule of a good people.[20] They appear in the cycle as a possible (but unlikely) victor over tyranny, but then collapse into tyranny themselves, and the rule of a good people is never recovered in the cycle given. Once kingship and the many have fallen, the two or three forms that any city will cycle through are tyranny, which succumbs to the rule of the few (either good men or daring, factious men), then back to tyranny via the factious, and so forth. Of course, it is possible that Cicero intends us to understand that his cycle circles around and starts over again with kingship, but he does not describe such a path in this writing. It is possible, perhaps, that the utter collapse of a republic—even if its people is still intact—might allow for the restoration of kingship. Scipio may be alluding to such a thing when he notes that when a few "good men" overthrow the tyranny that's arisen from the mob, this "recreates the city," perhaps allowing for the possible recovery of any of the regimes.[21] Scipio's language here suggests that the revolution of the few, good men effects a sort of re-founding, possessing in itself the fecund possibility of any of the regimes. Nevertheless, Scipio's history of Rome does not describe such a recovery either.

Fourth, an unarticulated but express fact is that the few, whether simply good men or proper aristocrats, are the most common means by which any unjust regime (whether tyrannical or of the multitude) is overthrown and righted into a good regime.[22] Kingship and popular rule are incapable of recovering themselves, and apart from the intervention of a few, there is only the continual vacillation between tyranny and faction. Notably, Scipio does not articulate a common fate of aristocracies; being a midpoint, they do not have an extreme to collapse into. *Presumably* the government of the few will decay into faction, but this assumption is not based on Scipio's express argument. Indeed, his failure to address the downfall of aristocracies should perhaps be considered a notable indication of an aristocratic sympathy on Cicero's part.

Fifth, Scipio gives us only one expressly articulated principle governing the cycle of regimes in his law of equal and opposite reactions: "So all excesses . . . are usually changed into their opposite; and [it] happens most in republics."[23] However, this principle does not govern without qualification, or once either a tyranny or a mob came to rule they would forever bounce back and forth between slavery and licentious freedom. As a principle, it is only moderately illuminating. What prevents the perpetual oscillation of extremes—the intervention of the few, either the good or the daring—is, however, quite interesting.

Sixth, Scipio's account of the cycle of regimes is somewhat scattered, but contrary to Kesler's opinion that "Scipio gives several accounts of the typical transitions of regimes that are inconsistent with one another,"[24] these accounts do line up when we understand them properly.[25] The appearance of inconsistency may be due to the fact that the cycle of regimes is not linear but rather presents a set of likely developments. The cycle of regimes seems never to revisit certain regimes once they have passed, and the primary cycle happens in a not-entirely-predictable fashion between and among tyranny, aristocracy, and faction.

Seventh, Scipio departs from Plato and Polybius, but follows Aristotle, in his description of the cycle of regimes.[26] The former two see a decline that runs logically from kingship through aristocracy to democracy.[27] Cicero's cycle of regimes is not based on abstract assumptions that chronological decay will follow a logical order, but on his observation of the varied developments in regimes, specifically in Roman history. Sometimes Cicero's cycle of regimes has simply been dismissed as a gloss on Roman history, and that it therefore does not offer relevant insight into the cycle of regimes generally. If this is the case, it would entirely belie Cicero's aim to reveal the "*ratio* of political things" and thus is unlikely to be his intention. Cicero means for us to understand the predictable way regimes do in fact change. Indeed, it is notable that Cicero's cycle of regimes aims to be more predictive of likely developments than determinative of a single, specific course like other theorists such as Plato and Aristotle who have commented on the cycle of regimes.

Although Scipio discusses the cycle of regimes in the context of the simple regimes, his analysis could also, presumably, apply to mixed regimes. Even in a mixed regime, there will likely be a preeminent element, or a vying among elements for preeminence, and hence the opportunity for an element to become corrupt and seize power leads to the logical conclusion that a cycle of regimes is relevant to the mixed regime as well. If Cicero identified or discussed this point, however, his commentary is not in the extant text. Yet, we will see an example of this cycle of regimes in Cicero's example of the mixed regime, the Roman republic.

THE INFORMAL CYCLE OF REGIMES

Scipio does not offer explicit advice regarding how to forestall changes in regimes, but rather endorses the mixed regime and the proper blending of elements such that the advantages of each simple type are given scope and the weakness of each regime is diminished. His history of Rome becomes a textbook for statesmanship when we see the pattern of regime change playing out under each given ruler. This pattern plays out under each of the Roman rulers except where the foresight of said ruler forestalls the decline, which in the Roman kingship happens in every case except in the kingships of Romulus and Tarquinius Superbus, who suffer the consequences of not preventing regime change from running its course. In other words, Scipio gives us the framework for understanding the decadent tendency of each regime and then gives us numerous, specific examples of Roman statesmen who succumbed to it or overcame it.

The passage which initially reveals the pattern comes just prior to Scipio's formal discussion of the cycle of regimes:

> When Tarquinius was driven out, the people exulted in a certain amazing exces-siveness of freedom. Then innocent men were driven into exile; then many per-sons had their goods torn away; then the rods were lowered before the people; then came [the allowance of] appeals in all matters; then the secessions of the plebeians; then, in short, most of the things done so that everything was [in the hands of] the people.[28]

These seven elements (demarcated in the text by *tum*) are generalized into a pattern that first repeats in Scipio's explicit discussion of the *cursus muta-tionem* and subsequently repeats itself persistently through each episode of Scipio's Roman history.[29] This, in other words, is a pattern Cicero regards as a matter of necessity given the contours of human nature. After a constitutional disruption or regal death:

1. Popular excess threatens turmoil
2. The people reject presiding authorities
3. In the anarchy, many people lose their authority, their property, or other good things
4. The people assent to new authorities
5. The people force these authorities to democratically humble themselves
6. The people fully force the laws to concede to their licentiousness
7. Finally, the mob rules

In the cycle of regimes described through Scipio's history, this pattern holds consistently through the middle step, at which point, if a good ruler comes to power and uses his power prudently, the final developments are curbed and so a prudent man may forestall the collapse into mob rule. The pattern plays out to the end unless some prudent action is taken to prevent mob rule and maintain the authority of the new ruler. As we will see, if a ruler cannot prevent the first step of popular excess, then it is virtually inevitable that every succeeding step will follow and that everything will hinge on the prudence of that new ruler. Everything, in other words, turns on whether "good men" or "factions" rise to the fore, as we saw in the formal cycle of regimes.[30] This new ruler, since he governs by the assent of the many, must always play to the people even while working to salvage the constitutional order and his own authority. Thus, even good men are typically forced through the fifth and sixth steps (of democratically humbling themselves and changing the law to concede to popular excess) while ultimately restoring constitutional balance in order to prevent mob rule.

We have already seen this pattern play out in the dialogue, in the "play within a play" of Book 1. Just as the opening act of Plato's *Republic* is a recapitulation of the trial of Socrates, so the opening act of Cicero's *De Republica* recapitulates the cycle of regimes. As the first three characters arrive at Scipio's estate, the conversation turns insistently to the topic of the second sun. Despite Scipio's objection to Tubero that he considers speculative conversations irrelevant, the younger, newer arrivals carry the day, insisting on continuing the conversation regarding the second sun (popular whim overcomes established rule and disregards his authoritative wisdom, steps 1, 2, and 3). When the magisterial Laelius arrives and is literally and figuratively placed at the center (step 4; a new ruler), the new assembly is pressed by its new governor to turn to more productive discussion—he is a "good man" and his sympathy aligns with the deposed good ruler. They resist, however, and Laelius, of necessity, concedes to the popular interest in cosmological inquiry (steps 5 and 6; the few concede to the many and the will of the many is allowed the pretense of rule), allowing the discussion to play out a little longer. Due to Laelius' politic pressing and conceding, however, the

discussion is modulated and moderated to pivot from purely speculative cosmology to politically-salutary theory. Thus the charioteer mildly subdued his
team and turned them onto a better way. Under Laelius' guidance, then, the
discourse becomes decidedly political rather than merely theoretical, which
is what the other characters (representing the *populus*) had initially wanted.

The political fable continues in the "play within a play" of Book 1. Rather
than dissolving into chaos, Laelius has mastered the multitude and consoli-
dates his authority: the initial, popular preference for discussing the second
sun has turned into the agreement of a prominent few—Philus, Manilius, and
Mummius—for discussing the question of the best regime, following Laelius'
suggestion.[31] The disordered curiosity of the many is productively reoriented
to salient and beneficent *political* concerns. Finally, the whole group recognizes Laelius' guidance and authority when he alone gives consent to Scipio
to proceed in discussing the republic. This little "revolt," in other words,
played out as it often will in the histories: with the first step (popular excess),
there is an inevitable slide to the fourth step (the institution of a new, naturally
authoritative ruler) who concedes to popular will insofar as is necessary to
gentle the crowd and turn its force away from indulgence into the course of a
new and balanced harmony.

Cicero's unpacking of the cycle of regimes, and specifically of the *cursus
mutationem*, helpfully reveals the way in which men, institutions, and societies are subject to predictable courses of development. Through his histories
of the kingship and the republic, discussed in chapter 8, Cicero will reveal
that this course has been surprisingly consistent. This means that the one who
knows—who has the insight to see these things and the knowledge of how to
right the ship of state—will be able to predict the way of political things, to
adjust his politics accordingly, and to preserve the regime in its best possible
condition, whether better or worse than the one he inherited.

NOTES

1. Cicero, DRP, 1.70.

2. Cicero, DRP, 2.3.

3. Cicero, DRP, 2.52. Lat. *"Ego autem, si quo modo consequi potuero, rationibus
eisdem, quas ille vidit, non in umbra et imagine civitatis, sed in amplissima re publica
enitar, ut cuiusque et boni publici et mali causam tamquam virgula videar attingere."*
It is a difficult sentence to render in English.

4. Cicero, DRP, 2.22.

5. Cicero, DRP, 2.22.

6. Cicero, DRP, 2.29.

7. Is it safe to say that this is Cicero's teaching on regimes if the argument is given in the mouth of Scipio, a character in the dialogue? Since it is my contention that Scipio does not speak for Cicero in a number of other ways, how can we know that he speaks for Cicero in this respect? My opinion is that he does. For better or for worse, Cicero is proud, optimistic, and insightful enough to believe that he can explain the meaning of political things well enough that it can be understood and be genuinely useful in caring well for souls and for cities. The noble and the useful, for Cicero, truly are the same (when we understand both properly, of course). Cicero is quite confident in the powers of the Master Rhetorician of Rome, confident in his own understanding, in his ability to make it known, and in the salutary benefit of this knowledge. His rhetoric, in this way, is more Aristotelian than Platonic.

The upshot of all this is that Cicero is revealing much more than he is concealing. This is perhaps the most significant ground of Cicero's disagreement with Plato. Thus, when Scipio is teaching us a conceptual vocabulary for political things (such as the definition of a republic), even as he subsequently modifies his definitions, we can reasonably take Scipio to be teaching us what Cicero thinks is true, or at least the best way of understanding things. Of course, the rabbit hole of political understanding goes a lot deeper than vocabulary, and so Scipio's opinion cannot be taken to be Cicero's simply. With respect to those deeper things, as argued in chapter 1, Cicero directs our gaze to more sublime truths through the productive tension between Scipio and Laelius.

8. Gallagher, "Metaphor," 513.

9. Cicero, DRP, 1.21.

10. Cicero, DRP, 1.13.

11. Gallagher, "Metaphor," 512.

12. Cf. *De Republica* 1.31, 33, 35.

13. Cicero, DRP, 1.45; my translation. . . . *deterrimus [or teterrimus] et ex hac vel optimatium vel factiosa tyrannica illa vel regia vel etiam persaepe popularis.* Since the beginning of the sentence is lost in a lengthy lacuna, translators cannot quite agree on how best to translate this passage. My translation largely follows Zetzel. *Pace* other interpreters such as Fott, Scipio is not giving us a description of the specific course of the cycle of regimes here, but is simply noting that the collapse of one form of the city leads to the rise of another form of the city. Fott prefers a translation that indicates a specific order of the cycle of regimes. If this is so, however, this cycle deviates from the order Scipio lays out later, and so it is sensible to read Scipio's statement more generally.

In addition, Fott is of the opinion that the "most offensive city" is that of the tyrant, which is reasonable given that *deterrimus* is applied to the tyrant in 1.65. However, the fact that the mob is the only regime missing from the list and that the discussion of the simple regimes tends to focus on the plagues of popular regimes, it is more likely Scipio is referring to the rule of the multitude instead.

14. Notably, kingship does not reoccur in the cycle of regimes, suggesting the possibility that when it is lost, it can never be recovered. Indeed, Scipio twice comments that when kingship falls that "type" of regime falls as well: "you see that through the injustice of one man [i.e., Tarquinius Superbus] that entire type [*genus*] of republic

fell" and "when the king begins to be unjust, that type [*genus*] perishes on the spot" (Cicero, DRP, 1.64–65; cf. 2.51). None of the other "types" of regimes are said to perish in this way. Kingship proper may be unrecoverable in the way that other regimes can recur. The "exception" to this, as noted below, is that kingship might recur on the basis of a re-founding and the formation of a new republic (and perhaps of a new people entirely).

15. Cicero, DRP, 1.65–67.

16. Cicero, DRP, 1.68. Notably, Scipio does not say the "good men" or the "daring men" are aristocrats proper, but they in some sense belong to "the few." As a *novo homo* himself, Cicero knew that aristocrat lineage or wealth were not the only pathways to influence. Cicero also often pairs the term *boni* with the idea of the *utile*, the good and the useful, which he says should not be separated, but too often are. Baraz helpfully notes that we should not "[divorce] . . . Cicero's continuous politically charged use of *boni* in promoting his vision of the positive elements within the state" (Baraz, *Republic*, 54).

17. Faction [Lat. *factio*] is Cicero's classification of oligarchs, the deviant rule of the few for their own benefit rather than for the common good.

18. Cicero, DRP, 1.68.

19. This corroborates the claim that Scipio joins Plato in considering the city of the mob to be the worst regime (see note 13).

20. Cf. Cicero, DRP, 1.64–65; 2.51.

21. Cicero, DRP, 1.68.

22. Cicero, DRP, 1.65 and 1.68.

23. Cicero, DRP, 1.68.

24. Kesler, *Natural Law*, 166.

25. Most importantly, we should see that the list at DRP 1.45 is simply a list of regimes, not a cycle of regimes. The cycle is not described until 1.65.

26. Aristotle, *Politics*, 1318a and Zetzel, *Selections*, 45.1.

27. Cicero's cycle also contrasts with Machiavelli, who is drawing from Polybius and possibly Cicero in his *Discourses on Livy* (1.2). Machiavelli sees a principate declining into misrule (through the prince's corrupt heirs), its overthrow by the aristocrats supported by the people, a decline of the aristocracy (again through corrupt heirs) into oligarchy, an overthrow and establishment of democracy, the decay of democracy, and the reinstitution of the rule of a prince.

28. Cicero, DRP, 1.62.

29. cf. Cicero, DRP, 1.65–68.

30. A critical feature in tempering the people is often the intervention of a naturally authoritative figure, such as a father or a father-in-law or an old man. It is worth recalling that this is the basis, too, of Scipio's concession to Laelius in the small circle, the greater age of Laelius.

31. Cicero, DRP, 1.34.

Chapter 8

The Histories of the Kingship and the Republic

De Republica, Book 2

When Laelius and Scipio conclude their discussion of the simple regimes—with Scipio reiterating his insistence that the regime truly worth discussing is the mixed regime—Book 1 draws to a close with Scipio's promise that he will illuminate what he has been saying with a historical illustration: the history of Rome, something which is "known to all, which we inquired about some time ago."[1] This history is useful precisely because it is already known and holds a venerable authority even greater than Scipio's glorious reputation. Having given them the tools for sifting regimes, Scipio now re-presents this history to his audience to allow them to discover the truth of what he has been saying for themselves. The histories that Scipio unfolds, then, are not records of the past simply so much as windows into the soul of citizen and city; as Schofield notes, "perhaps we might speak of theory nourished by history and history perceived in the light of theory."[2] Scipio elevates the telling of history into political philosophy by framing it to reveal fundamental truths about nature, cities, and men.

THE ROMAN KINGSHIP: ROMULUS

The beginning of Rome is indisputably the fabled founding of Rome by Romulus. Scipio tells the tale rather differently than is conventional, emphasizing the good and obscuring the ill. Generally, Scipio praises the founding of Rome by Romulus for his foresight in all respects, beginning with the formation of a people and the formal founding of a republic. Laelius, perhaps amused at this exorbitant praise, notes that Scipio "ascribe[s] to reason those things concerning the site of the city that Romulus established by chance

123

124 *Chapter 8*

or necessity."³ Scipio's design in so generously highlighting the reason of Rome's founding is to reveal in his history of Rome a paradigm, or *ratio,* of political things. This story begins with the organization of a people, continues with the people's grasp of their "thing," the republic, and finally with that kingly republic's political organization. Revisiting his definition of a republic in Book 1, Scipio said that it began with the assembling of a people ordered together in right and common advantage. This people, Scipio went on to say, then established a republic by finding a place, marking it as their own, and making places for men to meet with other men, past and present, and with gods ("shrines and common spaces").⁴ Scipio's discussion of the founding of Rome follows this pattern exactly.

First, Scipio delineates the way in which Romulus founded a people. Scipio nods to legend in citing the divine birth of Romulus and Remus, their abandonment by King Amulius, their being suckled by a she-wolf, and being reared by shepherds. Then, by virtue of his "bodily strength and fierceness of spirit," Scipio notes that Romulus so overawed and impressed nearby people that they followed him and "calmly and willingly obeyed him." He led them into battle against King Amulius, the tyrant, and killed him.⁵ In the terms that Scipio expressed in Book 1, Romulus has at this point gathered together a people, a "multitude being joined in agreement in right and allied in a community of mutual benefit."⁶ Notably, it's unclear what sense of "right" [*ius*] binds them (Cicero avoids mentioning that Romulus' band is a band of robbers and misfits) or what they consider their common advantage to be, but even a band of robbers is marked by its own sense of justice and its own species of flourishing. This is true even where there is no specific, articulated law or specific conception of justice that unites them, but even simply a shared orientation to right as expressed through Romulus' will and a common advantage in their survival as a people.

Second, his having defeated King Amulius, Scipio's account outlines how Romulus established a republic. He "first thought to found a city" and turned his attention to choosing a place to dwell. Here, in particular, Scipio describes in great detail the variety of reasons why Romulus' choice for a location evidenced his "excellent foresight."⁷ What Scipio highlights, possibly echoing Aristotle and Dicaearchus,⁸ is the need to insulate a city's culture and institutions from willy-nilly foreign influences that bring sea-changes to a republic with each turn of the tide. In particular, he highlights the troubles the Greeks experienced due to their maritime character, by virtue of which it was hard to avoid continual contact with other peoples. Rome, Scipio notes, managed to reap the benefits of contact with other peoples by virtue of its location on the Tiber, without running quite the same extensive risks as a seaside port.⁹ On land, Scipio grants Romulus a similar insight in how he built Rome in rugged country that insulated it to some extent from invasion, thus similarly providing land barriers to violent or corrupting alien forces.[10]

Having established themselves in a place—the first criteria of a republic—Scipio is forced to deviate briefly from the paradigm of how peoples become republics to deal with Rome's particular, peculiar history. He had blithely passed over the fact that Romulus' "people" were a band of misfits and robbers, all men, lacking the women and the homes they required to "people" in the fullest sense. Hence, Scipio now tells the tale of the seizing of the Sabine women and the subsequent war with the Sabines and their king, Tatius; the selection of the Fathers to help rule the newly intermixed people; the death of Tatius, which Scipio eventually concedes was a murder; and Romulus' subsequent, solitary rule over Rome.[11]

Before concluding the story of Romulus' rule, however, Scipio returns to the paradigm of the founding of the republic, discussing, third, the acts of enclosing the city and establishing it with religious and political orders and institutions. Specifically, Scipio notes that Romulus had "founded the city" after "taking the auspices himself" (he omits the murder of Remus), that he drew augurs "from each tribe" to participate in reading the signs, and that he ordered the people into "bodies of clients" governed by "fines" rather than by "force."[12] Scipio concludes this discussion by noting that these final accomplishments were the "two extraordinary foundations of the republic," namely, "the taking of auspices and the [establishment of the] senate."[13] This fulfills, in an emerging form, the final element in Scipio's discussion of the establishment of the republic: the building of a town or city "distinguished by shrines and common spaces."[14]

Although Scipio does not say so, there is every reason to think that we are supposed to consider Romulus not only the first king, but the first tyrant in Roman history. It is true that Scipio asserts that Superbus is the "first shape, appearance, and origin [*origo*] of a tyrant," but in making this point by means of the repetition of a key word he explicitly draws our attention back to the "'origin' [*originem*] of the Roman people" at the beginning of Book 2.[15] Romulus' overlooked murders and impieties, his consolidation of power, and his own eventual murder at the hands of the Fathers, all point the accusing finger. Cicero, in his alternately pious and brazen white-washing of the history of Rome, compels us to become Romulus' accusers ourselves, as we spy a tyrant through the text where he explicitly demarcated none; no doubt Cicero recognizes that his readers are well-versed in Rome's lore and will see that he is suggesting a new mythology more than recounting history.[16] It appears, in fact, that Scipio's cycle of regimes begins its turning from the first Roman king, as Romulus falls into tyranny and is overcome by the aristocratic Fathers. After reigning for nearly forty years, Scipio notes that Romulus "died," and eventually declares that he was "killed," but focuses

primarily on how Romulus' "force of talent and of virtue" readily contributed
to his divinization by the Fathers.[17] So early in the era of Roman kingship,
the seeds of the mixed regime are planted when Rome's Fathers take hold
of power long enough to choose Numa Pompilius to rule after Romulus, a
choice which is subsequently affirmed by formal popular accession.

COMMENT ON CICERO'S LITERARY STATESMANSHIP

The nature of Cicero's history of Rome comes into focus once we realize that
it is not first and foremost "history." Cicero simultaneously crafts a salutary
political mythology and teaches us about the meaning of political things. In
non-Ciceronian renditions, the kingship of Romulus is rife with the triumph
of force and will, full of necessity and calculation. There is a form of justice
in Romulus' Rome, but its tender shoot trembles before the polyphemic command Romulus exerted. These lurid facts are also truths of human nature, but
in their bruteness they stupefy us into ignorance regarding the fullness of the
nature of things, especially in its flourishing. They obscure from our view
the ordering toward reason and right that is inherent in all peoples, even in
Romulus' Rome.

In retelling Rome's founding, Cicero (through Scipio's persona) spins a
new political mythology that emphasizes the seeds of reason sown in Rome's
natal earth. In doing so, Cicero may obscure the brutal crimes of Rome's origin, but he simultaneously seeks to rejuvenate "right" as a genuinely *Roman*
element in republican life. Right and justice are not weak, foreign interlopers
attempting to ruin Roman triumph, but are Roman in themselves, even if
Romans never knew it. Nature compels the existence of these things. While
on the one hand this may mean Cicero's history is not a very good history,
on the other it may be something better, a form of wisdom literature: as a
true mythology it helps illuminate elements of the Roman character that had
been lost to itself, with disastrous consequences. Cicero's literary statesmanship deliberately preserves "the cause that gave birth to the city," the bond
of human fellowship which spontaneously blooms into an agreement in right
and a commitment to mutual benefit.[18]

Notably, Cicero does not attempt to propagate this political mythology in a
wholly serious way. Most of his contemporary readers would have found his
history obviously inaccurate in certain respects, and Cicero, through Laelius,
predicts their skepticism: "you [Scipio], ascribe to reason those things concerning the site of the city that Romulus established by chance or necessity."[19]
From Cicero's emphasis we learn, however, that he is determined to introduce
reason to Rome and to intertwine it with Roman character in fact through
his fiction.

THE KINGSHIP CONTINUED

The fact that we are studying a history of the kingship should not obscure the essential part that the Fathers play in Roman rule. Specifically, they committed tyrannicide and accomplished the transition from Romulus' unfettered rule to a more prudent mode. They accomplished the divinization of Romulus, thus completing the first founding of Rome, by compelling Proculus Julius to testify to his seeing the new god Quirinus. Subsequently, Scipio declares that "those leading men" "prudently" established a "plan" (Lat. *rationem*), making interim rule the ordinary practice in Rome, whereby any king's authority would depend on his "virtue and wisdom, not family," which they accomplished by instituting the practice of adopting rulers. Their deliberation led them to seek out Numa for Rome's second king.[20] The Fathers, in all their significance, are the second "rulers" of Rome in Cicero's telling.

These developments follow the path of the *cursus mutationem*, the informal course of change in regimes, in the Roman kingship. The pattern (as described in 1.62 and 1.66ff., and above) follows a standard course, as was said.[21] In the case of Rome, following the death of Romulus, (step 1) the people "did not tolerate" the rule of the Fathers and, (2) "did not cease to demand a king," forcing the Fathers from power. At this critical juncture, Scipio notes that those "leading men" "prudently thought out a plan [*rationem*]" so that no royal line would hold power perennially, intending that the question of rule would constantly be referred back to them and to the people. No mention is made of the people running amok and taking property or authority for themselves (3), but (4) the people proceed to select Numa as their new king under the guidance and "authority" of the Fathers.[22] Scipio says, dignifying chance with the mantle of foresight, that "[t]hose rustics of ours saw even then that regal virtue and wisdom, not family, ought to be sought." Following this, (5) Numa did not simply accept the people's invitation to rule, but, "[a]lthough the people . . . had approved him to be king," formally "provided a curiate law concerning his own power of command" in the *comitia curiata*, an institution representing both the popular and aristocratic elements in Roman life.[23] This act humbled the king, forestalled any fear of threat to the people's freedom, and dignified the authority of the *comitia*. The prudent action of the Fathers along with Numa's humble concession effectively redirected the *cursus*: the laws did not concede to popular excess (step 6) and mob rule was avoided (step 7).

Forestalling the wayward tendency of the people does not, in itself, make a constitution good, but rather the degree to which it hews to right (i.e., to *ius*). Indeed, Numa saw both the imbalance and the barbarism in the Roman lust for war and undertook a variety of reforms to soften and reorient the

Roman character. What Numa accomplished thereby was, in a modest way, a re-founding of Rome. The founding of a republic involves establishing a place for the city, cultivating and improving the surrounding land and defenses, and building homes and public works including "shrines and common spaces."[24] Numa de-centered martial Rome, reoriented men to the produce of their land rather than the lands of others, and invigorated the religious and civic life of Rome around peace rather than war. He did this by first distributing the various stretches of land Romulus had conquered to the citizens, diffusing the population from the city; second, in doing so, he made them masters of their own estates and farmers whose yield relied on their own diligent cultivation and self-government rather than on their barbaric strength.[25] Finally, Numa established more religious offices (new augurs, pontifices, Flamines, Salii, and Vestal Virgins), creating new places of honor to direct Roman ambition, and introducing a variety of religious rites along with "marketplaces, games, and all causes and celebrations for coming together."[26] By instantiating Rome's religious and public life in new and salutary rites, Numa deepened and strengthened the republic.[27] Scipio notes, indeed, that Numa had invigorated "the two most splendid things for the long life of a republic, religion and mildness."[28]

Despite a missing portion of text involving the next king, Tullus Hostilius, the pattern of change in regimes helps to interpret what we do know about him. Following the constitutional pattern, (1) upon Numa's death an unnamed "interim ruler" proposes Tullus Hostilius take up his station, (2) himself thus being replaced and (3 and 4) the people themselves formally approving Hostilius' rule. Notably, whereas prudence and circumstance had guided the series of events following Romulus' violent death and Numa's accession to rule, now this same process has, in effect, been regularized and constitutionalized. Just as dams and waterworks channel violent floods into placid canals, the *cursus mutationem* has been regularized and ordered, so that the people effectuate cathartic revolutions as a matter of course. Tullus, in several acts of public benefaction, (5 and 6) "consulted the people by division concerning his own power of command," used the proceeds from spoils of war to build up the Comitium and the Curia (the original Senate), limited the power of the kings to declare war, and—"so that you may observe how wisely our kings even then saw that certain things should be granted to the people," Scipio notes—Hostilius "would not even use the royal symbols except by order of the people."[29] Since each of these developments is accompanied by a concession to the people, the final stage of mob rule is not realized. Instead, the republic is strengthened throughout. Unfortunately, since we are missing more than half of the discussion regarding Hostilius, we cannot say precisely how Scipio might have said he improved the republic. We can speculate at best. Referring to Livy's writing,[30] it is possible that Scipio might have recorded how Hostilius and the Roman army were drawn into conflict in Alba and betrayed by the Alban dictator, Mettius Fufetius, and how Hostilius in a master stroke overcame the betrayal, had Mettius slain, and incorporated Alba into Rome, and subsequently conquered the Sabines. Both of these victories greatly enhancing the population, land, resources, and power of Rome, which would fit the paradigm Scipio has given us, though (once again) the content of these pages must remain speculative.[31] After two missing pages of text, Laelius concludes the discussion of Hostilius by noting that "in the conversation you have begun, the republic does [not] creep but flies into its best form."[32]

The next king of Rome is supremely praised by Livy but, in a surprising contrast, nearly ignored by Scipio. Livy writes that Ancus Marcius was "unsurpassed by any of his predecessors in ability and reputation,"[33] whereas Scipio severely downplays Marcius' accomplishments, identity, and significance.[34] The brief paragraph discussing how he came to rule, his reign, and his death is barely four sentences in translation.[35] What is emphasized in his spare biography is a discussion about Marcius' mysterious line of descent, with as little being known about Marcius' father as we are told about the son. Scipio's explanation of this ignorance is that "of those times little more than kings' names has been brought to light," which contradicts his earlier suggestion that learning flourished from the earliest days of Rome.[36] These things taken together—the conspicuous lack of a biography, the conspicuous lack of a father, and the notable contradiction in Scipio's account—indicate that in Scipio's opinion Ancus Marcius is irrelevant in the *ratio* of Rome we are being given. Marcius, it turns out, is simply a placeholder for another figure who enters Rome during his reign.

Having summarily noted Marcius' reign and death, Scipio goes on to explain that it was during Marcius' reign that learning entered Rome in the person of Demaratus of Corinth, a foreigner who contributed singly to the "overflowing river of . . . training and . . . arts" that now came to Rome from the Greeks.[37] This emphasis suggests that in terms of the constitutional order of Rome, Demaratus' learned influence is what is significant about Ancus Marcius' reign, at least so far as Scipio is concerned. What precisely Demaratus did that made him so important is unclear, since much of the conversation regarding his influence is lost in a lacuna. These details would have been instructive, but the broader point is more fundamental: contrary to Manilius, who was "content with the fact that we are accomplished not in arts that have been imported from overseas but in native, domestic virtues," Scipio sees learning (which by its nature involves an openness to the foreign and other) as integral to Rome's flourishing, first with Numa and now with Demaratus. As Zetzel notes, pointing to Demaratus' son, Cicero "places far greater emphasis than other accounts on Priscus as the source of Greek culture and learning."[38] Following the two missing pages of manuscript, the discussion turns from Demaratus to that son.

Upon Marcius' death, a sixth ruler is adopted—none other than Demaratus' son, only referred to by his Roman name, Lucius Tarquinius Priscus.[39] Before his death, Scipio reports that Ancus Marcius so trusted Priscus "that he was reckoned in all deliberations and, one might say, a partaker and companion in kingly rule."[40] Priscus, who was characterized by "the utmost benevolence toward all citizens," was chosen by the unanimous popular vote to be the next king. Like Numa, Hostilius, and Marcius before him, after the king's death (1 and 2) he turned to the Curia to endow his rule with the formal approval of the people (3 and 4). Scipio notes at this point that he insistently popularized himself (5) (or, "emulated the habits of this people in every respect") by using his Roman name rather than his original Etruscan name, Lucumo.[41] His concessions to the people (6) took the form of expanding the positions of honor by doubling the number of Fathers and the number of knights, albeit forestalling any offense to the aristocrats by distinguishing between the greater and lesser rank of the old and new members.[42] As the republic was growing in extent, a natural imbalance would emerge in the change of proportion between the many and the few, and Priscus thus prudently instituted reforms which broadened access to the aristocracy without diluting its authority, honor, or deliberation. He did not demean men of honor to satiate the people, in other words, but elevated the people to aspire to ranks of honor themselves. Scipio concludes by noting that Priscus added to Roman land by conquering the Sabines and that he confirmed Roman civil and political life by establishing the Ludi Romani and swearing that he would "make a temple to Jupiter the Best and Greatest on the Capitol."[43] Since each of these things is constituent in the development of a people into a republic, we ought to understand that Priscus is continuing the work of establishing the republic.

The seventh ruler was a boy not chosen by the ordinary means, effecting something of an extraordinary revolution in rule, but a revolution for the better. Indeed, Laelius makes the striking comment that Servius Tullius in some critical way "[saw] the farthest of all in the republic," superseding his predecessors in constitutional accomplishment.[44] His reign, also, follows the pattern of change in regimes. This boy, Servius Tullius, had a slave woman for a mother, but was treated by Lucius Tarquinius as a father, and so the people concluded that he had, in fact, fathered the boy.[45] When the jealous sons of Ancus Marcius, who had been overlooked in regal appointment, killed Lucius Tarquinius (1 and 2), then Servius Tullius—pretending Tarquinius was still alive and that he was only acting by his orders—proceeded to disburse gifts to the people, and to continue to dispense justice, winning the people to himself (3, 4, and 5). Eventually, when his father was finally buried, Tullius did not look for the approval of the Fathers, who might have prevented his nomination to the kingship, but instead went to the people to approve his rule, a mandate he received from them. Subsequently, to maintain constitutional form, Tullius followed his predecessors in formally submitting to the Curia for its approval.[46] Two missing pages obscure Scipio's recounting of Servius' exploits, but Livy supplies some of the likely details: Servius successfully waged war against the Etruscans, which reflected well on his glory, and made alliances by marriage at home to forestall jealousies and secure his throne. However, his primary accomplishment lies in his development of the Servian constitution.

The Servian constitution refers to the remarkable reorganization Servius made of the people to redistribute power and authority to better maintain the harmony of elements in the regime. In doing so, Livy notes, "he set himself to by far the greatest of all works in times of peace," a comment which echoes Laelius' earlier praise.[47] Under this constitution, the people were organized into a variety of centuries, with each century holding an equal vote. The centuries were clustered into groups, with the most honorable holding the right to vote first. The aristocratic and timocratic elements (nobles and knights), being a minority of the Roman population, made up a slim minority of centuries, being organized into eighty-nine groups, whereas the remainder of the populace was organized into 104 centuries according to various criteria, with groups voting in order of rank. In general, for example, the votes of the older were prioritized over the younger. Scipio optimistically assumed that the eighty-nine centuries of optimates would generally be united, so that despite their being outnumbered by the people, only eight centuries of the people would need to join them for them to carry the day. While it might appear to the people that they had the most electoral power, then, Scipio considered it most likely that the optimates would always carry the day.[48] Hence, Scipio particularly notes how the new model satisfied the people by extending electoral rights, but satisfied prudence in its distribution of authority: "no one was denied the right to vote, but the man who exerted the most influence in the vote was the one who was the most concerned for the city to be in its best form."[49] Although Cicero's account is perhaps doubtful with respect to historical detail, this basic idea, with a number of modifications, served as the model for the Comitia for centuries to come[50] and is the reason why Laelius expresses his admiration of Servius' far-sightedness.

Despite several critical gaps in the manuscript, Scipio tells us that Tullius is eventually murdered by Tarquinius Superbus, his own son-in-law, and that Superbus thus becomes the next ruler of Rome. However twisted his character becomes, Superbus initially accomplished several good things. He increased the territory and wealth of Rome through conquest, he built the temple to Jupiter on the Capitol, established colonies, and made religious observances.[51] Eventually, however, his reign was overcome by tyranny:

"resting on victories and riches," Scipio declares, Superbus "ran riot with insolence, and he could control neither his manners nor the lusts of his own [family]."[52] Thus, the cycle of regimes ran its course: "With [Lucius Brutus] as an authority and leading man, the city was aroused by this recent complaint of Lucretia's father and relatives and by the recollection of Tarquinius's haughtiness and the many injuries from him and his sons [step 1]; and it ordered the king himself, his sons, and the family of Tarquinians into exile [step 2 and 3]."[53] The remainder of the steps—the establishment of new authorities and their humbling before the many—become the foundation of the Roman republic.

THE ROMAN REPUBLIC

Since Book 1 plays out a rather insistent debate regarding the simple regimes, and since wrangling about kingship is one of the central elements of that debate, it is easy to presume that Cicero's history of Rome—beginning with the kingship and proceeding to the "Republic" proper—is a movement from simple regimes to mixed regimes in a two-act drama. This is true, but only partly. In a sense, there are no simple regimes, only mixed regimes, since every regime contains few and many, and what is politically possible in any given circumstance is severely delimited by their character and condition. Even a king only holds his authority formally, while in reality relying on the cooperation of the few and the many to sustain his authority and power. Hence, the mixed regime might be said to exist on a sort of spectrum. From this point of view, due to the early influence of the Fathers and the people, the mixed regime already emerges during Romulus' reign, at the birth of the kingship itself, and Rome waxes in strength and wisdom (in Cicero's telling), moving from strength to strength in a continually rebalancing, mixed regime, until the reign of Superbus. Yet, at the same time, as Scipio himself notes, "in a republic where there is one man with perpetual power, especially royal . . . that royal name is eminent, and a republic of this sort cannot be called, or be, anything but a kingdom."[54] The preeminence of kings is such an overawing fact that although they do rely on others to support their rule, there is, in fact, a qualitative change that takes place in the proper establishment of a mixed regime. In Rome's history, following the overthrow of Superbus, the elements of the regime are genuinely mixed to produce something that is fundamentally other than the tripartite, yet unmixed, ordinary constitution. As Scipio declares, eventually "the republic was established in its best form [*statu optimo*], which is a moderate blend of those three types [*tribus generibus*], the regal, the aristocratic, and the popular."[55]

The beginning of Scipio's discussion of the Roman republic is unfortunately obscured by sixteen missing manuscript pages, roughly equivalent to sixteen paragraphs. Our speculations about the content of the missing material are fortunately aided by the example of the cycle of regimes provided for us by Scipio at the end of Book 1. There, Scipio had declared:

> When Tarquinius was driven out, the people exulted in a certain amazing excessiveness of freedom. Then innocent men were driven into exile; then many persons had their goods torn away; then came annual consuls; then the rods were lowered before the people; then came [the allowance of] appeals in all matters; then the secession of the plebeians; then, in short, most of the things done so that everything was in [the hands of] the people.[56]

One of the vicious consequences of tyranny is that it simultaneously destroys the kingship and the character of the people over which it rules. Before the missing pages, Scipio notes that, due to the violence of Tarquinius Superbus, the people "could not bear to hear the title of king."[57] As Superbus gathered power unto himself, even while allowing the Senate the practice of deliberation and counsel, "the force, power, and royal name [were] conspicuous and eminent."[58] This looming power engendered "fear" in the people, which led them to scramble desperately for slavery's antithesis, or unfettered freedom. This reaction speaks to the hated nature of the tyranny carried out by Superbus, but it also suggests that his tyranny corrupted the people themselves, since they not only came to hate bad command but also the good, refusing kingship entirely. Hence, when Brutus and Collatinus overthrew Superbus and the formal tyranny, the disorder in the *res publica* established the licentious dominance of the multitude. As Scipio had stated earlier about democracy, "from this unbounded licentiousness . . . the minds [*mentes*] of citizens turn out so dainty and soft that if the slightest force of command is displayed, they become angry and cannot endure."[59] It was this critical state of affairs which Rome's first republican rulers needed to salvage after having deposed Superbus, and it is at this point where the extant manuscript picks up: "because of this state of mind [*hac mente*] our ancestors expelled both the innocent Collatinus, on account of suspicion from that kinship [to Superbus], and the remaining Tarquinii, on account of the offense from that name."[60] It is telling of Scipio's sympathy that he referred to Collatinus as "innocent": the people, in this case, were unreasonable and unrestrained, and the great task of statesmanship by good men such as Publicola was to becalm and recultivate the civil spirit of the Roman people.

In the midst of this turmoil, the statesmanship of Publius Valerius (that is, Publicola) is notable as an example of a good man who resisted tyranny and managed to stabilize the Roman *res publica*. Like a charioteer trying to bring a careening team of horses under his control, Publicola's handling of the people necessitated significant concessions, but his concessions were managed in such a way—with an intuitive, if not explicit, knowledge of the *cursus mutationem*—so as to moderate the people and establish harmony among the elements in the regime, which took on a mixed character as a result. Due to the popular excess (step 1), good men such as Collatinus were forced from rule (step 2) and his goods stripped from him by the overzealous mob (step 3), and consular rule devolved fully onto Publius Valerius (Publicola) as a result (step 4). To avoid aggravating "the same state of mind" (that is to say, the fear and licentiousness of the people), Publicola had the "rods . . . lowered when he had begun to speak in an assembly," moved his home to a more humble spot when its lofty location aroused the suspicion of the people, and also "ordered his own lictors to go over to [Spurius Lucretius][61] because he was older" (step 5).[62] Most significantly Publicola made it so that all Roman citizens were guaranteed the right of appeal to corporal or capital punishment (step 6).[63] This last thing Scipio cites as being "in the greatest sense" the reason why Publicola was known as the "'cultivator of the people,'" both referring to his cognomen "Publicola" (a combination of *publica* and *agricola*) and his rejuvenation of the people's moderation, an accomplishment which forestalled a decline into mob rule (step 7). Publicola, as Scipio declares in sum, "maintained the authority of the leading men more easily when he had given moderate freedom to the people."[64]

Publicola managed to turn the wild spirit of mob rule away from the destructive conclusion of the *cursus mutationem* by aiming at a becalming harmony. In terms of maintaining balance in the mixed regime, Scipio briefly emphasizes the simple key: "Hold on to what I said at the beginning: unless there is in the city an evenhanded balancing of rights [*ius*], duty, and service, so that there is enough power in the magistrates, enough authority in the deliberation of the leading men, and enough freedom in the people, this form [*statum*] of the republic cannot be preserved safe from change."[65] As Publicola took power, there was too much freedom in the people, consequently too little authority in the deliberation of the leading men, and no effectual power in the magistrates (such as Publicola himself). By assuaging the inflamed fear of the people, Publicola moderated their licentiousness and restored his own, constitutionally-limited authority, which thus created space for the deliberation of the Senate to assert itself. Scipio continues that, as a result, "in those times the senate maintained the republic in this form."[66] This control was ultimately maintained because "no [vote of an] assembly of the people would be valid unless the Fathers' authority approved it."[67] Hence, "all these things were maintained by the leading men possessed of the highest authority, as the people yielded."[68]

Curiously, twice in his short discussion of Publicola, Scipio notes that his discussion is not entirely historical. Indeed, with respect to establishing the right of appeal, Scipio points out that text and tradition deny that Publicola did any such thing: both the "books of the pontifices," the "Twelve Tables," and the "tradition" of the decemvirs show a preexisting right to appeal.[69] Publicola may not in fact, then, have moderated the people by instituting this right. Nevertheless, it is recommended to us by Scipio as the sort of thing that a statesman would do in order to satisfy the people. This sort of concession primarily satisfies the people, and it assuages the problem of their overzealous pursuit of freedom, by addressing the "fear" of the abuse of power that led them in such a reckless, headlong pursuit in the first place.[70] As in his discussion of the kingship, Scipio's unhistorical telling of history is intentional. The reason for this is clarified in the comment he gives in concluding his discussion of Publicola: "Now I do not repeat these things that are so old and so worn out to you without cause, but I clarify models [*exempla*] of men [*hominum*] and things [*res*] through familiar characters [*personis*] and circumstances [*temporibus*]—according to which the rest of my speech is arranged."[71] The term *personae* implies a reference to characters in a drama or play, suggesting that Cicero is telling a story to illuminate a truth about things, but not necessarily in a pedantic historical sense. This underscores the idea that the history of Rome we are reading is primarily pedagogical, not strictly chronological or historical; it is concerned with teaching the nature of political things, especially the course of change in regimes.

Scipio's narrative continues with a formulaic comment that is repeated three times in the text we have, and which was likely repeated several times in text we have lost: when "the republic" was "in this form [*statu*]."[72] These references preface the beginnings of a new section in the history of the republic, marking a point of conflict or turning in the constitutional order itself. The term *status*, of course, is a critical concept for Cicero, meaning both the formal order and the moral constitution of a particular republic. Whereas in the kingship Cicero demarcated developments in rule by the ruler, whose singular authority has overawing significance, in the republic he has Scipio demarcate significant shifts in the *status*. Since this phrase seems to be a device by which Scipio consistently marks developments in the republic, and since there are sixteen pages missing before 2.53 (the beginning of the discussion of the republic) and eight pages missing after 2.63 (missing pages which conclude the discussion of the republic), it is reasonable to think we could expect to have seen several more references to "the republic" being in a particular "form." The extant portion discussing developments in the republic is eight pages in length. If we assume that the discussion of each stage was roughly similar in length, we would expect six or seven total iterations of *in hoc statu*, suggesting that about half of them are lost due to the fragmentary text.

The next threat to the *status*—likely either the second or third—takes place in the form of the plebeian secession of 494 BC. Before that occurred, despite the exercise of power by the first dictator, Titus Larcius, the mixed regime enjoyed a proper balance according to Scipio: "all things were maintained by the leading men possessed of the highest authority, as the people yielded."[73] However, the people, after some time, demanded more authority in matters of right, and although this unbalanced the working of the republic, Scipio articulates the inevitability of this development: "Reason, perhaps, was lacking in this, but the nature of republics itself often overcomes reason."[74] Republics travel the *cursus mutationem* as a matter of some inevitability. The question is not whether a good citizen can forestall the first step; the question is whether he can prevent the last one.

In this particular case, the people generally had fallen under the burden of public debt and sought relief for themselves; prudent counsel did not foresee or forestall this development ("such a plan was overlooked") and so the people took matters into their own hands.[75] The riled people withdrew from the city, effectively overthrowing the authority of the Senate and consuls[76] and taking their authority for themselves (steps 1–3 in the *cursus mutationem*). As a result of their withdrawing from the city and refusing to return until their demands were met, the tribunate was created, an office which allowed the people to represent their interests to the Senate and check its action in a given moment (step 4).[77] Despite this theoretical check on the Senate, Scipio notes that "the wisest and most courageous men in arms and deliberation" continued to "[protect] the city," wielding authority without the people's objection due to their austerity: "they were eminent in honor far above others, [but] they had a smaller share of pleasures and a hardly larger one of wealth."[78] Each public figure was known, as a private man, to care "diligently" and beneficently for people as well (steps 5 and 6).[79] In other words, the institution of the tribunate satiated the people's lust for a greater share in *ius*, but the moderate, public-minded character of the leading men allowed them to maintain balance, preventing the final decline into mob rule.

The next iteration (when "the republic was in this form") begins with the attempt by Spurius Cassius, a consul, "to seize royal power."[80] The primary means by which Cassius attempted to do this was his proposal of the first agrarian law, a populist measure which called for a distribution of land to the plebeians (commencing steps 1–3 of the *cursus mutationem*). This law was opposed by the leading men and, ultimately, by the people themselves, who began to suspect Cassius' ambitions.[81] Scipio concludes this account by declaring that this matter was resolved when Cassius' own father, having discovered alleged treachery, took up his paternal right to govern over Cassius (step 4) and "punished [*mactavit*] [Spurius Cassius] with death, as the people yielded" (steps 5 and 6).[82] The word *mactavit* here can mean to punish, but it also means to honor or to offer as a sacrifice. It is a curious word choice that suggests the nature of the father's act: not as an individual or discrete exercise of judicial authority, but a political act of expiation, to which "the people yielded."[83]

The next development in the Roman regime (*in hoc statu*; the fifth or sixth iteration) involves a rather drastic attempt at re-founding. Under the Senate's guidance, "a plan was instituted" which would do away with the consulship and the tribunate and replace it with decemvirs, ten men with "maximum power immune to appeal."[84] This rejection of appeal attempted to roll back a concession Publicola had made to the people in tempering the popular revolt against Collatinus, which Scipio had previously criticized as a step in the decline to mob rule.[85] Although the original set of decemvirs used their power well, seeming to justify the constitutional innovation, Scipio notes that the second set "were not similarly praised for trust and justice."[86] These men refused to give up their power after one year, establishing a *de facto* factional tyranny. "When the republic was in this form," Scipio declares, the regime became unbalanced since "the entire republic was in the possession of the leading men."[87] As a result, "from the injustice of these men a very great disturbance and a change of the entire republic suddenly arose."[88] Rather than ruling humanely, stooping to popular concerns, they "ruled over the people lustfully, pitilessly, and avariciously" and added two tables of law which, among other things, denied intermarriage between patricians and plebeians.[89] Cicero's manuscript breaks off again at this point and does not resume for sixteen pages, but we can reconstruct the remainder of the story. The haughty, tyrannical conduct of the decemvirs led to anger in the people and their rejection of the decemvirs' authority in the so-called second secession of the plebeians (steps 1–3). Popular leaders Lucius Valerius and Marcus Horatius mediated between the people and the Senate, ultimately establishing the Valerio-Horatian laws, which dismantled the decemvirate and restored the consulships and tribunate (step 4).[90] As necessary concessions to the people, a new plebiscite was established which allowed the plebeians themselves to pass laws binding on the whole people (steps 5 and 6). Thus, Rome was once more spared from an utter collapse into mob rule, albeit through granting greater authority to the people generally; this would have left the republic on more precarious footing, though stabilized for the time being.

The extensive gap in the remainder of the manuscript swallows up the remainder of Scipio's discussion of the Roman republic. Given that the constitutional changes Scipio describes in the extant manuscript only spanned the time period from 509 BC to 449 BC, it is unlikely that the remainder of his discussion brought him remotely close to the date of the dialogue, which is set in 129 BC. Rather, based on an educated guess, it is not unlikely that Scipio would have wrapped up his discussion of the history of the republic relatively quickly at this point, perhaps after the founding of the office of the consular tribunes (which would reference the tribes established by Romulus and the legalization of marriages between patricians and plebeians in the Lex Canuleia, both of which took place in the 440s BC.[91] The remainder of the eight missing pages would have given some consideration to the springs of flourishing and failure in the republic, and particularly how it served as a model of the best regime. We might now consider what Scipio (and ultimately Cicero) meant to reveal as a teaching on the *ratio* of political things.

NOTES

1. Cicero, DRP, 1.70.
2. Schofield, *Cicero*, 79.
3. Cicero, DRP, 2.22.
4. Cicero, DRP, 1.41.
5. Cicero, DRP, 2.4–14.
6. Cicero, DRP, 1.39; my translation.
7. Cicero, DRP, 2.5.
8. See Zetzel, *Selections*, 162–63.
9. Cicero, DRP, 2.5–10.
10. Cicero, DRP, 2.11.
11. Cicero, DRP, 2.12–14.
12. Cicero, DRP, 2.16.
13. Cicero, DRP, 2.17.
14. Cicero, DRP, 1.41.
15. Cicero, DRP, 2.51, 2.3.
16. Zetzel comments, to the contrary, that "the reason for this [pious] approach" of Cicero's is that he "eschews the personal and the sensational in favour of constitutional and institutional matters" (Zetzel, *Selections*, 160). It is true that Cicero is interested in the constitutional and institutional, but Cicero does not leave out Romulus' crimes because they are sensational, but because the traditional telling would mar Rome's origins.
17. Cicero, DRP, 1.20.
18. Cicero, DRP, 1.41.
19. Cicero, DRP, 2.22.
20. Cicero, DRP, 2.20–25.
21. To reiterate: following some upset, (1) the people become restive or wild, (2) good men are forced from rule, (3) good things (whether property or authority) are seized from their owners, (4) new authorities are established, (5) these new authorities are forced to humble themselves before the people, (6) the laws concede fully to popular excess, and finally (7) mob rule is established—unless, that is, a prudent,

statesmanlike intercession is made at some point to curb the careening excesses of the mob.

22. Cicero, DRP, 2.25.
23. Cicero, DRP, 2.25.
24. Cicero, DRP, 1.41.
25. Cicero, DRP, 2.26.
26. Cicero, DRP, 2.27.
27. Cf. Cicero, DRP, 1.41.
28. Cicero, DRP, 2.27. Immediately following this is a brief discussion between Scipio and Manilius on the question of Pythagoras' alleged influence on Numa. Scipio explains that this was impossible given Pythagoras' later birth, and notes that the philosopher was, rather, a contemporary of Tarquinius Superbus, the tyrant (Cicero, DRP, 2.28). Pythagoras is first mentioned in the prologue and the significance of his mention here should not be overlooked. We will consider the significance of this interjection in the discussion of Superbus.

This third ruler, Numa Pompilius, is noted as a "foreigner," one of the Sabines, who undertook significant attempts to reform the martial soul of Rome (Cicero, DRP, 2.25–29). Somewhat amusingly, despite the fact that Numa is Sabine, Manilius comments agreeably at this point that he is "content with the fact that we are accomplished not in arts that have been imported from overseas but in native, domestic virtues" (Cicero, DRP, 2.29). The centrality of foreign influence to the Roman project will be explored more fully in Chapter 8.

29. Cicero, DRP, 2.31.
30. As Schofield shows, Cicero and Livy can be fruitfully compared to gain insight into their purposes in writing. What is most notable is the different emphases, and in some cases different details, reported by each (*Cicero*, 46–47). These differences mean, of course, that we can't rely on Livy to fill in the gaps in Cicero's telling of the history, at least not in the same terms that he would. Nevertheless, with discernment, Livy can help supply in broad strokes some of the history that would have filled those gaps.

31. Livy, *Ab Urbe Condita*, 1.22–30.
32. Cicero, DRP, 2.33.
33. Livy, *Ab Urbe Condita*, 1.35.
34. Cicero, DRP, 2.33–34.
35. In Fott's translation, Marcius' name is not even mentioned in those first few sentences except in a footnote. This exclusion appears to be an error, however, since the original manuscript discovered by Cardinal Angelo Mai appears to contain Marcius' name (Vat.lat.5757, 170).
36. Cicero, DRP, 2.33; 2.18.
37. Cicero, DRP, 2.34.
38. Zetzel, *Selections*, 188.
39. Cicero, DRP, 2.35.
40. Cicero, DRP, 2.35; my translation. Lat. *"ut consiliorum omnium particeps et socius paene regni putaretur."* Fott's translation ("a partner in all deliberations and almost an associate in the kingdom") is a bit more vague than Cicero's Latin.

41. Cicero, DRP, 1.35 and n.39.
42. Cicero, DRP, 2.35–36.
43. Cicero, DRP, 2.36.
44. Cicero, DRP, 2.37.
45. Cicero, DRP, 2.37.
46. Cicero, DRP, 2.37–38.
47. Livy, *Ab Urbe Condita*, 1.42.
48. Cicero, DRP, 2.39–40.
49. Cicero, DRP, 2.40.
50. Cf. Zetzel, *Selections*, 194–96.
51. Cicero, DRP, 2.44.
52. Cicero, DRP, 2.45.
53. Cicero, DRP, 2.46.
54. Cicero, DRP, 2.43.
55. Cicero, DRP, 2.frag 5.
56. Cicero, DRP, 1.63.
57. Cicero, DRP, 2.52.
58. Cicero, DRP, 2.50.
59. Cicero, DRP, 1.67.
60. Cicero, DRP, 1.53.
61. Note that Spurius Lucretius is the father of Lucretia and the father-in-law of Lucius Junius Brutus. He was, in other words, a revered figure for his role in the overthrow of the tyrant Superbus. According to Livy to speculate about the missing content (and in this case it is quite likely that some of the same events would have filled the gap in the manuscript preceding this), Lucretius played an important role in convincing Collatinus to leave his consulship and Rome:

> "At first Collatinus was struck dumb with astonishment at this extraordinary request; then, when he was beginning to speak, the foremost men in the commonwealth gathered round him and repeatedly urged the same plea, but with little success. It was not till Spurius Lucretius, his superior in age and rank, and also his father-in-law, began to use every method of entreaty and persuasion that he yielded to the universal wish. The consul, fearing that after his year of office had expired and he returned to private life, the same demand should be made upon him, accompanied with loss of property and the ignominy of banishment, formally laid down the consulship, and after transferring all his possessions to Lanuvium, withdrew from the state" (Livy, *Ab Urbe Condita*, 2.2).

62. Cicero, DRP, 2.55.
63. Cicero, DRP, 2.53.
64. Cicero, DRP, 2.55.
65. Cicero, DRP, 2.57.
66. Cicero, DRP, 2.56.
67. Cicero, DRP, 2.56.
68. Cicero, DRP, 2.56.
69. Cicero, DRP, 2.53–54.
70. Cicero, DRP, 2.50.

71. Cicero, DRP, 2.55.

72. Cicero, DRP, 2.56, 2.60, 2.62.

73. Cicero, DRP, 2.56.

74. Cicero, DRP, 2.57.

75. Cicero, DRP, 2.59.

76. Due to the crisis, the consuls Verginius Tricostus and Veturius Geminus were superceded by the dictator Manius Valerius Maximus. He was the brother of Publicola and ultimately sided with the people. These details satisfy the second step of the *cursus mutationem* in particular, though none of these details are mentioned by Cicero (cf. Livy, *Ab Urba Condita*, 2.28–32).

77. Cicero, DRP, 2.59.

78. Cicero, DRP, 2.59.

79. Cicero, DRP, 2.59.

80. Cicero, DRP, 2.60.

81. Livy, *Ab Urbe Condita*, 3.41.

82. Cicero, DRP, 2.60.

83. Cicero, DRP, 2.60.

84. Cicero, DRP, 2.61.

85. Cicero, DRP, 1.62.

86. Cicero, DRP, 2.61.

87. Cicero, DRP, 2.62.

88. Cicero, DRP, 2.63.

89. Cicero, DRP, 2.63.

90. Livy, *Ab Urba Condita*, 3.49–54; cf. Zetzel, *Selections*, 222.

91. Cicero, DRP, 2.14, 2.63.

Chapter 9

The Guide

One of the most significant and most enigmatic contributions to political theory Cicero makes in *De Republica* is the concept of the Guide, the *rector rei publicae*. This figure dominates the imagination of his readers, which is all the more notable given how little we know about him. Because of the fractured nature of the text, leaving only two brief discussions of this figure, we need to tease out Cicero's teaching on the matter from the scant details we have. Although oblique references to the Guide are peppered throughout *De Republica*, he is formally introduced when, in Scipio's recounting of the Roman kingship, the tyrant Superbus comes to power. This early discussion provides a good place to begin a fuller inquiry. Scipio summarizes both the tyrant Superbus and the Guide in this way:

> So let this be the first shape, appearance, and origin of a tyrant, which we have discovered in the republic that Romulus founded after taking the auspices . . . how Tarquinius, who obtained no new power but unjustly used what he had, overturned the entire kingly type of city. Let there be opposed to this man another, who is good, wise, and knowledgeable about the advantage and reputation of the city, a protector and manager, so to speak, of the republic. Let those be the names for whoever will be a guide and helmsman of the city. Make sure you can recognize this man, for it is he who can protect the city by judgment and effort. And since the title has been used less often in our conversation so far, and in the rest of our speeches we will have to treat more often the type to which this human being belongs.[1]

There are a number of important points, and several critical questions, that arise from this brief text. First, as a counter to the trauma imposed by the tyrant Superbus, who overturned "the entire kingly type [*genus*] of city," Scipio prescribes the rule of a "type" of man. What is a "type" of man, and what type is the Guide? Second, when Scipio admonishes his fellow interlocutors to "[m]ake sure you can recognize this man," he is not merely giving good counsel, but suggesting that one of the critical characteristics of a good citizen is to be able to recognize this type.[2] Scipio is introducing a new thing into Roman political understanding—a great man who is not a king or general or otherwise great by standards of conquest, family, or wealth—and knowing the characteristics of this type is essential to seeing him and to becoming him. Third, we must discern whether Scipio is referring to a figure who holds political office or not.

THE TYPE OF THE *RECTOR REI PUBLICAE*

The first point to consider is Scipio's suggestion that there are "types" of men just as there are "types" of regimes, and that the Guide is a distinct type. How many types of men Scipio believes there are—if there is a list—is not spelled out, though Schofield notes that Cicero identified kings, magistrates, critical officials, or leading citizens.[3] Two broad categories that Cicero seems to have in mind based on a comment in Book 3 are "those men [who] nourished the first gifts of nature by words and arts" and "these men [who] did so by institutions and laws."[4] The contrast seems to be between the poet on the one hand and the lawgiver on the other, but several sentences later the speaker, Philus, goes on to note the contrast between "the quiet plan of life spent in the best studies and arts" and "the political way."[5] Whatever other types there may be, two of them are the lives at the center of the active and contemplative ways of living. The exemplar of the active life is our Guide, the statesman, whereas the contemplative life is exemplified by the philosopher.

In describing the Guide, Cicero suggests a political figure, though not a narrowly political one. He is the opposite of a tyrant, Scipio notes, "who is good, wise, and knowledgeable about the advantage and reputation of the city, a protector and manager, so to speak, of the republic."[6] This figure concerns himself with maintaining good order in the city and "is always armed against things that upset the form [*statum*] of the city."[7] This vague description of an ideal type is, as Walter Nicgorski suggests, an intentional abstraction. In *Orator*, Cicero describes an orator "who likely never was and never will be . . . , mak[ing] with his mind the perfect type" to serve as a model for citizens seeking "imperfect approximations."[8] In doing so, Cicero provides a particular model of a man—not a king, nor an aristocrat, nor a citizen simply—who transcends any particular regime.[9]

THE CHARACTERISTICS AND WORK
OF THE *RECTOR REI PUBLICAE*

When Scipio admonishes the citizens of his little gathering to "[m]ake sure you recognize this man," the Guide, he is impressing upon them one of the responsibilities of good citizenship. Knowing the characteristics of this man is critical, then, particularly because the kind of man Cicero has in mind has no parallel in Greek or Roman political theory, although Roman history provides numerous notable examples of such figures (Scipio himself being one). To help us identify this man, Cicero borrows a variety of words (*tutor, procurator, rector, gubernator*) to indicate the outlines of a wholly new concept in political theory.[10] In pointing us to such a figure, Cicero necessarily confronts the Roman assumption that demarcates leading men by their military glory or wealth or family status exclusively. Romans might not be quite so quick to spy a good, wise, and effective man (such as Cicero) who is not riding on a chariot or known by a family name. Rather, it is the Guide's comprehensive vision, his well-rounded virtue, his rhetorical ability, his knowledge of right, and ultimately his prudence that set him apart from other men and other citizens.

The ultimate aim of the Guide appears to be "the happy life of citizens," construed broadly.[11] In a fragment derived from one of Cicero's letters to his friend Atticus, Cicero declares that the "director of the republic" aims at this happiness "in order that it may be steady in resources, opulent in provisions, distinguished in glory, honorable in virtue."[12] This simple goal is hardly a modest one. Given that the truth about the soul means that Earth is aimed at Heaven and the Heavens have, in some real sense, occupied the Earth with Reason, one might ask whether a statesmen is fundamentally concerned with guiding men on Earth or to Heaven—or perhaps to both. The obvious field of our statesman's work is the political community, but a man's home is not merely his castle or his city or his fatherland, but the cosmos itself, if the Dream of Scipio is to be believed, and how men live as citizens is also relevant to their lives beyond the city in the celestial realm. The Guide is never merely a statesman, then, but also a psychagogue leading souls toward the afterlife. The instance Scipio describes in Book 1 in which Gallus enabled virtuous courage in his men by alleviating their superstition regarding eclipses is a singular example of how guides of men may well need to teach men how the heavens go in order to teach them how to live well, which is to say, how to go to heaven.[13] Speculation regarding the workings of the heavens belong to the natural philosophers; machinations regarding the city belong to the politicians; but Cicero has in view men like Scipio and Laelius—political philosophers and philosopher politicians, political guides who are at least as active as they are contemplative.

Given the comprehensive scope of the Guide's work, Cicero emphasized that good leaders must also be virtuous men. The scale of Roman endeavor meant that Roman politics was mass politics, requiring political actors to master the stagecraft requisite to win favor as well as the statecraft needed to use power well. Indeed, politics in Cicero's Rome was enacted on a stage with relatively few critical actors, though these men had scores of ambitious understudies vying to replace them. The power of leading politicians flowed significantly from their ability to embody and direct popular opinions and passions. Cicero's interest in rhetoric was not ultimately for the sake of sophistic manipulation of the Senate and people of Rome, but because true rhetoric—rhetoric that makes truth visible to the soul—preserves right, common benefit, and human fellowship in political society. Given the visibility of the Guide, Cicero emphasizes that he must serve as a model, not simply enacting the people's will, but reflecting the good order he has cultivated in himself into them as they gaze upon him. In a remarkable passage, Africanus comments, "for [the Guide] there is almost only one [duty], for almost all the others are in this one: that he never cease instructing and observing [*contemplari*] himself, that he call others to the emulation of himself, that he show himself to his fellow citizens as a mirror through the brilliance of his spirit and life."[14] The guide is truly a tutor of peoples, then.[15]

Recalling the beautiful orrery Gallus described in Book 1, which was placed in the Temple of Virtue and well known for its craftsmanship, we see Cicero making the point that the people know and participate in what is good and true through its radiance made visible. "The good" in abstract is hard to hold before the mind's eye and harder to remember in the middle of difficult trials. In the turmoil of mass life, the people bring their thoughts, their hopes and fears, and their blundering intimations of the good into focus through the clarifying lens of a great or prominent man. The examples of good men, in particular, strike us with their nobility and the power of their example, and we naturally measure ourselves by them. The soul of *this* man, then, is the soul of the city in particular. It has the potential to be, and it ought to be, for which reason this most active of men can least of all afford to abandon philosophy and wisdom, even while he least of all has time to indulge it. "For what," Cicero says in his preface to Book 3, "can be more splendid than when the handling of, and experience in, great matters are combined with the studies and investigation of the corresponding arts?"[16]

Two of the books almost entirely missing from *De Republica* are thought to have been concerned with the Guide and with the education of citizens in particular, specifically Books 4 and 5. Cicero's *De Legibus* provides further fascinating insight into the shaping of civil and religious laws for cultivating virtue. Despite the missing material in *De Republica*, it seems clear that Cicero emphasized the right orientation of both the hearts and minds of citizens. Hearts should be oriented by honor, minds by knowledge of right. Hence, in a comment from Cicero's fragmented preface to Book 3, he notes that the "guide of republics increased [the sense of shame] through opinions and fully developed it through institutions and training so that shame, no less than fear, kept citizens from transgressions."[17] Shame, in Cicero's view, is not merely society's punishment of the inner man for transgression of cultural mores; in well-formed citizens, who prioritize what is honorable (Lat. *honestum*), shame at failure to live honorably arises from the self, from within, rather than being enforced from without. The shame that Cicero has in mind, then, is a gift which "nature has given to a human being as a kind of fear of disparagement that is not unjust."[18] This implies that citizens, no less than the Guide, will have a way of knowing what justice is, a fact which should remind us of the overlapping modes of revelation of Gallus' spheres (see chapter 4).

Cicero's discourses on the higher, natural law in *De Republica* and *De Legibus* are meant to help unveil the principles of right to common view, or at least to render them visible for lawmakers, as J. J. Barlow suggests.[19] Lawmakers, and especially the Guide, can make the higher law visible through institutions, displays, and practices that cultivate right action and insight into what is right. Figures like Numa Pompilius and Publicola did precisely this as a way of stemming the destructive course of the *cursus mutationem*. Numa, for example, transformed the warlike character established by Romulus by instituting "sacred rites," which required that "many things . . . be learned thoroughly and observed, but without expenditure," along with festivities and celebrations, thereby "'calling up' to humanity and gentility the reasoning souls of men who were then savage and even feral with a passion for warring."[20] Similarly, when the Roman people were still inflamed by Superbus' tyranny and deeply suspicious of right authority, Publicola made a number of significant concessions to the people, such as guaranteeing a right of appeal, deferring to the elder, venerable Spurius Lucretius, and removing the axes from the fasces, which were the symbols of supreme authority.[21] Such actions not only maintained order in the republic by establishing a balance among its elements, but also cultivated habits of heart and mind both human and divine.

Yet, although Cicero considers an education in natural law critical to wise governance, it does not transplant the primary need for prudence. "Perhaps you seek a prudent man?" Laelius asks Scipio as Book 2 turns to the discussion of the Guide. Knowledge of natural law counterfeits wisdom and serves as a guide in the dark, but it is not the same thing as wisdom and may not always be a trustworthy guide. Natural law is like a navigator's compass, pointing due north; prudence is more akin to a trustworthy map in the hands of an experienced traveler, laying out courses that navigates to true north around obstructions and dangers that could otherwise prove fatal. In other words, natural law dictates a way that is very often consistent with wisdom, but it may not help in revealing the most fitting action in every moment. Prudence results from experience and goodness, and thus Nicgorski rightly emphasizes that the "model statesman is neither a god who descends among men nor a fabrication to be made," but that he is cultivated "by sound customs and laws" and subsequently becomes a protector of those same institutions.[22]

Prudence can also be cultivated through knowledge of the experience of others, however—including through books like Cicero's own *De Republica*. Hence Scipio declares that "the source of political prudence, with which this entire speech of ours deals, is to see the paths and bends of republics so that when you know how each thing inclines, you can hold it back or run to meet it first."[23] For this reason, Scipio apologizes to his audience at one point for rehashing the history of Rome that they are so familiar with, but he does it, he says, "to clarify models of men and things through familiar characters and circumstances."[24] Cicero's reliance on literature is not incidental to his project. In what he intends to be a criticism, Charles N. Cochrane notes that Cicero undertook "the deliberate substitution of literature for mathematics in what had been the characteristically Platonic combination."[25] In Cochrane's view, this resulted in an anti-Platonic turn to aestheticism, prioritizing beautiful words over mathematical rigor. Whether or not Cicero intended to deprecate the importance of number in philosophy, his turn to literature and the literary is an attempt to get at wisdom from the human side of the equation, through the cultivation of prudence, rather than by means of the abstract realm of sacred number. In Cicero's view, a philosophy that cultivates knowledge without cultivating virtue is, at best, unhelpful, but probably much more malignant. Beautiful rhetoric makes men good through its revelation of truth more capably than abstract figuring does. One of Cicero's singular contributions in cultivating prudence, then, is his turn to the literary.[26]

Finally, if the prudent man—the man who sees and does the right thing in the right moment—is necessarily a good man, it is important to know how he becomes good. Certainly, good citizens and good statesmen are formed by customs, laws, and institutions—but how are these good? Perhaps more importantly, how may the prudent statesman know how to elevate or transform a city's ways to orient them more fully to right? As J. J. Barlow states, "[The Guide] must both stand apart from the horizon of the citizen and yet remain within it."[27] The civic education that enables him to do this includes natural law, but ultimately must include the philosophical skepticism that characterizes Cicero's way. Thus, the Guide must "never cease instructing and observing [*contemplari*] himself," not because he doubts that he knows anything, but because he supposes he can know everything better.[28] Hence, Nicgorski aptly concludes,

> This is no finished incorruptible philosopher-king nor a Stoic perfect wise man of whom Scipio speaks. It is a model on a more attainable, human plateau; yet the very incompleteness, the opening in this model to self-monitoring and self-improvement, reveals the usefulness of a concept of the model statesman/ orator. . . . As long as the perfect model includes the injunction to self-examination and self-improvement and as long as the central and most important virtue of this model statesman is prudence, the model has a built-in protection against a corruptive and smug closure and against a dangerous stretching of the self toward an unrealistic and inappropriate personal standard. One cannot have too much prudence.[29]

Cicero's Guide, therefore, is politically effective precisely because he is also philosophic.

OFFICIUM, OFFICE, AND THE *RECTOR REI PUBLICAE*

A final matter to consider is whether the Guide, as Cicero conceives him, is necessarily a figure who holds political office or whether he may simply be a teacher of statesmen—perhaps, even, a simple writer. Cicero's polemical assertion against men who are inactive in political life early in *De Republica* should temper our speculations. He says, that the "citizen who compels of all persons, by official command and by penalty of laws, what philosophers by speech can scarcely persuade a few persons [to do], should be given precedence over the teachers themselves who debate these things."[30] Quite obviously, Cicero will not grant license to "teachers" to dawdle in their schools under the pretense that their lectures are the best they can do for the republic. Yet, Cicero's commendation of the Seven Sages, his deep respect for Plato, and his own attempt to compile a comprehensive philosophic and academic corpus in Latin for Romans clearly indicates his respect for good teaching and good teachers as well. We should not presume too hastily that the one "who can protect the city by judgment and effort" is always an explicitly political figure.[31] The statesman is a guide *par excellence*; but that does not mean he is the only one who can offer guidance. Required, sometimes, as Schofield says, is the "exceptional action by a dictator or a single private citizen . . . who will possess the ability in a crisis to seize the initiative—whether in an authorized official capacity or otherwise—in order to restore the system to proper functioning."[32] Nevertheless, there is a place in Cicero's economy for the serious, philanthropic philosopher.

That Cicero sees philosophic guidance as relevant—if not always as pressing or as urgent—is a point we can discern both in his affirmation of the importance of philosophical education and via subtler literary arguments. In narrating the final act of the Roman kingship, Scipio noted that "that circle will now come round—the natural motion and revolution of which you must learn to recognize from the beginning."[33] In describing the downfall of Superbus' tyranny, Scipio brings together the cosmological language of "revolutions" with the language of the "political prudence, with which this entire speech of ours deals."[34] Recounting the infamous rape of Lucretia, Scipio marks the rise of Lucius Brutus, "a man preeminent in talent and virtue," who drove the Tarquins out of Rome.[35] Scipio presents Brutus to us as a good man in an unqualified sense, virtuous and energetic, acting correctly at the correct moment. Thus, when Scipio subsequently begins his discussion of the *rector rei publicae*, the "Guide of the Republic," who is "opposed" to the tyrant, there is a natural parallel to Brutus, this good man, possessing insight, who acts at the critical moment to save the republic.[36] He is in some ways the linchpin of Cicero's teaching on the republic. However, in keeping with the subtle elevation of the philosopher, Brutus is not the only figure we are meant to associate with the Guide.

Though he is not mentioned in the immediate context, Cicero means for us to view Pythagoras in association with the Guide along with Lucius Brutus. "Let there be opposed to this [tyrannical] man another," Scipio had said, "who is good, wise, and knowledgeable about the advantage and reputation of the city."[37] Only a few pages earlier, during the unfolding of Numa's reign, there is an unexpected aside in which Manilius wants to know whether Pythagoras was a contemporary of Numa Pompilius, as he has heard. There is not much reason, in context, for Cicero to include this aside here, nor does it seem to have been a pressing matter in the day. Notably, this very mention by Cicero is the earliest Roman text in which we have reference to the alleged connection between Numa and Pythagoras, and Michael Humm concludes that, in fact, "the myth of the relationship between Numa and Pythagoras was already dead by around the mid-first century BC" when Cicero is writing.[38] In other words there does not seem to have been a question of a connection between Numa and Pythagoras when Cicero penned *De Republica*, and so Scipio's detailed chronology correcting the misapprehension primarily serves to pinpoint and highlight Pythagoras' presence in Italy during the reign of Lucius Tarquinius Superbus.[39] The mention of Pythagoras draws our attention to his presence at precisely the point in time at which the prudent man who knows how to save regimes is brought to our attention.[40] Scipio's reference to the "other" man whose arts may yet save the city seems to be meant to cast our thoughts back to Pythagoras.[41]

In being directed to Pythagoras, we are meant to think of what Pythagoras represents, which is the philosophic insight of Plato in particular, but of philosophy more generally.[42] We are not meant to think that Pythagoras himself somehow had a hand in Superbus' downfall. Notably, near the end of Book 2, Scipio's description of the work of the Guide takes on a distinctly Pythagorean air: "As with lyres or flutes, so also with song itself and voices, a certain harmony must be maintained from distinct sounds, and trained ears cannot bear for it to be changed or discordant; yet this harmony is made concordant and congruent by the moderation of very dissimilar voices."[43] This section is a clear literary parallel to the Dream of Scipio where the elder Africanus notes that "educated men, having imitated this [heavenly] place with strings of musical instruments and songs, have opened for themselves a return to it, just like others who have cultivated divine studies in human life with preeminent talents."[44] This Pythagorean vein running through *De Republica* is not intended to hint at some secret Pythagoreanism on Cicero's part. At least in the histories, it is useful to him because Pythagoras already intersects with Roman history, whereas Plato does not. Pythagoras thus serves as a vehicle for inserting a Platonic or philosophic figure into a Roman context at the precise moment when Cicero wants to point to certain subtleties. After all, it is philosophical insight that is capable of grasping the *ratio* Cicero threads through Scipio's history and knows how to deploy it in political life. Most particularly, this reference brings us back to the insight into the *cursus mutationem*, the course of changes in regimes. This is guidance for the Guide, and insight which enables him to be a guide.

Following the pattern laid out across *De Republica*, we should not be surprised that when Cicero presents us with the Guide—this preeminent man in the republic—he presents us with two figures, and it should not be surprising that they represent two ways or lives. Here it is helpful to recall the contrast Scipio makes between the active Socrates and the philosophic Plato, or the question of the two suns, or the two spheres of Gallus from Book 1, one of which is impressive on its face and one of which is impressive to those who seek insight. Junius Brutus is the active, virtuous man whose deed overthrew a tyrant and restored the possibility of Roman liberty, and his popularity leads to his selection as one of Rome's first consuls. On the other hand, it is questionable whether this Brutus could give a genuine account (a *ratio*) of virtue, goodness, or wisdom; it is doubtful whether Brutus fully understands the qualities that constituted his great success, and it is unsure whether he could accomplish his deed if tyranny wore a different face or loomed in different circumstance. This capacity for insight, which must form an essential part of capacity for judgment of the Guide depends on a philosophic mind which is nevertheless unafraid of action. If this were not true, there would be little value in providing a *ratio* of political things.

The Guide, then, need not have an office—though he likely will—but he must be capable of insight and persuasion, shaping passions and opinions and communicating by his rhetorical powers his own insight to those who struggle to see. Cicero the senator may serve as a Guide, then, but also Cicero the author.[45] Both are critical, in fact—one to undertake the prudent deed in a particular time, and the other to illuminate it for all time. Generally, however, the present moment usually needs more good men than it has, and Cicero's rhetoric is thus also meant to encourage political action, albeit appropriately philosophic in tenor.

NOTES

1. Cicero, DRP, 2.51; the rest is lost.
2. Cicero, DRP, 2.51.
3. Schofield, *Cicero*, 88.
4. Cicero, DRP, 3.4; Z7.
5. Cicero, DRP, 3.5; Z6.
6. Cicero, DRP, 2.51.
7. Cicero, DRP, 6.2; Z1.
8. Nicgorski, "Cicero's Focus," 238.
9. Nicgorski, "Cicero's Focus," 243.
10. Cicero, DRP, 2.51.
11. Cicero, DRP, 5.2; Z8.
12. Cicero, DRP, 5.2; Z8.
13. Cicero, DRP, 1.23.
14. Cicero, DRP, 2.69.
15. J. Atkins highlights the centrality of the Guide's virtue and reason to pursuing a good political order in Cicero's conception of politics (see especially *Politics*, 71–72). W. Nicgorski highlights this in his magnum opus on Cicero as well (*Cicero's Skepticism*, see especially Ch. 5, "The Socratic Statesman").
16. Cicero, DRP, 3.5; Z5.
17. Cicero, DRP, 3.3; Z5.6.
18. Cicero, DRP, 3.3; Z5.6.
19. Barlow, "Education," 372. Cicero's understanding of natural law is a major topic in Cicero studies. To crack the lid on it would invite questions and discussions we cannot afford to take up here. Cicero's most particular discussions of the natural law take place in *De Republica* Book 3 (most of which is lost), *De Legibus* Book 1, and throughout *De Officiis*.
20. Cicero, DRP, 2.27; my translation. Fott's translation captures the gist of the text but is a little looser than best in this case. He misses the martial joke: Numa "called up" Romans to be human beings as one might call a soldier up to do his duty.

21. Cicero, DRP, 2.53–55.

22. Nicgorski, "Cicero's Focus," 244.

23. Cicero, DRP, 2.45.

24. Cicero, DRP, 2.55.

25. Qtd. in Barlow 355.

26. In considering the relevance of the Dream of Scipio for the education of states-man, J. Atkins capably discerns the most significant lessons that Cicero's readers, whether philosophically inclined or not, can glean from the dialogue's climax: the "gap" between the orderly heavens and the disorderly earth, the discovery of true glory in its cosmic context, the "god-given duty" of political service, the "hope" that dutiful action will have rewards beyond terrestrial life, and finally that the statesman can, through wise reason, do something to cultivate the harmony of the heavens in earthly realms through attending to men's souls (*Politics*, 76–78).

27. Barlow, 359.

28. Cicero, DRP, 2.69.

29. Nicgorski, "Cicero's Focus," 243.

30. Cicero, DRP, 1.3.

31. Cicero, DRP, 2.51.

32. Schofield, *Cicero*, 89.

33. Cicero, DRP, 2.44.

34. Cicero, DRP, 2.44; 2.46.

35. Cicero, DRP, 2.46.

36. Cicero, DRP, 2.51.

37. Cicero, DRP, 2.51.

38. Humm, "Numa," 36–37.

39. Cicero, DRP, 2.28.

40. Cicero noted in discussing Superbus' downfall that the "circle will now come round," perhaps (in an additional detail) meaning to echo the name of the school, the "semicircle," founded by Pythagoras in Croton (Cornelli, *In Search of Pythagorean-ism*, 63).

41. Cicero in his *Tusculan Disputations* associates Brutus and Pythagoras as well: "Pythagoras, who was pre-eminent for the fame of his wisdom, lived in Italy at the same time that L. Brutus, the founder of your famous house, set his country free" (4.2; trans. by J. E. King 1945).

42. Cf. Cicero, DRP, 1.16.

43. Cicero, DRP, 2.69.

44. Cicero, DRP, 6.23; Z19.

45. Appian notes that Cicero "had held supreme power after Caesar's death, as much as a public speaker could" (*The Histories*, 4.19).

Chapter 10

The Mixed Regime

The figure of the Guide is one of Cicero's memorable contributions to political theory, but we should not let our view of this remarkable figure obscure the importance of the mixed regime to Cicero's political thought. Walter Nicgorski rightly notes that "Cicero appears to be more decisive [than Plato or Aristotle] in asserting the primacy of statesmanship among the responsibilities of this human life," but it is important to add that Cicero's emphasis on the statesman is not meant to downplay the importance of the mixed regime.[1] Indeed, Cicero conceives of politics as capable of accomplishing philosophic goods that philosophy proves incapable of guaranteeing, and while the statesman is critical, his success depends in large part on the well-mixed regime.

We are understandably tempted to see the Guide as being at the center of Cicero's political thought, impressive and mysterious as he is, but Cicero emphasizes the mixed regime for good reason.[2] Although a good deal of Cicero's discussion regarding this mixed regime has been lost, Scipio's initial definition gives us a great deal to work with. The mixed regime is a regime that "has been brought to a condition of equilibrium [*aequatum*], and tempered from the three primary modes of republics."[3] Cicero's emphasis here is not on the static, hierarchical ordering of the regime, but on the balance of its elements, regarding which Scipio declares later on: "unless there is in the city an evenhanded [*aequabilis*] balancing of [right], duty, and service, so that there is enough power in the magistrates, enough authority in the deliberation of the leading men, and enough freedom in the people, [it is not possible to preserve unchanged the constitution (*statum*) of this republic]."[4] Cicero's discussion of the simple regimes in Book 1 of *De Republica* echoes many points made by Aristotle and other classical political thinkers, but the importance of the mixed regime becomes notable in light of Aristotle's discussion of the citizen. In Book 3 of his *Politics*, Aristotle notes that good citizens concern themselves with "preservation of the partnership," and hence with the preserving the regime (*politeia*) that forms the partnership.[5] Given that regimes differ, however—especially since there are good and bad regimes—a good citizen is not necessarily the same as a good man. Indeed, Aristotle identifies a single case in which the two coincide, namely where a good man is also an excellent ruler in a good regime, since only a ruler is able to exercise the virtue of prudence.[6] Cicero's mixed regime, in a revolutionary way, breaks down the distinction between the good man and the good citizen because it introduces a dynamism into the regime that assumes change in the political order rather than attempting to bracket it out.

Aristotle's teaching regarding the regime involved a teaching on the soul: the way of a people is a way of being, and some ways of being correspond to virtue more than others. To be a good citizen—to support one's city and people—might or might not be the same as being a good man. "This city" and "the good city" are not always, or often, or almost ever, the same. The difficulty that Aristotle's important question raises implies that the political life and the good life are often, in the end, largely incompatible. Of course, we might be tempted to argue that one could be a good man while being a bad citizen—that is, perhaps by refusing to participate in vicious political acts. This is part of virtue. Yet, insofar as man is separated from his city, he is distanced from himself, from the fullness of human flourishing, since man is a political animal. The contemplative way of life is a tempting alternative in considering how to be whole, since the divine transcends the city, but as man is more than a beast, however, so is he less than a god. He is always still man and still a political animal. The political life lays a claim on him that renders a simple escape into the contemplative or away from the city both impossible and impermissible.

Cicero's adoption of the mixed regime makes way for a resolution to this profound problem. Thus, the mixed regime is more than a clever alternative to the political inflexibility of the simple regimes. Whereas Aristotle conceives of the simple regimes (with variations, especially in a polity) as the only possibilities, and of each type of regime as establishing a horizon which in most cases will fall well short of justice, Cicero conceives of the mixed regime as a prism which is able to reveal the light of the true horizon in contextually appropriate ways. Aristotle's political teaching in *The Politics,* Book 4, gives guidance in principle about how one might modify a given regime to maintain it, but there is an inflexibility in Aristotle's thinking that, in Cicero's view, makes the mixed regime preferable since it can adapt its form without necessarily resorting to revolution. The fundamental principle of justice in the simple regimes is the maintenance of the hierarchy specific to each city. Justice in such a city is thus parochial by nature; the regime compels it to be so. However, the mixed regime has no rigid form, but primarily a balance. It is not a static institution, but a dynamic one, more akin to Aristotle's discussion of the middling regime, but without that city's foreshortened horizon. It permits the city to restructure the republic, as was accomplished by the

Servian constitution, without doing violence to the fundamental constitution, but rather as a way of maintaining it.[7] The republic, which exists to preserve the bond of human fellowship, is able through prudent guidance to be drawn more and more into alignment with right. When necessary, it is able to make "concessions to human desires," as J. Atkins says, without the need for revolution;[8] and if those concessions are not ultimately wise, it is able to adjust the balance between constitutional elements to maintain relative political harmony. This flexibility highlights that the mixed regime is an important element of uniting the active and contemplative lives not only for one man, but in orienting a whole people in duty toward right.

TWO TROPES: FOREIGN LEARNING

Two tropes that pervade *De Republica* address this question of change in the regime and help illustrate how Cicero resolves this difficulty. The first theme is the tension between foreign influences and domestic order that appears throughout the work in various forms. In his own voice and in the voices of Scipio and Manilius, Cicero explicitly criticizes foreign learning for being irrelevant.[9] However, in the history of the kings, foreign learning comes to have an obvious influence over Rome in the persons of Numa Pompilius and Demaratus of Corinth.[10] In the introduction of the Guide, furthermore, Cicero subtly directs our attention to the relevance of philosophy for a true understanding of the common good in presenting the example of Brutus and implying the significance of Pythagoras (as a representative of philosophy generally). This trope is finally echoed in the Dream of Scipio, which also serves to emphasize the salutary benefit of foreign learning to homespun virtue. Scipio, the Roman, has this dream when he has gone to visit King Masinissa, an African.[11] In the dream itself, Scipio's perspective is continually drawn to and from his fatherland in a way that ultimately shatters the distinction between foreign and domestic. Rome is Scipio's home—but, to quote Philus from the beginning of the dialogue, "[our home] is not the one that the walls of our houses surround but this whole universe, which the gods gave us as a domicile and a fatherland in common with themselves."[12] This trope underscores that Rome will always be Rome, but as her "guides and preservers" strive in virtue toward right in human fellowship, they will also establish themselves in their universal home.[13]

Another way in which Cicero gestures toward the significance of foreign learning is in the literary correlation he subtly constructs between the nine heavenly spheres and the nine rulers in the Roman kingship. Because of the way in which Cicero organized his discussion of rulers in the kingship, there are seven kings, but nine rulers.[14] It is at the ends and the center that this cosmological parallel has its greatest significance. In considering the parallel of figures and spheres, first to last, it is natural and appropriate to associate Romulus, the man as he was, with Earth; yet, the Romulus of Scipio's account is foresighted beyond reckoning, ordering all things in his founding for the benefit of Rome in future ages, and this divine man is also properly connected with the Heavens.[15] This dual association reflects Scipio's dual association with both Heaven and Earth as well. The Sun, which in the description of the Dream of Scipio is given as "the leader, chief, and director of the other lights," corresponds to the fifth figure in Scipio's account of rulers, and despite the fact that Ancus Marcius is the fifth ruler in line, the discussion of his reign places all the emphasis on Demaratus of Corinth, the man who truly brought learning and reason to Rome. In his literary treatment of Marcius' reign, Cicero strove stubbornly to associate Demaratus with Rome's fifth ruler so that he could be associated with the Sun. The upshot of this is not that Demaratus is a secret puppeteer behind the Roman kings as the Sun is "the leader, chief, and director of the other lights," but that Greek learning and philosophy abide at the heart of this benign, guiding influence. This correlation is Cicero's literary, albeit somewhat esoteric, way of emphasizing the centrality of this learning, which is nearly always associated with foreign influence. The trope of foreign influence in domestic affairs is thus Cicero's clever way of simultaneously emphasizing the role of philosophy and education in a good political order and paying homage to Plato, his intellectual light.

To briefly expand on this unusual literary device, it seems clear that Cicero strove to extend the number of Roman rulers in the kingship to nine and that he undertook some artistic calisthenics to see to it that Demaratus of Corinth was at the center, the position occupied by the Sun. Cicero likely did not mean for every figure to parallel with a planet. If he did, it is not entirely clear from which end he intended the correlations to happen, and there are reasons to suppose this is intentionally ambiguous, as I have suggested. There are, however, a variety of ways to connect other characters with certain planets: Superbus, the man who slew his own father to take up rule, is naturally associated with Saturn, or Cronos, who was himself guilty of patricide. Servius Tullius, the king that Superbus overthrew, is described as *optimi regis* by Scipio,[16] and corresponds to Jupiter, whom Scipio had formerly described as *Iovis optimi*, declaring, "Why should I call a human being who desires to dominate or have sole command . . . a 'king' . . . instead of a 'tyrant'?"[17] Lucius Tarquinius Priscus who ambitiously reorganized the Roman Senate and knights and conquered the Sabines, is associated with Mars. Passing over Demaratus, who is discussed in the text, Tullus Hostilius would presumably be associated with Venus (for unclear reasons), Numa Pompulius with Mercury, the messenger of the gods, who brings religion to men, and the Moon, one-half terrestrial and one-half divine, which is associated with the Fathers who divinized Romulus and brought Numa the religious man to moderate Romulus the war-like god-man.

This use of numerical patterns by Cicero is partly an homage, in his mind, to Plato, and not a sign of a secret Pythagoreanism on Cicero's part, but there may be some further significance. It is a matter of no small importance whether Cicero thinks the analogy between the spheres and the characters in *De Republica*, but more importantly the cycles of kings and the republic that he outlines, is merely *useful* as a literary device, a metaphor, for pointing us to political wisdom or whether he thinks that there is a true relation between earthly and heavenly things such that a knowledge of the spheres actually could give one knowledge of political things. In other words, is there such a direct continuity between practical activity and theoretical knowledge that the one who knows (i.e., the philosopher) would be equipped for public life by virtue of his theoretical knowledge alone? Is the realm of change below the orbit of the moon—the terrestrial sphere—in actual fact only a region of *apparent* change, like the realm of the Heavens, which are governed in their perfect motions by divine Mind? The planets appear to change, but theoretical knowledge reveals that they are engaged in a sacred and harmonious rhythm that lies beyond easy mortal apprehension, but is flawless nonetheless. Indeed, in this dance all stars eventually return to their starting places at the elapse of an "astronomical year," a span of more than ten thousand years.[18]

The radical view that the realm of change is in fact entirely subsumed into the theoretical, and that philosophy thus prepares one for politics, is not Cicero's view, however. There are indications that he finds the cosmological paradigm a helpful one for illuminating the elements of harmony and order, but he does not mean to reduce all things to fate and number. He is not a Stoic nor a thoroughgoing Pythagorean.[19] Cicero is quite serious in his prefatory criticism of the philosophers who excuse their uncivic philosophizing by claiming that philosophy will prepare them for politics.[20] He will have none of it. J. Atkins insightfully concludes that the terrestrial analogy to heavenly cosmology is the complex of human psychology.[21] Human psychology is, ironically, almost more predictable in its irrationality than in its rationality, but in both cases is amenable to the experienced guidance of the wise. Prudence of a requisite greatness does not come readily, however, and so Cicero very much agrees with Scipio, who declares that "it is for some great citizen and almost divine man, while governing the republic, to foresee those that threaten and to direct its course and power."[22] This great citizen, by analogy, stands in as the sun in the cosmos, which is itself "the leader, chief, and director of the other lights, the mind and balance of the universe."[23] It seems likely, however, that Cicero anthropomorphized the activity of the sun in this case in order to theomorphize the activity of the Guide. Cicero's treatment of the sun in *De Natura Deorum*, in contrast, describes its motion without attributing any agency or mind to it.[24] This suggests that Cicero's Dream of Scipio is more like a myth intended to re-enthrall the statesman with the divine significance of his work than to suggest that the terrestrial is only an infinitely-complex extension of the heavenly sphere.

TWO TROPES: ADOPTION

A second trope Cicero makes use of in *De Republica* is adoption, a theme that overlaps considerably with "foreign and domestic" issues but suggests an easier rapprochement. Adoption takes something foreign and stamps it with the mark of authentic belonging, but adoption always follows from a prior and often greater attachment or commitment. Adoption is a way of formalizing in a specific time and place a commitment that transcends what was established by circumstance. There is a sense, then, in which adoption hearkens to a higher law, to a higher good, than the natural or terrestrial order. This theme is evident in Rome's adoption of foreigners and commoners as kings, as with Numa Pompilius, Tullus Hostilius, and Tarquinius Priscus.[25] It is emphasized in the discussion regarding Gallus' orreries, where the orbs were acquired by the Grandfather Marcellus, when it is not Marcellus' natural son Marcus but the stranger Gallus who grasps and communicates the significance of the seemingly-dull sphere; it is emphasized all the more explicitly in the Dream of Scipio in the different emphases communicated by the natural father Paullus and the adoptive grandfather Africanus. In critical ways, this theme culminates in the literal adoption of Scipio by his adoptive grandfather Scipio Africanus, a figure who represents the true glory that transcends, and yet saves, the city. It transcends the city in the sense that the magnificence of the courage and prudence that enabled the elder Africanus to defeat Hannibal at Zama and the younger Africanus to overcome the great Carthage is awe-inspiring and nearly divine. Hence, the narrator in *De Republica* notes that, when "abroad," Laelius "worshipped Africanus as a god because of his outstanding glory in war."[26] This glory saves the city as well, however, since it is for the sake of the city. Yet, the narrator goes on to say, "when they were in Rome Scipio saw Laelius as a parent because he came first in age," thus demonstrating moderation and justice as well.[27] Coriolanus, then, was wrong: man becomes a beast when he tries to transcend the city. Caesar was also wrong: man merely shows himself to be a failed god when he makes the city the source of transcending glory. But Scipio, who knows how to live beyond the city as well as within it—who is native to both, adopted by both, depending on one's point of view—overcomes the futility of Coriolanus and Caesar by living *in ordo* in the Heavens and on the Earth.

These tropes are an important way that Cicero deals with the challenge of change to the political order by rightly embracing it. These tropes suggest that change is endemic to political order as it is to life, and the frequent injection of foreigners into Roman political rule suggests that adoption is in fact part of Rome's domestic order. Novelty can threaten established orders by encouraging change for change's sake, but Cicero's conception of political order is not premised on maintaining a static regime "just so" (be it one, few, or many). The mixed regime, as Scipio had said, is the regime that "has been brought to a condition of equilibrium [*aequatum*], and tempered from the three primary modes of republics."[28] This equilibrium is in the constitution of the city, which consists primarily in the proper balancing of the three elements that, when they individually dominate, make up the simple regimes—namely, the one, few, and many, corresponding to the kingly, aristocratic, and popular regimes (and their deviant forms). Cicero highlights the admirable characteristic or quality of each in declaring that the city depends on "an evenhanded [*aequabilis*] balancing of [right], duty, and service, so that there is enough power in the magistrates, enough authority in the deliberation of the leading men, and enough freedom in the people, [it is not possible to preserve unchanged the constitution [*statum*] of this republic]."[29] In a fragment from Book 3, Laelius and Scipio affirm that when any of these three elements is pushed out, then there is no more "'thing' of the people," and what remains is for a dutiful people to recover their "thing."[30] It is in weathering changing circumstances in a ship of state which has balanced its three constituent parts well that right may stand at the center of human affairs.

Human beings come together, Cicero believes, because we are inhabited by a desire for society and for virtue. We seek others out and form communities with them, but not merely for the sake of fellowship—although that is good—but out of a genuine desire to care well for others.[31] In heeding this call, men become a people by "being joined in agreement in right and allied in a community of mutual benefit" and form a republic to fulfill that calling.[32] Cicero's broad definition allows for people who are quite different from one another—as different as the band of nine men gathered at Scipio's house—to form a people and a republic, and to maintain it even if their understanding of right and benefit changes over time. The good republic may or may not embody right perfectly—indeed, a good republic may be far from perfectly just—but it may still be good if it preserves the nascent elements of authority, deliberation, and freedom in their proper proportion and in their proper place. When a change comes to the regime by way of threat or growth, Cicero's model allows for change to the regime without threatening the fundamental order that makes a people, a regime, or a republic. This is fortunate for Cicero, since it means that he is not undertaking an act of violence against Rome by attempting to elevate her through the introduction of philosophy;

rather, he is undertaking an act of care. Aristotle had suggested that only in the best regime would it be possible for the best man and the best citizen to be the same thing: Cicero emphasizes that what makes a man "good" is not orthodoxy or wisdom, but the love and pursuit of wisdom, which most fundamentally begins with a life oriented to the good. There is a philosophical way of life that undertakes this, but also a much more practical, "constitutional" way of doing so that is outlined by *officium*. The mixed regime facilitates a people's political life both by providing stability and by providing the possibility of political improvement without undermining the regime. Through the prudence of the Guide and the mixed regime, then, Cicero envisions a city which permits the broadest possible overlap of the contemplative and active lives.

NOTES

1. Nicgorski, *Skepticism*, 167.

2. Cicero scholars have done admirable work developing the importance of this idea in Cicero and in relation to political theory generally. J. Atkins' (2013) extended treatment offers a good exploration of the idea in Cicero and in scholarship more generally through his book.

3. Cicero, DRP, 1.69.

4. Cicero, DRP, 2.57. The end of this critical sentence is often poorly translated. Fott renders the Latin *non posse hunc incommutabilem rei publicae conservari statum* as "this city cannot be preserved safe from change," but his translation overlooks Scipio's use of the word *status*, or constitution. Change is endemic to Cicero's understanding of the city, but change in the equilibrium of the constitution should not be.

5. Aristotle, *Politics*, 1276b25.

6. Aristotle, *Politics*, 1277a15.

7. Cf. Cicero, DRP, 2.39–41.

8. J. Atkins, *Politics*, 114.

9. Cf. Cicero, DRP, 2.29.

10. Cicero, DRP, 2.25, 29.

11. Cicero, DRP, 6.13; Z 9.

12. Cicero, DRP, 1.19.

13. Cicero, DRP, 6.17; Z 13.

14. The rulers are Romulus, the Fathers, Numa Pompilius, Tullus Hostilius, Ancus Marcius/Demaratus of Corinth, Lucius Tarquinius Priscus, Servius Tullius, Tarquinius Superbus, and Lucius Brutus. The spheres are given in Book 6 as the Heavens, Saturn, Jupiter, Mars, Sun, Venus, Mercury, Moon, and Earth, but the ones that warrant significant attention in the Dream are the Heavens, the Sun, and Earth.

15. This "doubling," which is a feature of Cicero's work, is repeated in other cases. Brutus and Pythagoras, forming a model of the Guide as a pair, are likewise readily associated both with Earth and with the Heavens.

16. Cicero, DRP, 2.45.
17. Cicero, DRP, 1.50.
18. Cicero, DRP, 6.28; Z 24.
19. It is relevant to note that Cicero deviates from Pythagoras and Plato in his cosmology, preferring the Chaldean ordering of the spheres over the Egyptian one. See P. R. Coleman, "Music," 237n.9. J. Atkins, noting the analogy between the "guide of the commonwealth" and the sun, suggests Cicero may have preferred the Chaldean ordering since it places the sun "closer to the middle than the Platonic ordering" (*Politics*, 67).
20. Cicero, DRP, 1.4 and 1.9.
21. J. Atkins, *Politics*, 69ff.
22. Cicero, DRP, 1.45.
23. Cicero, DRP, 6.21; Z 17.
24. Cicero, DND, 2.49–50.
25. Cicero, DRP, 2.25, 30, 35.
26. Cicero, DRP, 1.20.
27. Cicero, DRP, 1.18.
28. Cicero, DRP, 1.69.
29. Cicero, DRP, 2.57.
30. Cicero, DRP, 3.35; Z 43–45.
31. Cf. Cicero, DRP 1.1, 1.39.
32. Cicero, DRP, 1.39, 41.

Conclusion

The Meaning of Political Things

There is something of a danger in explaining ancient thinkers or perspectives to readers in modern times, or to any times other than the original ones. In Cicero's case, two thousand years encompass many different ages. Taking for granted that the unchanging things do not shift, the things of the world do, very much, and we are unavoidably enmeshed in our own times. Gaining wisdom from the ancients will always require inflecting their knowledge to accommodate our different circumstances, and so Cicero does not only need someone to translate his Latin, but also to translate his insight.

This translation of Cicero's insight into our own moment is fraught, however. There are at least two difficulties: firstly, as has been mentioned, the changed circumstances mean it can be hard to apply Cicero's insights directly—once they have been understood, which is the second and more difficult problem. More importantly, it can be hard to know with complete confidence what Cicero fully meant to say. All translation involves interpretation, and all interpreters have their own mind about things. In pretending to share the enlightened expressions of greater, ancient minds, we might simply be smuggling in our own small opining under the cover of their great names—and, worse, we might not even know we are doing it.

Given our limitations and these different times, can Cicero be for us an ancient guide to good politics today? In the end, it is reasonable to conclude that he certainly can, in two ways, if we are careful of our own shortcomings. At the very least, his particular actions, understood in their particular context, can help us develop our own political instincts, much as Cicero's orations served to help cultivate the style of writers from St. Augustine to John Adams. However, this is not Cicero's most valuable bequest to us. In *De Republica* and in his entire corpus, Cicero, ever the Academic skeptic, models the philosophic way statesmen ought to hold themselves with regard to justice, and the politic way philosophers should pursue truth.

The reason politics and philosophy are so inexorably tied up together is that political things—law, virtue, deliberation, justice, and so forth—form a particular nexus between earthly and heavenly things. Cicero's express wish in composing *De Republica* was to imitate Plato, but he likewise wished to reveal justice in the soul as well as in the city for the mutual benefit of both. He desired to use the things that pass away to reveal the things that *are* perennially. Cicero intimated this ambitious project in his preface to Book 1 when he notes, modestly or immodestly, that he has a "certain ability to expound the meaning [or, way] of political things [*ratio rerum civilium*]."[1] Scipio uses this phrase again toward the end of Book 2 when he says that Plato "brought about a city . . . in which the meaning of political things [*ratio rerum civilium*] could be examined," and he notes furthermore that he himself "[applied] the same considerations [*ratio*] [that] he saw [to the history of Rome]" in order to "touch, as with a wand, the cause of each public good and bad thing."[2] Cicero, like Plato, hoped to illumine foundational things for those who wished to see them, things related to human nature and purpose and action as they touch on things divine. To honor and illumine Cicero's ambition, this concluding chapter will highlight certain elements at the heart of Cicero's political philosophy gleaned from *De Republica* as a whole.

Much of Cicero's foundational teaching about the way of political things is artfully woven into his first book in the play between the various characters, although this teaching is repeated and made more or less explicit subsequently. It begins with a problem: the nature and meaning of things is not very clear. When the characters meet, each interlocutor in turn is brought into the query about the second sun that was seen in the Senate, and not only can they not agree about what it means, they cannot agree that it matters. Either way, they do not know: the question of the second sun undermines, even shatters, the characters' expectation of understanding of the order of things. Notably, however, their ignorance does not undermine their assumption that there is a cosmic order, nor does the second sun lead any of the characters to doubt that its appearance is in keeping with the nature of heavenly things. Yet, since there is something in the cosmic order that resulted in the second sun, it becomes clear that they not only do not understand the second sun, but their ignorance is broader than they knew before: they do not, perhaps, even understand the first sun, nor the cosmos it governs. They do not know what they do not know. They seem, in the end, fundamentally divided on whether they should even pursue knowledge of such a rarified nature.

If things in the heavens are difficult to know, it is arguably the case that earthly things are more difficult to know, at least with certainty, given the flux and apparent randomness of human action. The orbs of the stars move about, but at least their courses, lying in an appointed perfection, do not change. The troubling exceptions seem to be the wandering planets which vary in speed and orbit, hurtling forward but then sometimes slowing, pausing, and even reversing themselves for a time. Nevertheless, these changes do not seem to be deviations from a fundamental order, but rather expressions in obedience to a mindful cosmic dance. In seeming contrast, the affairs of human beings on Earth are marked by chaotic change and apparent disorder. But a broader view begins to reveal a different picture. Although things on this terrestrial orb are changeable, unlike among the spheres in the heavens, it turns out that they are, in fact, broadly predictable. The predictability of human actions, especially taken en masse, makes it possible to give an orderly account even of irrational or nonrational things, and so there is a fixity in terrestrial affairs that allows for a fruitful analogy to the music of the spheres and their harmonies.[3] This orderliness results in no small part from the fact that all human action and choice, to echo Aristotle, seems to aim at some good; and even if the goods we aim at are varied or at odds, our endeavoring as human beings inevitably leads us into philosophical and ethical realms as we ask, "What is *good* for us to do?" Even if we are continually drawn to pursue self-satisfying appetites, we are likewise continually gripped by wondering what would be truly best, and whereas Machiavelli counsels us to take Chiron, the beast-man, as our guide to human things, Cicero offers us the Guide, the philosopher-statesman, instead.[4]

The philosopher-statesman is focused on the well-being of the things below, but he cannot, it turns out, be indifferent to the things above. The impulse to investigate the second sun's meaning is natural for human beings and, to some degree, necessary to leading a well-ordered life. Granted, an intractable sort of uncertainty clouds the inner workings of nature; the difficulty of discovering any final knowledge of nature is so great that what beckons to us as so worthy an endeavor simultaneously seems to mock us, at least potentially, as a fool's errand. This difficulty could lead to a pragmatic turn, or an antitheoretical, anti-philosophic turn, but such a reaction, Cicero believed, went too far. None of Cicero's main interlocutors in the dialogue, particularly Scipio, Laelius, and Philus, are ultimately desirous of making such a turn themselves, despite early inclinations to the contrary (see chapters 2–4 for further, related discussion). The difficulty of knowing the true and unchanging things—a recognition central to Cicero's Academic skepticism—should, yes, chasten our impulse to pursue a theoretical life to the exclusion of practical concerns, but the worthiness of the prize, and its relevance to living well, nevertheless counsels continual inquiry over dogmatic or utilitarian determinations of truth or justice. Even if it is difficult to know the truth about things, the world is filled with false opinions that mislead men with respect to justice and right, and this fact alone means that we should not be put off from pursuing the truth about man and the cosmos, regardless of the difficulty. Yet, each action must be undertaken at the right time. What cannot be delayed at any expense is living well now as best we know how. Yet praxis, it turns out, informs reflection in a way that is particularly conducive to philosophical insight.

By embracing the appropriateness of praxis, as Cicero does, we come to see that the nature we know—human nature, human society, this Earth we inhabit—are things we can see and touch and make tolerably reliable judgments about the goodness of. We can discern that things are crooked that should not be, literally as well as figuratively. There is in fact a beneficent, flourishing order possible for the things below, and this order seems, at bottom, to share in a unity with the goodness of the starry things above. Hence, for Cicero, nature is obscure, but not opaque, especially the natures in front of us.[5] Reflection shows that we live well, in light of cosmic things, by attending seriously to the life before us, especially writ large in political society. And as life in political society involves us in deliberation about justice, reflection on truth, and enjoyment of the good, Plato's endeavor to find justice for man—in the world, and thus in the cosmos—by looking to the city proves all the more credible. What we learn by caring for human things ends up illuminating our understanding of the divine things more reliably, perhaps, than the other way around. Political philosophy thus emerges as the citizen's guide to securing a life worth living and the philosopher's most accessible window into nature. It provides us with the knowledge of right in our time and in all time. Cicero's approach in *De Republica* embodies this approach, although, appropriately, Cicero the skeptic refuses to give it to us as a final teaching.

The two spheres of Gallus described in Book 1 by Philus simultaneously affirm and undercut the primacy of political philosophy. The two orbs describe one majestic, heavenly reality, but they look quite different and communicate different aspects about that reality. The orb placed in the Temple of Virtue displays the impressive and alluring face of the beautiful: it makes plain to common sight what was beyond human vision, and is wonderful to the many, at least until they get bored. The other, mundane orb is unimpressive on its face, but it is in reality a mechanical wonder capable of imitating and revealing the motions of the heavenly spheres. To the wise it is worthy of sustained attention and reflection and reveals sublime truths about the nature of things. The two orbs of Gallus prove two things to be true, but they do not point in the same direction: on the one hand, human nature is powerfully animated by an element of reason that spontaneously recognizes and responds to the truly beautiful and the truly good; yet, at the same time, the workings of reason in human beings are so foreshortened that unless the truth is rendered attractive or useful, it has little appeal to men, in general, and will often seem irrelevant to human life. Most of us dwell happily all our lives in the land of seeming. In this anecdote, as well as in the subsequent story about Gallus' overcoming his soldiers' superstition by reason, Cicero holds these two facts in tension: the high capacity for insight and dignity in man and its stubbornly low realization. There are, in fact, profound things for wisdom to grasp, but the wise, beholden to the many, do not wield natural authority in temporal affairs. Wisdom needs auxiliaries; it needs power in the form of good deeds, fine speeches, and loyal friendship.

Beyond this, Cicero insists that there are fixed springs of action in human affairs which, when understood, make it possible to anticipate the courses of men just as it is possible to predict the courses of the wandering planets. These fixed realities may include things such as the cyclical scarcity and abundance imposed by Earth's seasons, but more so the "necessity for virtue" and "love of defending the common safety [*salutem*, or well-being]" that Cicero had identified in his preface.[6] Cicero is unabashed and remarkable in his insistence that some degree of virtue and civic dutifulness are nigh compulsions for men. (Notably, virtue and the common safety are directly analogous to the two principal elements of the formation of a people Cicero had identified, a shared commitment to right and communion in shared benefit, since *ius* is the foundation of *virtus* and *utilitas* the ground of *salus.*)[7]

In the chaotic flux of political life, it is all too easy even for good men to justify the way of the passions, and all too tempting to disregard the moral good of order in oneself and in one's city, to act without respect to *fines malorum et bonorum*. However, in his discussion of human nature, Cicero strikingly insists that beneficence abides at the heart of the human impulse.[8] What we spontaneously seek is driven by and driven to the human good in the most comprehensive sense, even if it often falls short. The structure of being itself is oriented toward flourishing, and this undergirding reality turns, directs, and compels us throughout our terrestrial sojournings. The tumult that appears to characterize human life is not, in fact, a genuine chaos, but instead a disordered and disorganized realizating of the good toward which we are all naturally spurred. It is in following this forceful direction of nature that men naturally form communities ordered toward right and for their common benefit, which is nature's desire for them (see also chapter 6). These communities are as different in custom as men are different, yet there are startling ways in which they are all alike, which allows us to distinguish between differences arising from custom and those arising from nature.

Nature's persistent contributions to human life seem to result, always and everywhere, in the creation of dual goods which should remain well-balanced but often collapse into competition.[9] Nature's spur persistently drives sociable human beings to come together in communities with others, and to persist in piety and community with the gods. No sooner do we enter society, however, than we are confronted with the emergent distinction between the native and the "other," the foreigner. As chapter 10 notes, for Cicero, Rome's success came because of her ability to incorporate foreign learning and to adopt as leaders foreign-born sons who had the insight to care for the Roman body politic best; but the dialogue also makes clear that these influences were only welcomed when they no longer seemed foreign. The balance between "ours" and "not ours" was thus maintained, precariously, to the benefit of Rome— but this was not always the case. Other dualities, besides, plague human life when they fall out of balance, most notably of all being the balance between *theoria* and *praxis* (discussed extensively in chapters 1–5). There are other particular political dualities as well, however, such as the continual contest between the people and the aristocracy (the many and the few); the natural roots of authority seen in the veneration given to one's ancient *patres* and in the reverence granted to *gloria* in its many novel appearances (things ancient and known, things tempting and new);[10] the desire for recognition that animates all human beings with its intimations of transcendence, and the stirring resentment of persons or people who are insufficiently honored, and the need, then, for each element in a regime to share meaningfully in the life of the city, or to feel that it does (the critical importance of honor, envy, and differing forms of equality); the cancerous danger of haughtiness and contempt on the part of rulers, and the pernicious "fear" of the people which, when awakened (as it often is by demagogues), terrifies them into preferring mob rule, and then tyranny or dictatorship, to any more moderate forms of government, good or bad.[11] Experience initiates us into some degree of intuitive understanding of many of these things; articulating and knowing them helps in remembering them and bringing them to bear on political affairs. Cicero, via his literary statesmanship, seeks to embody these things *in verba* to make them more clear.

As Cicero's express wish is to give a teaching that will help in the founding or preserving of regimes, these insights all come to bear particularly in the teaching on the *cursus mutationem*, the course of change that takes place in all regimes over time. Cicero suggests that every regime is subject to series of threatening developments beginning with popular turmoil and ending, if all goes badly, in mob rule. On the one hand, this set, predictable *cursus mutationem* is a sign of the lack of reason in human life, but its predictability means that it is subject to foresighted intervention. Cicero embodies in his histories of the Roman kingship and the Roman republic the examples of rulers who had this insight and those who did not. Those who did not inevitably lost their rule, and the body politic, to faction and mob. Those who had this insight, by instinct or understanding, were able to use this rule to the end of stabilizing and conserving the body politic. Superbus Tarquinius serves as an infamous example of the former, and Servius Tullius serves as an excellent example of the latter.

A great part of the work of rule involves cultivating in the people a sense of confidence and unity, and more importantly a knowledge of the good and just. A people's being united in *iuris consensu* (see chapter 6) is the necessary foundation of common life, but it is not the same as standing in *ius*, in "justice" or "right," itself. Philosophers come to understand who and what they are and how they should live through inquiry, but a people grasp these same things through political mythology and religious life, dimensions which were largely fused in Cicero's ancient world. The specific ways in which Cicero retells Roman history helpfully reveal something regarding foundings. He downplays the infamously brutal and violent elements of Rome's history (e.g., of Romulus' character and deeds), imputes to particular rulers an intention and foresight that it is doubtful that they had (specifically with respect to Romulus),[12] and describes very ancient times as being characterized by insight or learning that was unlikely to be true (as in speaking of the learnedness of early Romans).[13] Cicero's highlighting emphasizes his understanding that beginnings are uniquely important to a people's self-understanding, since they discern their ends in their beginnings, and so he tells a story of Roman origins that emphasizes the elements he most wishes Rome to grow in. Right reason and learning should be priorities for *true* Romans, Cicero asserts: they are not deviations from the Roman character nor mere concessions to foreigners. They are part of the Roman fabric because Romans too are men. Cicero's history merges with elevated myth in certain respects, not because he wants to hide Rome's true history—he makes it plain to his readers that his "history" is not entirely accurate—but because his writing, especially in Book 2 of *De Republica*, is in itself a work of literary statesmanship, something akin to a re-founding.

All of these truths about human nature lead Cicero to propose the superiority of the mixed regime based on his particular learning and insight, a regime which most readily allows for the counterbalancing of elements within a constitutional order. With the collapse of a simple regime into bad rule, the possibility of good government comes to rely entirely on the attempt and success of a few good citizens to overthrow the inevitable tyranny. In the cycle of regimes, however, neither the rule of a good king or a good people are likely to reemerge, and this only highlights the mixed regime for its stability and its ability to realize the civic good through institutional balance even where the elements of the regime may not be entirely virtuous. Each element must be given its due: power to the magistrates, judgment to the aristocracy, and freedom to the multitude.[14] Should this equilibrium be lost, the mixed regime will undergo the same *cursus mutationem* that directed the course of the simple regimes, with the people forwardly seizing power for themselves and some new authority establishing himself only through prudently humbling himself before the multitude. In the history of the kingship, everything depends on the prudence of good rulers; in the history of the republic, Cicero highlights the value of a well-balanced constitution to weather troubled waters.

Over the course of *De Republica*, Cicero serves as pedagogue and psychagogue, attempting to inculcate wisdom about human nature and society as well as to spark a virtuous care for these things in his readers. He is a statesman and founder, attempting to stir up civic virtue and civic wisdom in citizens and political leaders, while also recasting Rome's founding in a light more amenable to reason. He is an author and admirer, not only of the Good he is writing about, but of the Teacher, Plato, he is emulating in ways large and small. Nevertheless, we see Cicero as his own man undertaking a project that reflects his own unique insights into politics and into Rome. The one who knows—who has the insight to see these things and the knowledge of how to right the ship of state—will be able to predict the way of political things, to adjust his politics accordingly, and to preserve the regime in its best possible condition, whether better or worse than the one he inherited. And this seeking wisdom and doing justice is how a good man should live, and if need be, how he should die.

NOTES

1. Cicero, DRP, 1.13.
2. Cicero, DRP, 2.52.
3. See also J. Atkins, *Politics*, 69ff.
4. Cf. Niccolò Machiavelli, *The Prince*, Ch. 18.
5. Cf. Walter Nicgorski's excellent discussion of "effective criterion" throughout Cicero's Skepticism, but especially in chapter 1, "Skepticism, Politics, and a Philosophical Foundation."
6. Cicero, DRP, 1.1.
7. Cf. Cicero, DRP, 1.39.
8. Cicero, DRP, 1.3.
9. Cf. J. Atkins posits that *De Republica* is shaped by "five pairs of contraries." These are practice and theory, the ideal city in speech and Rome as the ideal city in deed, the "best conceivable ideal" and the "best possible," the "rational and the irrational," and "the divine and human" (*Politics*, 65–66). In the list below, my examples will correspond with Atkin's insightful list sometimes and add to it at others.
10. Cf. Cicero, DRP, 1.18, Scipio's authoritative glory; 2.5, Romulus attains glory and then founds a city; 2.31, Tullus Hostilius' "manifest" glory; 2.36, the augur Attus Navius prevents Lucius Tarquinius from changing the names of the original three tribes.
11. Cf. Cicero, DRP, 1.62, the haughtiness of rulers (*inportunitas et superbia*): "because of the harshness and haughtiness of one man, Tarquinius, the royal title fell into hatred among the people"; 2.50, the fear of the people resulting from inequity with respect to land and honors.

12. Cicero, DRP, 2.21
13. Cicero, DRP, 2.18
14. Cicero, DRP, 2.57.

Bibliography

Altman, William H. F. "Altruism and the Art of Writing." *Humanitas*, Vol. 22, No. 1–2 (2009): 69–98.

Appian. *The Histories of Appian*. Trans. Horace White. Harvard University Press, 1912 and 1913.

Aristotle. *Nicomachean Ethics*. Trans. Robert Bartlett and Susan Collins. University of Chicago Press, 2012.

Aristotle. *The Politics*. Trans. Carnes Lord. University of Chicago Press, 1984.

Asmis, Elizabeth. "A New Kind of Model: Cicero's Roman Constitution in *De republica*." *The American Journal of Philology*, Vol. 126, No. 3 (Autumn, 2005): 377–416.

Atkins, E. M. "*Domina et Regina Virtutum*: Justice and Societas in *De Officiis*." *Phronesis*, 1990, Vol. 35, No. 3 (1990): 258–89.

Atkins, J. W. *Cicero on Politics and the Limits of Reason: "The Republic" and "The Laws."* Cambridge University Press, 2013.

Baraz, Yelena. *A Written Republic: Cicero's Philosophical Politics*. Princeton University Press, 2012.

Barlow, J. Jackson. "The Education of Statesmen in Cicero's "*De Republica*." *Polity*, Vol. 19, No. 3 (Spring 1987): 353–74.

Brouwer, René. "'Richer than the Greeks': Cicero's Constitutional Thought." *Ciceros Staatsphilosophie*. Ed. Otfried Höffe. CPI Books, 2017: 33–46.

Caspar, Timothy. "*Recovering the Ancient View of Founding*." 2006. Claremont Graduate University, PhD dissertation.

Cicero, Marcus Tullius. *Academica*. Trans. H. Rackham. Harvard University Press, 1967.

———. *Cicero on Old Age* (or, *De Senectute*). Trans. W. A. Falconer. Harvard University Press, 1923.

———. *Letters to Atticus* (Vols. 1–3). Trans. by E. O. Winstedt. G. P. Putnam's Sons, 1919.

———. *Letters to Friends* (Vols. 1–3). Trans. by W. Glynn Williams. Harvard University Press, 1958.

———. *Letters to His Brother Quintus*. Trans. by Evelyn S. Shuckburgh, 1908–9. Perseus Digital Library. http://www.perseus.tufts.edu/.

———. *The Nature of the Gods*. Trans. Horace C.P. McGregor. Harmondsworth: Penguin Books, 1972.

———. *On Divination*. Trans. by W. A. Falconer. Harvard University Press, 1923.

———. *On Duties*. Trans. E. M. Atkins. Cambridge University Press, 1991.

———. *On Friendship*. Trans. by W. A. Falconer. Harvard University Press, 1923.

———. *On Moral Ends*. Trans. Raphael Woolf. Cambridge University Press, 2001.

———. *On the Republic and On the Laws*. Trans. David Fott. Cornell University Press, 2014.

———. *The Republic and the Laws*. Trans. Niall Rudd. Oxford University Press, 1998.

———. *Tusculan Disputations*. Translated by J. E. King. Harvard University Press, 2001.

———. *Tusculan Disputations*. Translated by C. D. Yonge. New York: Harper & Brothers, 1877.

Coleman-Norton, P. R. "Cicero and the Music of the Spheres." *The Classical Journal*, Vol. 45, No. 5 (Feb. 1950): 237–41.

Cornelli, Gabriele. *In Search of Pythagoreanism*. Göttingen: Hubert & Co, 2013.

Fott, David. Introduction. *On the Republic and On the Laws* by Marcus Tullius Cicero. Cornell University Press, 2014.

Fox, Matthew. *Cicero's Philosophy of History*. Oxford University Press, 2007.

Frank, William. "Cicero, Retrieving the Honorable." *Studia Gilsoniana* 3 (2014): 63–83.

Gaius. *Institutes*. Trans. by Edward Poste. Oxford: Clarendon Press, 1904.

Gallagher, Robert. "Metaphor in Cicero's *De Republica*." *Classical Quarterly* 51.2, 2001: 509–12.

Hale, J. R. *The Literary Works of Machiavelli*. Oxford University Press, 1961.

Hariman, Robert. *Prudence: Classical Virtue, Postmodern Practice*. Pennsylvania State University Press, 2003.

Humm, Michael. "Numa and Pythagoras: The Life and Death of a Myth." *Classical Studies*, 2014: 35–51.

Jones, Robert Epes. "Cicero's Accuracy of Characterization in His Dialogues." *The American Journal of Philology*, 60.3, 193: 307–25.

Kesler, Charles. *Cicero and the Natural Law*. 1985. Claremont Graduate University, PhD dissertation.

Lévy, Carlos. "Philosophical Life versus Political Life: An Impossible Choice for Cicero?" *Cicero's Practical Philosophy*, edited by Walter Nicgorski. Notre Dame Press, 2012: 58–78.

Livy. *Ab Urbe Condita*. Trans. Rev. Canon Roberts (1905). en.wikisource.org/wiki/From_the_Founding_of_the_City.

Long, A. A. "Cicero's Plato and Aristotle." *Cicero the Philosopher*, edited by J. G. F. Powell. Oxford UP, 1995: 37–61.

Lovejoy, Arthur. *The Great Chain of Being: The Study of the History of an Idea*. Harvard University Press, 1964.

Nicgorski, Walter. Appendix. *Cicero's Practical Philosophy*, ed. Walter Nicgorski. Notre Dame Press, 2012: 242–82.

————. "Cicero's Focus: From the Best Regime to the Model Statesman." *Political Theory*, Vol. 19, No. 2 (May, 1991): 230–51.

————. Appendix. *Cicero's Skepticism and His Recovery of Political Philosophy. Palgrave Macmillan, 2016.*

Plato. *The Republic*. Trans. Allan Bloom. Basic Books, 1991.

Poste, Edward. Interpolated commentary. *Institutes* by Gaius. Oxford: Clarendon Press, 1904.

Powell, J. G. F. "Cicero's *De Republica* and the Virtues of the Statesman." *Cicero's Practical Philosophy,* ed. by Walter Nicgorski. Notre Dame Press, 2012: 14–42.

Schofield, Malcolm. *Cicero*. Oxford University Press, 2021.

Stein, Joshua. "Cicero's Cosmos: The Universe as Metaphor." Paper delivered at The Inspiration of Astronomical Phenomena. Dec. 2000. https://shifterspeak.files .wordpress.com/2014/02/a-2.pdf/.

Strauss, Leo. Cicero course transcript. The Leo Strauss Center at the University of Chicago. 1959. leostrausscenter.uchicago.edu/cicero-spring-1959/.

Vatican Manuscript Vat.lat.5757. DIGIVATLIB. spotlight.vatlib.it/palimpsests/about /vat-lat-5757-inf/.

Vitruvius. *De Architectura*. Perseus Digital Library. Trans. by B. G. Teubner, 1912. http://www.perseus.tufts.edu/hopper/text?doc=Perseus:text:1999.02.0072.

Wirzubski, Ch. "Cicero's *CVM Dignitate Otium*: A Reconsideration." *The Journal of Roman Studies*, Vol. 44, 1954.

Wood, Neal. *Cicero's Social and Political Thought*. University of California Press, 1988.

Zetzel, James E. G., *De Republica: Selections*. Cambridge University Press, 1995.

Index

Cornelius Scipio, Publius. *See* Scipio
  Africanus (grandfather), Publius
Cornelli, Gabriele, 153n40

De Republica:
  alternating centers, 54, 59–60, 81,
    84, 157ff.;
  fragmentary nature, 1, 14;
  historical reliability, 28, 43n2,
    43n7, 135;
  motives for writing, 2, 13–14, 23,
    62, 77, 111–12;
  naming of, 98–9;
  pedagogical ambiguity, 62;
  setting, 28, 29, 43n1, 48, 65n51;
  use of Platonic images, 52, 57,
    71, 75–6, 85–6, 111–12
Demaratus of Corinth, 129–30, 157–58
The Dream of Scipio, 5–6, 14, 36–8,
    47–9, 52–4, 56–9, 66n52, 78, 81–6,
    94, 145, 151, 153n26, 157–160
Duty. *See officium*

Earth, 1, 14, 17, 36, 38, 47–9,
    56–9, 66n52, 66n59, 81–6,
    87n9, 145, 153n26, 158, 160,
    162n14-15, 167–68
Education:
  Civic, 75, 146–148, 153n26, 158;
  Philosophic, 30, 91,
    99–100, 150, 158
  Epicureanism, 1, 3–5, 37–8,
    65, 70, 92;
  Ciceror's criticism of, 15–7, 24,
    25n32, 42, 85
Fannius, Gaius, 52, 57–8, 65n51,
The Fathers, 3, 125–27, 130, 132,
    134, 158, 162n14
Fott, David, xi, 25n32, 55, 77, 83,
    88n13, 92, 95–6, 104, 121n13
Founding, 4, 113, 116, 121n14,
    137, 170–2;
Founding of Rome, 123–8.
  See also The Regime, origins

Foreign learning, 15–6, 82, 113, 124,
    126, 129, 157–58, 160, 169–171.
  See also Demaratus of Corinth
Fox, Matthew, 43n7-8
Furius Philus, Lucius. *See* Philus,
  Lucius Furius

Gallagher, Robert, 74, 113–14
Gallus, Gaius, 36;
  orbs of, 6, 70, 73–7, 104–5, 145–
    47, 151, 160, 168
Glory, 15, 47, 53, 56, 62, 82–4, 102–3,
    143–45, 153n26, 160, 172n10
The good man:
  and the good citizen, 13, 15, 18,
    156, 122n16;
  and the cycle of regimes, 115–6
The Guide, 7, 26n37, 59, 74, 100–2,
    104–5, 143–152, 155, 157, 159, 162,
    162n15, 163n19, 167;
  Genus (type), 143–44;
  Purpose of, 145.
  See also The Statesman; The Sun

Haughtiness (*superbia*), 137,
    170, 172n11.
  See also Tyranny
The Heaven(s), 1, 5–6, 14, 36, 47–53,
    56–9, 60, 72, 78, 81–7, 87n9, 145,
    159–60, 162n14, 166–68
Honestum, 18–19, 40, 109n69, 147
Honor and shame:
  in the Roman histories,
    128, 130, 136;
  pedagogical use of, 147;
  rhetorical use of, 17–9
Hostilius, Tullus, 128–29, 158, 160
Human nature:
  beneficence of, 20, 169;
  and the city in speech, 166;
  natural spur to duty, 21;
  potential of, 168;
  and the regime, 113, 118, 171–72
Humm, Michael, 150

Index of Passages in *De Republica*

About the Author

Moryam VanOpstal is professor of history and government and dean of students at The Cambridge School of Dallas, where he has taught political theory and history for nearly a decade. He earned his doctorate in politics from the University of Dallas, and has taught there from time to time. His ongoing research interests include Cicero and his influences, American political history, democratic theory and classical education.